"Let's Swallow
Switzerland"

"Let's Swallow Switzerland"

Hitler's Plans against the Swiss Confederation

Klaus Urner

Translated by
Lotti N. Eichhorn

LEXINGTON BOOKS
Lanham • Boulder • New York • Oxford

LEXINGTON BOOKS

Published in the United States of America
by Lexington Books
4720 Boston Way, Lanham, Maryland 20706

12 Hid's Copse Road
Cumnor Hill, Oxford OX2 9JJ, England

British Library Cataloguing-in-Publication Information Available

Library of Congress Cataloging-in-Publication Data

Urner, Klaus, 1942–
   [Schweiz muss noch geschluckt werden!. English]
   Let's swallow Switzerland! : Hitler's plans against the Swiss Confederation / by Klaus Urner.
     p. cm.
   Includes bibliographical references and index.
   ISBN 0-7391-0255-9 (alk. paper)
   1. World War, 1939–1945—Switzerland. 2. Germany—Military relations—Switzerland.
3. Switzerland—Military relations—Germany. 4. Neutrality—Switzerland. 5.
Switzerland—Defenses. 6. Military planning—Germany—History—20th century. 7. Hitler,
Adolf, 1889–1945—Views on Switzerland. I. Title.

   D754.S9 U76 2001
   940.53'494—dc21
                                                         2001029299

Printed in the United States of America

Contents

Foreword

Professor Klaus Urner makes an important contribution to the English-speaking world with the translation of his historic account of Hitler's designs on Switzerland during World War II. Until Urner's research, many erroneously believed Switzerland was never seriously threatened and viewed its often declared neutrality as a color-blind and valueless posture designed to shield the country from the dangers threatening the rest of Europe. Urner reminds us that in reality Switzerland took the requisite steps to deter Nazi Germany's military planners from invading and turning Switzerland into the last of the European neutrals to be made part of Hitler's Reich.

The reasons for Switzerland's survival as an independent state during the Second World War should be recalled. It was largely the result of prudent military preparedness and the Swiss' deeply rooted determination to defend the homeland. A credible capability and the will to resist were the grist of a genuine and successful deterrent. As Professor Urner documents convincingly, Switzerland's conflict avoidance was assured by both the Third Reich's conflicting priorities and the Swiss' determination to fight if need be.

We in the West owe much to Switzerland's steadfastness not only during World War II but indeed throughout the Cold War. As NATO commander during the height of the Cold War and later as U.S. secretary of state, I came to appreciate firsthand the core values embodied by our Swiss friends which have consistently been compatible with Western standards. Occupying an important strategic position, Switzerland historically has been a democratic country subtly sharing the Western world view and safeguarded by strong military capabilities.

Contemporary political-military commentators, historians, and most importantly, foreign policymakers should take cognizance of the essence of modern Swiss history. Professor Klaus Urner's insights and revelations aid us in analyzing not only the central focus of his work but in understanding the universal importance of a strong, democratic Switzerland to Europe's continuing security needs.

General Alexander M. Haig Jr.

Preface

Until the late 1980s little was known of Hitler's plans of action against Switzerland. Instead, it was simply assumed that the German leadership never seriously contemplated an occupation of the country. Was there ever in fact any danger for Switzerland's continued existence during World War II? Those who base their judgment solely on the considerable financial and economic services Switzerland rendered to the Axis powers and who regard National Socialist Germany simply as a questionable but reliable business partner fail to recognize such a threat. A study widely distributed in 1997, titled "Under Hitler's Protective Hand,"[1] viewed the German dictator as a kind of "protector" of Switzerland, yet the work leaves unanswered the question of the dangers from which he was supposedly protecting the country.

The business relationship on which the close cooperation between Switzerland and the German Reich was based consisted during the war years of a staggered use of promises and services as well as of pressures and extortions. It was Hitler himself who created the preconditions to squeeze out of Switzerland all there was to take. As late as August 18, 1944, when the German troops were retreating in the Rhône valley and along the border areas southwest of Switzerland, Hitler gave strict orders "to keep Switzerland surrounded as long as possible."[2] This was his last attempt to maintain pressure on Switzerland by means of a German encirclement. A short time later the advances of the Allied forces relieved this blockade, bringing one of the most successful extortion operations of World War II to an end.

This had begun in June 1940 when, shortly before France's capitulation, Germany and Italy tried to use a surprise cut-off maneuver to bring Switzerland fully under their control. The progress of this operation and, when it failed, the dramatic increase in tension at the Führer's headquarters, the rapid

ix

advances of the 12th Army with nine divisions towards the western border of Switzerland, and the preparations for what the Germans described as the "Special Task" of subduing Switzerland are explored for the first time in this study. As the sources show, the operational designs directed against Switzerland during the summer and fall of 1940 were not just fictitious preventive plans, drawn up by a staff looking for something to do, but rather continuously revised proposals for attack that were updated according to the availability of troops.

When the armistice with France was signed and sustained and England became the next target for occupation, a fierce competition ensued for the control of the last secret passages that Switzerland was able to maintain in the border area with Upper Savoy. The second part of this book discusses the German and Italian efforts to seal these important back doors to the Allies, an undertaking that met with unanticipated obstacles. The story of the gap near Geneva ended on November 11, 1942, when the occupation of Vichy, France, fully closed the Axis Powers' ring around Switzerland.

Since the mid-1990s, three generations, among them the generation that was on "active military duty" during the war, are debating anew, and perhaps for the last time, how to assess the behavior of Switzerland during World War II. Late in time, but all the more intensively, the last dark realms of the Swiss past are being subjected to scrutiny. The question of how well Switzerland used or failed to use opportunities to counter pressures of extortion requires detailed responses. Whatever may be brought to light by this self-critical analysis, the fact remains that from the National Socialist point of view multicultural Switzerland was an anachronism—an island whose continued existence was only a matter of time—that was useful during the war but for which there would no longer be any justification after German world domination had been achieved.

"Collaboration" did not mean a guarantee of survival. Even as useful business partners, Switzerland and Sweden would not have survived a final victory by Germany. As Nazi Propaganda Minister Joseph Goebbels noted in his diary on December 18, 1941: "[I]t would be a veritable insult to God if they would not only survive this war unscathed while the major powers make such great sacrifices, but also profit from it. We will certainly make sure that this will not happen."[3]

Switzerland's inescapable predicament during World War II is not to be understood as an excuse for questionable behavior. Instead, a critical but realistic examination needs also to address the difficult situation created by the blockade and counterblockade. A full assessment of Switzerland at that time must include understanding the pressures and threats to which the country was then exposed. The current study intends to contribute to that goal. It was published first in 1990 by the Verlag Neue Zürcher Zeitung; a French edition of 1996 also found a positive response in western Switzerland. I thank Dr. Ernst Piper and Pendo Publishers that the study is now available in paperback as well. Additional documents and remarks, for which I am particularly indebted to Mrs. Ingeborg Meier and Division Commander (ret.) Denis Borel, clarify the insights gained and have been utilized for this edition.

Switzerland, "the eye of the Hurricane," as journalist Urs Schwarz fittingly called it, survived World War II thanks to the military efforts and the victory of the Allies. However, in 1940, after France's capitulation, there were forces in England and, later, particularly in the United States, that already counted Switzerland out, wanted to cut it off from all essential supplies, and surrender it fully to the Axis powers. They thus played into the hands of the radical tendencies on the German side which aimed at eliminating the small countries in order to remove the last operational bases in central Europe from use by Allied spies. Switzerland therefore owes even greater gratitude to those individuals who defended the existence of a small country out of principle. Among them is Dingle Foot, parliamentary secretary of the Ministry of Economic Warfare in London, who stated in a memorandum on September 21, 1940 that: "There are substantial advantages in preserving so far as we can the social and political stability and therefore the independence of one country in the middle of the general ruin."

After 1945, and again since the middle of the 1990s, Switzerland was and has been sharply criticized, particularly in the United States, for its stance during the war. Now that the mistakes and weaknesses of that time have been scrutinized in numerous research papers, there is a new readiness even in the English-speaking world to reevaluate the survival strategy pursued by Switzerland, then located at the center of the Axis powers. Thanks to the American Swiss Foundation and its president, Ambassador Faith Whittlesey, as well as Georg Gyssler, chairman of the U.S. Advisory Council, this book now appears also in English. I am grateful to Lotti N. Eichhorn for her carefully done translation and to John Gardner, Don Hilty, and Leo Schelbert for their labors.

This book was originally published in German by NZZ in 1990 and Pendo Pocket in 1998, under the title "Die Schweiz muss noch geschluckt werden!" Permission to publish in English has been generously granted by Verlag Neue Zürcher Zeitung of Zürich, Switzerland. Gratefully acknowledged is partial funding by Presence Switzerland (PRS), Pro Helvetia Arts Council of Switzerland, and the Sophie and Karl Binding-Foundation of Basel, Switzerland.

Klaus Urner
Zurich, June 1998/February 2001

NOTES

1. Fred David, "Unter Hitler's schützender Hand.Wie Adolf Hitler per Führerbefehl für schonenden Umgang mit seinem wichtigsten Wirtschaftspartner sorgte: Der Schweiz," *Cash* 32 (August 1997): 38ff.

2. Percy Ernst Schramm, ed., *Kriegstagebuch des Oberkommandos der Wehrmacht (Wehrmachtsführungsstab), geführt von Helmut Greiner und Percy Schramm*, vol. 4, bk. 1 (Frankfurt a. M.: Bernard & Graefe Verlag für Wehrwesen, 1961), 471.

3. Elke Fröhlich, ed., *Die Tagebücher von Joseph Goebbels,* vol. 2, bk. 2 (Munich: K. G. Saur, 1996), 536; Klaus Urner, *Zur Bedrohung der Schweiz im Zweiten Weltkrieg. Forschungsstand, Kontroversen, offene Fragen,* ed. Hans Werner Tobler, Kleine Schriften, no. 32 (Zurich: ETH, 1997), 9–15.

Introduction:
The Search for New Sources

At first it was quite uncertain whether any new insights about Hitler's possible plans for Switzerland could be discovered, as there had been keen interest in attempting to clarify this matter immediately after the war. The first impetus to engage in additional research, however, came from doubts concerning the interpretation of the German plans of attack that had been worked out during the summer and fall of 1940 against Switzerland and which supposedly had been made without any particular goal in mind. These plans, consisting of more than a half dozen drafts, personally involved the chief of the general staff of the army as well as two field marshals. However, no analogous attack scenarios against Sweden were known. In 1942 Hitler was supposedly sorry about not also having marched into Sweden at the time of the occupation of Norway two years earlier; but concerning the question about corresponding studies by the general staff, the Swedish military historian Carl-Axel Wangel stated succinctly: "No German plans of attack against Sweden have ever been found."[1] Earlier oral and written communications to my colleague Hans Rudolf Humm and to me that had been provided already by General Franz Halder as well as the now deceased Generals Walter Warlimont and Hermann Böhme indicated that much more lay behind the planning zeal against Switzerland than earlier had been assumed. Concerning its origin, it had only been known that the planning dated back to the time before the armistice of June 1940. This provided a starting point for the current study. In order to trace origins of planning, it was necessary to determine on the basis of German sources if and to what extent Hitler and his military command concerned themselves in June 1940 with Switzerland. For this purpose it was above all necessary to consult documents which would shed light on the internal events in the

Führer's headquarters as well as within the supreme command of the armed forces and the German army's high command.

One of the great obstacles encountered in the current study was that, if one desired to go beyond the source documents that had already been published, in many important instances the relevant documents were missing. The fire at the department of military science of the army's general staff in February 1942 had caused great losses, and in April 1945 the archives of the army in Potsdam were totally destroyed. To this must be added the failure of Brigadier-General Walter Scherff who was unqualified for his task as "representative of the Führer for recording military history" and who subsequently committed suicide. At the end of his tenure, he transferred the documents of the highest military authorities to Kufstein and Reichenhall and had both repositories burned at the end of the war.[2] The gaps caused by these losses are huge. Additional documents attributed to Field Marshal Walther von Brauchitsch, for example, would have been an important source for this work. Yet review of the "personal papers of the head of the army high command" yielded only militarily irrelevant correspondence between him and his adjutant's office regarding invitations and other letters.[3]

However, apart from these kinds of failures, there were also some initial successes. A revealing indication in the unpublished writings of Wilhelm Keitel, chief of the Armed Forces High Command, confirmed that the research could be expanded to other sources. In addition, the scope had to be extended beyond the summer of 1940. These other sources included the archives of Army Group C, the tank group led by Guderian, and the supreme command of the 12th Army as well as those of individual army corps and divisions which had advanced to the western border of Switzerland during the final phase of the French campaign or which would have been available for a possible attack after the armistice. As the question of an occupation of Switzerland was primarily a political decision, it was necessary to take into account all aspects which might provide information about Hitler's intentions. Individual events assumed a completely new meaning in the overall context. A threat was also posed by the counterblockade with which the Axis powers pressured Switzerland. What were its goals? In this research, internal Swiss concerns are discussed only if they were perceived by the German leadership and played a role in their considerations.

It was impossible to predict in advance that this research would turn into a veritable journey of discovery. It was hoped that additional knowledge would be gained, but to my own great surprise the research revealed that Hitler himself began to agitate against Switzerland and, even before the armistice, set in motion a military cutoff operation which, with its consequences, requires a new evaluation of the situation during the summer and fall of 1940. What resulted, and in what manner the total encirclement of Switzerland was continued by means of economic warfare, will become clear from what follows as well as from the documents given in the Appendix. It also emerges that Italy was accorded only a secondary role which, however, became more important as an unintended result caused by the German handling of the counterblockade after mid-1941.

Partial results of research for the first section were published in the *Neue Zürcher Zeitung* in June 1990 on the occasion of a retrospective on the fiftieth anniversary of the threat.[4] At that time I still relied on circumstantial evidence, but in the meantime, additional source material has provided certainty. Through the good offices of Dr. Heinrich Tanner it was possible to locate the private records of the officer who drew up the first studies of attack against Switzerland in the operational section of the general staff of the army. I am grateful to Dr. Dietrich Wilhelm von Menges who allowed me to see the documents of his cousin Otto Wilhelm von Menges, killed at Stalingrad, and who provided additional explanations. I also received valuable help from Mr. Georges Wüthrich, who conducted detailed research regarding German troop movements on the other side of the Swiss border. The documents which he put at my disposal made my own targeted research at the Federal Archive-Military Division in Freiburg i. Breisgau much easier. In my search for documents there I received expert assistance from Mr. Brün Meyer and Mr. Werner Loos. Mr. Michael Müller also offered suggestions, and I am grateful to him for information based on his own research.

NOTES

1. Carl-Axel Wangel, "Verteidigung gegen den Krieg," in *Schwedische und schweizerische Neutralität im Zweiten Weltkrieg,* ed. Rudolf L. Bindschedler et al. (Basel: Helbing & Lichtenhahn, 1985), 42; Josef Ackermann, *Heinrich Himmler als Ideologe* (Göttingen: 1970), 190–91.

2. Schramm, ed., *Kriegstagebuch,* 1825–1826; older documents and personal papers were excepted from being destroyed, according to the "Merkblatt zu den Schriftgut-Verlusten der ehemaligen deutschen Wehrmacht" of the Bundesarchiv-Militärarchiv, Freiburg i. Br.

3. BA-MA, RH 1/v. 27a, b; 28a, b.

4. "Juni 1940-Hitler's Krieg gegen die Schweiz hatte schon begonnen," *Neue Zürcher Zeitung,* nos. 126, 131, 143, 149, June 1990.

Abbreviations

A.Ausl./Abw.	Amt Ausland/Abwehr im OKW [Foreign Office/Defense in the OKW]
AA	Auswärtiges Amt oder Aufklärungsabteilung [Foreign Ministry or Reconnaissance Section]
Abt., Abtlg.	Abteilung [Section, Division]
Abw.	Abwehr [Defense]
ADAP	Akten zur Deutschen Auswärtigen Politik [Documents on German foreign policy]
AfZ	Archiv für Zeitgeschichte, ETH Zürich [Archives of Contemporary History, Swiss Federal Institute of Technology, Zurich]
AHQu.	Armeehauptquartier [Army Headquarters]
AK	Armeekorps [Army Corps]
Anl.	Anlage [Enclosure]
AOK	Armee-Oberkommando [Army Supreme Command]
ASMZ	Allgemeine Schweizerische Militärzeitschrift [General Swiss Military Journal]
Ast.	Abwehrstelle [Defense Position]
Aufkl.	Aufklärung [Reconnaissance]
Ausl.	Ausland [Foreign Affairs/Abroad]
BA-MA	Bundesarchiv-Militärarchiv, Freiburg im Breisgau [Federal Archive-Military Archives, Freiburg/Breisgau]
Batl., Btln.	Bataillon [Battalion]
BIZ	Bank für Internationalen Zahlungsausgleich [Bank for International Settlements]
Brig.	Brigade

Büro Ha	Büro Hausamann [Office Hausamann]
DDI	Documenti Diplomatici Italiani [Italian Diplomatic Documents]
Dg. Pol.	Dirigent (stellvertretender Leiter der politischen Abteilung des AA) [Deputy (Deputy Chief of the Political Section of the AA)]
dgl.	desgleichen [idem]
Div.	Division, Divisionen [Divisions]
Doss.	Dossier [File, Folder]
dt.	deutsch [German]
EPD	Eidgenössisches Politisches Departement [(Swiss) Federal Department of Foreign Affairs]
ETH	Eidgenössische Technische Hochschule Zürich [(Swiss) Federal Institute of Technology, Zurich]
EVD	Eidgenössisches Volkwirtschaftsdepartement [Swiss Federal Department of Commerce]
FHQ	Führerhauptquartier [Führer's (Hitler's) Headquarters]
Flak	Flieger-Abwehrkanone [Air Defense Gun]
Geb. Brig.	Gebirgsbrigade [Mountain Brigade]
Geb. Div.	Gebirgsdivision [Mountain Division]
Gen.	General
Gen. Kdo.	Generalkommando [General Command]
Gen. Qu.	Generalquartiermeister [Quartermaster General]
GenSt., GenStab	Generalstab [General Staff]
Genst., Gen. St., d. H.	Generalstab des Heeres [General Staff of the Army]
Ges.	Gesandter [Envoy/Ambassador]
gez.	gezeichnet [signed]
H. Kdo., Höh. Kdo.	Höheres Kommando [Higher Command]
H.Qu.	Hauptquartier [Headquarters]
HaPol	Handelspolitische Abteilung, AA [Section for Trade Policy of the AA]
HGr., H. Gr.	Heeresgruppe [Army Group]
HPA	Handelspolitischer Ausschuss [Committee for Trade Policy]
Hpt., Hptm.	Hauptmann [Captain]
HKW	Sonderstab "Handelskrieg und wirtschaftliche Kampfmassnahmen" im OKW [Special Staff "Trade Warfare and Economic Warfare Measures" in the OKW]

i. A.	im Auftrag [on orders from]
I.D., J.D.	Infanterie-Division [Infantry Division]
i.G.	im Generalstab [On the general staff]
I.R., J.R.	Infanterie-Regiment [Infantry Regiment]
I.R. "Gr.D."	Infanterie-Regiment "Grossdeutschland" [Infantry Regiment "Greater Germany"]
IKRK	Internationales Komitee vom Roten Kreuz [International Committee of the Red Cross]
IMT	Internationales Militärtribunal (Nürnberger Prozesse) [International Military Tribunal (Nuremberg Trials)]
Inf.	Infanterie [Infantry]
K-Organisation	Kriegsorganisation [War Organization]
Kdr.	Kommandeur [Commander]
Komp., Kp.	Kompanie [Company]
KTB	Kriegstagebuch [War Diary]
Kw.	Kraftwagen [Car]
Kw. Tr., Trsp., Rgt.	Kraftwagentransportregiment [Motorized Transport Regiment]
lei., l.	leicht [light]
Lt.	Leutnant [Lieutenant]
M.G.	Maschinengewehr [Machine Gun]
M.G.Btl.	Maschinengewehr-Bataillon [Machine Gun Battalion]
M.G. Kp.	Maschinengewehr-Kompanie [Machine Gun Company]
Mdl.	mündlich [oral]
MF	Mikrofilm [Microfilm]
Mil. Befh.	Militärbefehlshaber [Military Commander]
Mob.	Mobilmachung [Mobilization]
mot.	motorisiert [motorized]
NA	National Archives, Washington D.C.
NSDAP	Nationalsozialistische Deutsche Arbeiter Partei [National Socialist German Workers Party]
NL	Nachlass [Papers]
NZZ	Neue Zürcher Zeitung
o.D.	ohne Datum [without date]
OB	Oberbefehlshaber [Supreme Commander]
ObdH.	Oberbefehlshaber des Heeres [Supreme Commander of the Army]
Oberstlt.	Oberstleutnant [Lieutenant-Colonel]

OKH	Oberkommando des Heeres [Supreme Command of the Army]
OKW	Oberkommando der Wehrmacht [Supreme Command of the Armed Forces]
Op.	Operation [Tactical Military Movement]
Op.Abt.	Operationsabteilung [Section of Tactical Military Movements]
Oqu.	Oberquartiermeister [Chief Quartermaster]
Org.	Organisation
OSS	Office of Strategic Services
PAB	Politisches Archiv des Auswärtigen Amtes Bonn [Political Archives of the Foreign Ministry, Bonn]
Pak	Panzerabwehrkanone [Antitank gun]
Pi.	Pioniere [Engineers, Sappers]
Pi.Btl.	Pionier-Bataillon [Sapper Battalion]
Pol. I. M.	Politische Abteilung I-Militär des AA [Political Section I-Military of the AA]
Pz.	Panzer [Tank]
Pz. Gr.	Panzergruppe [Tank Group]
Pz. Jäg.	Panzerjäger [Tank Hunters]
Pz. Jäg. Abt.	Panzerjägerabteilung [Tank Hunters Division]
Pz. Sp. Wg.	Panzerspähwagen [Armored Scout Car]
Qu.	Quartiermeister [Quartermaster]
RAM	Reichsaussenminister [Foreign Minister of the Reich]
Rgt.	Regiment
RLM	Reichsluftfahrministerium [Aviation Ministry of the Reich]
RWM	Reichswirtschaftsministerium [Reich's Ministry of Commerce]
SD	Sicherheitsdienst [Secret Service]
SdST	Sonderstab [Special staff]
sFH	schwere Feldhaubitze [Heavy field howitzer]
SS	Schutzstaffel der NSDAP [Protective Formation of the NSDAP]
SS "A.H."	Leibstandarte SS "Adolf Hitler" [Bodyguard SS "Adolf Hitler"]
SS "T"	SS-Panzerdivision "Totenkopf" [SS Tank Division "Skull"]
St.S.	Staatssekretär [Secretary of State]
U.St.S.	Understaatssekretär [Undersecretary of State]

V.L.R.	Vortragender Legationsrat [Presenting Legation Counselor]
verst.	verstärkt [reinforced]
W	Wehrmacht [Armed Forces]
WFA	Wehrmachtführungsamt im OKW [Armed Forces Command Office in the OKW]
WFST	Wehrmachtführungsstab im OKW (ab August 1940) [Armed Forces Command Staff in the OKW (as of August 1940)]
Wi	Abteilung Wehrwirtschaft im Wehrwirtschafts- und Rüstungsamt im OKW [Section Economic Defense in the Office of Economic Defense and Armament in the OKW]
WiRüAmt	Wehrwirtschafts- und Rüstungsamt im OKW [Office of Economic Defense and Armament in the OKW]
Wwi	Wehrwirtschaftliche Abteilung im Wehrwirtschaftsamt, OKW [Section of Economic Defense in the Office of Economic Defense in the OKW]
z.b.V.	zur besonderen Verwendung [for special use]
z.Zt.	zur Zeit [at present]
Ia	Erster Generalstabsoffizier der Führungsabteilung [First Officer of the General Staff of the Command Division]
Ic	Dritter Generalstabsoffizier (Feindaufklärung) [Third Officer of the General Staff (Enemy reconnaissance)]

Part I

HITLER'S PLANS AGAINST SWITZERLAND: SUMMER 1940

Chapter One

Overlooked German Plans for Invading Switzerland

The armistice with France of June 25, 1940, took effect under traumatic circumstances. Within only six weeks continental Europe had become totally dependent on the Axis powers: The Netherlands, Luxembourg, and Belgium were occupied by the Germans; France was conquered and would in the future be divided into two zones, the British had fled back across the Channel; and Switzerland was almost fully encircled by the Axis powers. Even those who drew hope from Great Britain's unshakable will to survive had to concede that this new power structure would continue for some time to come.

The Swiss defense arrangements had also collapsed. Because of multiple misjudgments the Swiss army command and its defense strategy suffered a disaster without even having been tested, the catastrophic effect of which can barely be overestimated. Instead of French Army Group 3, from which General Guisan, based on his secret agreements, had expected protection of the western flank and direct support in case of a German attack, Guderian's dangerous tank group and soon also other German fighting units were stationed at the Jura border as of June 16–17.

As an added strain, the last units of the French forces which had been expected to offer assistance had instead to be interned in Switzerland under unfavorable conditions. Between June 16 and 21, nearly 43,000 soldiers and about 7,500 civilians sought refuge; the troops of the 45th Army Corps under General Daille alone, which crossed over with full equipment in the night of June 19-20, consisted of 29,700 French and Algerian soldiers and 12,500 Poles.[1] Now that Italy had also joined the war on June 11 to satisfy its territorial ambitions, there was a potential threat of incalculable proportions from all sides.

How the Swiss Army had let itself be led astray in preparation for the Western offensive ("Fall Gelb") has been discussed in detail by Christian

3

Vetsch.[2] In May 1940, contrary to the assumptions at that time, there was no danger of attack; in retrospect the troop movements observed in the area of southern Germany turned out merely to have been successful deceptive maneuvers which misled the French supreme command to make faulty deployments of their troops.

Given the totally changed and extremely precarious conditions after the middle of June 1940, the possibility of acute danger for Switzerland in the days before the armistice must be reexamined. The Swiss Army, overtaken by the course of the war, was then still oriented mainly towards the north by its completed defensive positions, whereas the border regions with France were insufficiently fortified and only sparsely occupied despite the meager shifts of troops.[3] All signs indicate that a continued sudden German advance towards the Swiss flank in the west and southwest, now deprived of French protection, would have reached its goal in a very short time.

On June 25 Pilet-Golaz, then president of the Swiss Confederation, made a controversial address which was supposed to provide orientation to the shocked people, but was instead itself an expression of deep insecurity. History also connects that date, however, with an event then kept strictly secret: the completion by the German army's general staff of the first draft of a plan of attack on Switzerland in the series of the so-called "Tannenbaum" plans. This sketch of attack served throughout July as the current plan; it was revised on August 8 and 12 and adapted to ongoing changes. Until October further drafts were elaborated on various staff levels.

The German plans of operation against Switzerland have been studied repeatedly, particularly by military historians. The pioneering work was that of Hans Rudolf Kurz, supplemented in 1973 by Alfred Ernst, while Werner Roesch presented in his 1986 dissertation *Bedrohte Schweiz* the most thorough evaluation to date of the relevant "Tannenbaum" documents.[4] It focuses mainly on the studies of attack elaborated between August and October which for military strategists were far more comprehensive and revealing than the earliest draft, which consisted of only five pages. The Swiss capability to resist was judged to be stronger in these scenarios. Today the code name "Operation Tannenbaum" is used generally for all plans of that time, although this designation did not appear before September 1940 in conjunction with a draft from within Army Group C.

Since it has been impossible until now to clarify what prompted the preparation of these invasion plans, the first draft with the title: "1. Vortragsnotiz über Angriff gegen die Schweiz [First Presentation-sketch Concerning an Attack on Switzerland]" is of particular interest in this context. The coincidence is more than just obvious: On the very day on which the armistice became effective, the Operational Division I of the Army's General Staff apparently had nothing more urgent to do than to prepare a rough draft for an attack on Switzerland! Is this, as Werner Roesch assumes, truly a mere coincidence without further meaning? The sketch of attack does not indicate when and by whom it was ordered. It simply reads: "A short study should be made of the possibilities of a surprise occupation of Switzerland by German troops from France and Germany with the assumption that Italian troops will simultaneously attack Switzerland from the south."[5]

Thus the order requested a short and thus also quickly presentable basic exploration which could be enlarged as events required. The draft presented by Captain von Menges—for its operative assumptions one may consult Kurz and Roesch[6]—presents a number of facts which permit a first set of conclusions: By means of a "surprising rapid invasion from several directions" the "enemy" army was to be crushed to such an extent that continued resistance and an orderly retreat to the Alpine region would be rendered impossible. A second goal was the rapid occupation of the capital as well as the center of the armament industry around Solothurn for "political and moral reasons." Finally seizure of the most important and intact train and road junctions should be achieved, "to make the country usable as soon as possible as a region of transit for all transports to southern France." This last aim has special importance because it shows particularly well how the integration of this plan of attack fits into the conduct of the war at that time. It is not the Gotthard connection with the Axis partner Italy which is emphasized, but rather Switzerland as a "region of transit" for the continuation of the war up to the complete occupation of southern France.

Franz Halder, chief of the General Staff of the Army, within whose area of competence the study of attack was prepared, had already expressed a desire a week earlier to use Switzerland as a transit country. On June 16—just when the tank troops of Guderian were occupying Besançon—Halder asked the Foreign Ministry to demand "that through diplomatic channels immediate permission should be obtained from the Swiss Government that sealed military trains would be allowed to travel through Switzerland, that is from Germany in the direction of Besançon."[7]

Allegedly, it was not troops but army supplies and food with the required escort personnel that would be transported through neutral Swiss territory. However, Ernst von Weizsäcker, the undersecretary of state in the Foreign Ministry, had reservations about presenting such a request in Bern and delayed the matter. The request to make the Swiss transport system available to the German armed forces was mentioned again as one of the three main goals in the attack sketch, though now as part of the continuation of the war in southern France.

The possible invasion of Switzerland thus bears a direct relationship to the alternative plans which were current before the armistice became effective on

June 25 at 1:35 a.m., German summer time. It must also be kept in mind that the armistice agreement between Germany and France signed on June 22 could still have failed up to the last minute because of Italian demands. Fighting continued until an agreement could also be reached in separate talks between Italy and France. The planned armistice would only take effect six hours after an Italian message about the successful conclusion of an agreement had been received. On June 24 the commander in chief of the army Walther von Brauchitsch took preventive steps in case the attack against the rear of the French alpine fortifications and in the direction of the Mediterranean coast would have to be continued. Within the framework of these plans—as is already evident from the attack sketches—the question of an occupation of Switzerland also grew in importance. However, the background information to these plans and thus the exact connections to the "Tannenbaum" documents is unknown.

Although the shock caused by the collapse of France at first had a strong effect on the Swiss people, there was at least hope in the conviction that after the conclusion of the German-French armistice negotiations the immediate danger for Switzerland would be past. As the excellent biography by Willi Gautschi demonstrates, General Guisan conferred on June 22 with his corps commanders; among other things, he was already worried about the coming partial demobilization and believed that the Germans would now "scarcely contemplate military action."[8] At no other time during World War II would a German-only surprise attack have had such disastrous effects as during these days of paralyzing insecurity and improvised transition.

The sketch of June 25 proves that the German general staff had clearly recognized the weaknesses of the Swiss defense plans. Zurich, Lucerne, and Bern were to be occupied by German troops no later than the second day. The Swiss people's will to resist was considered battered. There was even speculation about a "cold" annexation: "With the current political situation in Switzerland it is possible that it will accede peacefully to the ultimatum demands so that after a warlike border crossing a quick transition to a peaceful invasion may be assured."

Compared to later operational studies, only the smallest number of forces was deemed necessary during this most critical phase. Nine divisions divided into four army corps were planned for use under one supreme command. There are no detailed plans for Italian troops; it is stated only that the invasion of the corner around Chur-Davos would be left to them "for reasons of terrain." Both Alberto Rovighi and Hans Senn have shown that the plans directed against Switzerland by the Italian general staff were intensified after June 1940.[9]

It is remarkable that Swiss military historians in particular adopted the overly optimistic view that the German operational plans were connected neither to an acute threat nor to the involvement of Hitler himself. In 1951 and 1957 Hans Rudolf Kurz claimed that "Operation Tannenbaum" as well as another draft by the leadership staff of the armed forces were "purely studies of the type that the general staffs of large armies are in the habit of composing—and if only for the operational training of their general staff officers."[10]

In 1973 he further elaborated on this evaluation in his "Operationsplanung Schweiz": In May and June "when there was no imminent danger for us," Switzerland was militarily fully prepared while during the mid-summer and fall of 1940, when "Case Switzerland" was discussed by the Germans, Switzerland had entered a dangerous time of weakness.[11] Alfred Ernst intimates that according to a written statement of General Warlimont made on April 27, 1972, it was possible that Hitler had given orders for the attack study, but this track was subsequently not pursued further.[12]

In 1986 Werner Roesch essentially repeated the conclusions offered by Kurz and Ernst. He refers to Hitler's striving for hegemony and to his strengthened position with the generals and comments: "This situation may have led the operational division of the supreme command of the army to contemplate also the planning of such an action." It is scarcely possible to formulate the plan's historical origin more vaguely. Although Roesch wants to take the "Tannenbaum" plans "as preparations one has to take seriously for an eventual 'Action Switzerland,'" he was unable to find any direct or indirect influence of Hitler in his sources.[13]

Walter Schaufelberger recapitulated in November 1989 the overall evaluation of the German operational drafts from the point of view of military history: "They were certainly no longer sandbox-exercises by members of the general staff looking for something to do. However, they could have been activities by overly eager military command posts without the involvement of the political leadership."[14]

In view of these opinions, it should not be surprising that military aspects lost importance in attempts to explain why Switzerland survived World War II territorially undamaged, while aspects that had been much neglected for too long gained in significance. Today, economic factors, particularly the supply of arms, financial and gold transactions, and also transit traffic, are assigned decisive importance.

Some argue that the services rendered by Switzerland were so profitable for the Axis powers that an attack on Switzerland was not necessary; a division of the country would only have caused additional problems for Germany and Italy. Also cited are factors such as the usefulness of Switzerland for foreign intelligence services, humanitarian aid (ICRC) and, depending on location, the military and moral defense, the "Réduit," the stalling tactics of Pilet-Golaz in foreign policy, and still other aspects.

Before the vote on the initiative to abolish the army held on November 24–25, 1989, the various degrees of significance assigned to these "factors of salvation" provoked lively disputes between historians and journalists in Switzerland. Where the only goal was to produce arguments for or against retaining the army in the future, this *Historikerstreit* is already itself history. However, is it possible to accept those evaluations concerning the threatening situation of 1940 which have become dominant in current historical interpretations of divergent ideological origin? Are they not, despite all their differences in interpretation, based on an overestimation of the importance which is assigned to the posture Switzerland then assumed?

It makes little sense, for example, to try to document the high fighting strength of Swiss soldiers by means of German assessments from the time of the Third Reich. Although there is no lack of attestations of respect from the ranks of the German armed forces, what finally counts is the conclusion summarized as follows in the revised study of attack, dated August 12, 1940: "We can occupy the part of Switzerland assigned to us within about 3–4 days (if the demarcation line runs across the Bernese and Glarus Alps), otherwise within 4–5 days."[15] If it proved impossible to cut off the retreat of the Swiss army to its alpine positions, it would become difficult to calculate the time required: "It depends on the success of the surprise and on the unpredictable course of fighting in the mountainous terrain."[16] This remark in the "Operational Draft Switzerland (Tannenbaum)" of October 4, 1940, also makes it clear that from the viewpoint of the attacker the greatest risk was related to the "Réduit," which at that time was still being constructed.

To do without its own army and to rely on collaboration was not an option for the Swiss people during World War II. The various factors which were important for the survival of Switzerland carried different degrees of significance depending on the time of the war and the military situation. What remained constant was Hitler's evil mentality. To him, Switzerland and Sweden remained two "kleine Dreckstaaten," two small "muck-states," with no right to independent existence, even though he recognized their temporary usefulness for the German war economy. Thus to absolutize or minimize to irrelevance particular factors which allowed the survival of Switzerland becomes a futile undertaking.

Such a process of elimination, however, underlies the theories of the historian Jakob Tanner which imply that General Guisan's service consisted in "having withdrawn the army as a risk factor in domestic and thus also foreign policy just in time and in such a manner that it could not be misinterpreted abroad as an open display of readiness to capitulate." The retreat to the "Réduit" thus becomes a "brilliant chess move" which reduced the army to a myth.[17] "Historical research," according to this 1989 interpretation, "has shown in the meantime that the retreat into the mountains was logical from an economic point of view. The strategy of the concentration of strength, the largely unprotected surrender of the most important demographic agglomerations and industrial centers in the *Mittelland* [the Swiss lowlands] enabled the Swiss industrial and banking establishments to optimize the external trade relationships with the Axis countries."[18] This exaggerated counterposition which declares the army a risk and claims collaboration as the decisive factor in preserving Switzerland's security severely underestimates the danger of the National Socialist regime with its totalitarian strategies of demand and suppression.

Models based on a cost/benefit calculation assume that the protagonists of the Third Reich were rationally calculating people. The defenders of a Swiss policy of accommodation during the war years had already based their assumption on the fateful error that Hitler's intentions concerning Switzerland could be tempered by good behavior. It would be a paradoxical misinterpretation to assign success in hindsight to this policy of supposed collaboration as though it had been the primary factor responsible for the survival of Switzerland rather than the external factors deriving from the general progress of the war.

The 1985 dissertation of Jürg Fink, titled "Die Schweiz aus der Sicht des Dritten Reiches 1933–1945 [Switzerland from the Perspective of the Third Reich 1933–1945]," has contributed considerably to the erroneous assessment of Hitler's plans.[19] Unfortunately this topically important work limits itself despite many merits to an enumeration of individual statements of well known National Socialists regarding Switzerland. Fink's interspersed comments often do not go beyond what this or that comment might have meant. As Hitler's remarks are analyzed only as separate comments rather than within the context of his monstrous, all too well known ideas already, Fink reaches an ambivalent conclusion.

Thus grave misjudgments endure to the present time because of Fink's improper handling of a key quotation. Subsequently his "discovery" became the principal proof that Hitler did not threaten the existence of Switzerland, but rather protected it because he promised himself a greater benefit from keeping the country intact. Thus during the decisive summer of 1940 Hitler is said to have firmly prohibited any invasion. For this assertion, Fink refers to the following note by Henry Picker who temporarily recorded the table conversations with Hitler at his Führer-Headquarters (FHQ):

> When the German tank corps of General Guderian reached the Swiss border near Pontarlier on June 17, 1940, Hitler emphatically prohibited any invasion of Switzerland. He told us at the FHQ concerning the problem of Switzerland that this country was

incomparably more useful as a protectorate and as international junction for diplomatic activities, espionage, financial transactions, and the delivery of goods in short
supply (e.g., war materials and raw materials for war purposes) than as a satellite.[20]

"The meaning of this note by Picker cannot be underestimated for our investigation," Fink comments, without noticing that his main witness was neither on June 17, 1940, nor on any other day at the Führer-Headquarters near
the Belgian-French border. Rather it would be almost two years until Picker
would listen to Hitler's table conversations on March 21, 1942, at the FHQ
"Wolfsschanze" in East Prussia under quite different circumstances!

In any event, the earliest recording of Hitler's table conversations began
only on July 5, 1941, and were made by Heinrich Heim. Picker served as his
replacement from March 21 to July 31, 1942, at the FHQ. Werner Jochmann
has already pointed out the errors, particularly in Picker's personally revised
edition of 1976, which Fink also used.[21] In this edition, Picker inserted his
own italicized comments and additions, written many years after the war, into
the midst of the recorded text.

In this instance Picker mixed pieces of arguments that appeared in 1942 but
could also have been read into the record after the war or could have been received in some other way, in such a manner that leaves the impression that all
of it was Hitler's original statement made on June 17, 1940! In fact, Picker
inserted his attempted explanation, which he had cobbled together from individual elements for his 1976 edition, as commentary to the conversation notes
of July 5, 1942. A comparison with the 1951 edition by the Freiburg historian
Gerhard Ritter confirms that such an insert in "Hitler's Table Conversations"
did not exist.

A simple analysis of the content discloses that the given statements could
not have been made at that time. "The world will be redistributed and those
who don't take part will be shortchanged"; thus is reflected the then prevail-
ing euphoria of victory on June 16, 1940, in Goebbels' diary. Hitler, however,
was supposed to have worried at that moment about financial transactions,
about the delivery of unavailable Swiss goods and armaments for which Germany had shown no interest until that May. The author of an authoritative
monograph should not have missed the fact that this "petty stuff" could not
have been of any importance during those weeks when Hitler had acquired
enormous additional resources and was waiting only for the acquiescence of
England to realize his plans for world domination.

In addition, Fink leaves out the first half of Picker's remarks: "An important reason that General Henri Guisan, the Swiss commander in chief from
1939 to 1945, kept Switzerland out of World War II was the fact that he made
the country militarily strong, like a porcupine. To conquer it would have cost
any attacker valuable divisions, tanks and planes without reaping a commen-

surate value."[22] This part of Picker's retrospective wisdom apparently did not fit into Fink's concept.

Another piece of evidence which supposedly confirms Picker's remarks proves to be a false assumption. On June 17, 1940, Guderian's tank troops did not turn northeast after reaching the Jura border because Hitler—as Fink suggests—was interested in sparing Switzerland, but because the purpose of this pincer operation was to enclose the considerable French forces in Alsace-Lorraine in cooperation with the 7th Army. It is said that Guderian captured 150,000 prisoners with this advance alone.[23]

In the publication by Markus Heiniger "Dreizehn Gründe warum die Schweiz im Zweiten Weltkrieg nicht erobert wurde [Thirteen Reasons Why Switzerland Was Not Conquered during World War II]" (Zurich 1989), the ominous citation by Picker is even used on the back cover. In the euphoria of victory of June 1940, according to Heiniger, "the Führer decided expressly against a violation of Swiss territory. He prefers an undamaged Switzerland which would produce for him."[24] Heiniger has indeed spectacularly displayed this alleged citation by Hitler, but he is not alone in its unverified adoption; the constant repetition has had its effect on the public.

Thus it is no coincidence that so far no evidence exists that proves a special interest by Hitler in the Swiss economy during 1940. Until the attack in the West, the Third Reich had shown itself—with some exceptions—remarkably disinterested in acquiring Swiss war material. At that time the Swiss export capacity for armaments was almost fully exploited by the Allies for their own needs. This was impressively demonstrated by the numbers published by Robert U. Vogler concerning the War Department: By March 20, 1940, France and Great Britain had placed orders for Swiss war material of about 264 million francs; the corresponding orders from Germany were 149,504 francs.[25] That Switzerland after the defeat of France had to reorder its war-related exports was an obvious consequence of the Axis Powers' policy of counterblockade which became effective by the encirclement of the Swiss Confederation. A basis for the forced commitment of the Swiss economic and financial potential in favor of the German war economy was established by the agreement of August 9, 1940. Only in November 1940 did Germany approach the Swiss government with new credit requests; tough negotiations ensued regarding the contrary positions of the two sides which, after a provisional agreement, lasted until mid-July 1941. When the German war economy became overtaxed due to the conduct of war on several fronts, the interests of the Third Reich with regard to Switzerland changed considerably. An all-too-static evaluation which projects subsequent developments back to the summer of 1940 is bound to lead to an exaggerated assessment of the importance which the German leadership then accorded to this small country.[26]

In June and July 1940 Germany had other priorities. At that time the German leadership assumed that after the acquiescence or elimination of England, Switzerland would anyhow lose its importance. According to Article 15 of the German-French armistice agreement of June 22, 1940, it was even expected that Germany would become less dependent on the Gotthard transit route. The article states that "the French government assumes the obligation to execute the transit traffic of goods between the German Reich and Italy which runs through the unoccupied areas at the volume demanded by the German government."[27] The German hopes attached to this regulation were, however, not fulfilled; but for the time being the importance of the Gotthard for transit traffic was temporarily diminished as a dissuasive factor during the summer of 1940.

In addition, the multiple services rendered by Switzerland as financial center to Germany in 1940 led Walter Funk, the economics minister of the Reich, merely to state that in the case of an eventual involvement of Switzerland in the war, the headquarters of the Bank for International Exchange (Basel), that is "the BIZ itself should be specially protected and shielded." His hesitant approach to Ernst von Weizsäcker, undersecretary of state of the Foreign Ministry, disappeared in the form of a note in the dossiers of subordinate offices. To oppose Hitler was then as far from Funk, who was also President of the Reichsbank, as was his "Führer's" interest in Switzerland as a financial center.[28]

The critical analysis of familiar interpretations offered here regarding the situation in the summer of 1940 shows that individual insights have not yet been convincingly harmonized in this complex puzzle. Important details are missing; occurrences within the German leadership remain particularly obscure. The background for the plans of attack cannot be traced from military sources alone. I have already indicated that in my opinion the first attack sketch of June 25 shows that the situation of danger for Switzerland had intensified significantly before the conclusion of the armistice. Can such a development actually be detected? To track it down requires an expanded basis of inquiry which, as will be seen, leads to surprising results.

NOTES

1. Jürg Stadelmann, "Juni 1940: 50,000 Flüchtlinge kamen in die Schweiz," *Basler Zeitung,* 19 June 1990; *Neue Zürcher Zeitung* [hereafter cited as NZZ], 16–17 June 1990, 23–24; Willi Gautschi, *Henri Guisan. Die schweizerische Armeeführung im Zweiten Weltkrieg,* 3rd edition (Zurich: Verlag Neue Zürcher Zeitung, 1989), 196ff.
2. Christian Vetsch, *Aufmarsch gegen die Schweiz. Der deutsche "Fall Gelb"– Irreführung der Schweizer Armee 1939/40.* Olten: Walter Verlag, 1973.

3. See the corresponding assessment of Hans Senn, "Schweizerische Dissuasion-sstrategie im Zweiten Weltkrieg," in *Schwedische und schweizerische Neutralität im Zweiten Weltkrieg,* ed. Rudolf L. Bindschedler et al. (Basel: Helbing & Lichtenhahn, 1985), 202–3: "The army's north-east position at the river Limmat in any case had no rationale. Although it had been extended westward, there were no fortifications ready in the area and the wide arc of defense which now encompassed the whole [Swiss] *Mittelland* was too large in order to wage war credibly with the available means."

4. Werner Roesch, *Bedrohte Schweiz. Die deutschen Operationsplanungen gegen die Schweiz im Sommer/Herbst 1940 und die Abwehrbereitschaft der Armee im Oktober 1940.* Dissertation Universität Zurich; (Frauenfeld: Verlag Huber, 1986). Hans Rudolf Kurz, *Operationsplanung Schweiz. Die Rolle der Schweizer Armee in zwei Weltkriegen;* (Thun: Ott Verlag, 1974.) Alfred Ernst, "Die Bereitschaft und Abwehrkraft Norwegens, Dänemarks und der Schweiz in deutscher Sicht," in *Neutrale Kleinstaaten im Zweiten Weltkrieg.* Schriften der Schweizerischen Vereinigung für Militärgeschichte und Militärwissenschaften, Heft 1 (Münsingen: Buchverlag Tages-Nachrichten, 1973), 7–73.

5. "1. Vortragsnotiz über Angriff gegen die Schweiz," Generalstab der Armee, Operations-Abteilung (I), 25. Juni, 1940, gez. v. Menges, in BA-MA, RH 2/465 Schweiz, Band A oder Mikrofilm NA T 78, Roll 649, 2097/376-80. To reduce the notes, the exact identification of the folders of the microfilms in the National Archives in Washington, DC (NA) and of the corresponding identifications in the Bundesarchiv-Militärarchiv in Freiburg i. Breisgau (BA-MA) have been added below in the "List of Sources" which also identifies those documents which I have examined in the original in Freiburg i. Breisgau. This will ease the finding of materials in the BA-MA and also of the corresponding microfilms in the NA which are available also in the Archiv für Zeitgeschichte at the ETH [Federal Institute of Technology] in Zurich. Also in the BA-MA many folders that have been damaged by fire contain only photocopies.

6. Roesch, *Bedrohte Schweiz,* 11ff; Kurz, *Operationsplanung,* 36ff.

7. Aufzeichnung, Berlin, 16. Juni 1940, signed Kramarz in: AA, Büro des Staatssekretärs, Schweiz, Bd. 1, 14 May–30 June 1941; microfilm NA T 129, roll 177, 86167.

8. Gautschi, *Guisan,* 203, 216.

9. Alberto Rovighi, *Un secolo di relazioni militari tra Italia e Svizzera 1861-1961.* Roma: Ufficio Storico, Stato Maggiore dell' Esercito, 1987; Hans Senn, "Die Haltung Italiens zum 'Fall Schweiz' im Jahr 1940," in NZZ, 14–15 June, 1988, 25.

10. Hans Rudolf Kurz, *Die Schweiz in der Planung der kriegführenden Mächte während des Zweiten Weltkrieges* (Biel: Schweizerischer Unteroffiziersverband, 1957), 41.

11. Kurz, *Operationsplanung Schweiz,* 34.

12. Ernst, "Bereitschaft," in *Neutrale Kleinstaaten,* 62.

13. Roesch, *Bedrohte Schweiz,* 75–76.

14. Walter Schaufelberger, "Militärische Bedrohung der Schweiz 1939/40," in *Kriegsmobilmachung 1939. Eine wissenschaftlich-kritische Analyse aus Anlass der 50. Wiederkehr des Mobilmachungstages von 1939.* Ed. Roland Beck i. A. der Abteilung für Militärwissenschaften der ETH (Zürich: 1989), 42; also "Die militärische Bedrohung der Schweiz im Zweiten Weltkrieg," in NZZ, 14 November, 1989, 23. The military historian of Zurich offers there for the first time hints which point in a totally different direction than the differentiated summary of previous insights: "Yet there could also have been initiatives of overly zealous staff and commando personnel without an existing serious cause for them."

15. "Der deutsche Angriff gegen die Schweiz, Neufassung infolge neuer Nachrichten über die Schweiz," Teil I, Genst. d. H., Op. Abt. (I), 12 August, 1940, signed von Menges, in Schweiz, Bd. A (Entwürfe, Lageberichte), BA-MA, RH 2/465.

16. "Operationsentwurf Schweiz (Tannenbaum)," H. Gr. C. Ia, 4 October 1940, in "Schweiz," Bd. B, Op. Entwurf H. Gr. C "Tannenbaum," BA-MA, RH 2/465.

17. Jakob Tanner, "Der Gotthardgranit," *Wochenzeitung*, 1 September 1989.

18. Jakob Tanner, "Kriegswirtschaft-Hand in Hand mit den Nazis," *Bilanz*, no. 10, 1989, 346–52; quotation, 348.

19. Jürg Fink, *Die Schweiz aus der Sicht des Dritten Reiches 1933–1945. Einschätzung und Beurteilung der Schweiz durch die deutsche oberste Führung seit der Machtergreifung Hitlers.* (Zurich: Schulthess Polygraphischer Verlag, 1985).

20. Fink, *Schweiz,* 24; Henry Picker, *Hitlers Tischgespräche im Führerhauptquartier,* 3rd expanded edition (Stuttgart: Athenäum-Verlag, 1976), 420.

21. Werner Jochmann, ed., *Adolf Hitler Monologe im Führer-Hauptquartier, 1941–1944. Die Aufzeichnungen Heinrich Heims* (Hamburg: Albrecht Knaus, 1980).

22. Picker, *Tischgespräche*, 42.

23. Heinz Guderian, *Erinnerungen eines Soldaten*, 11. Auflage (Stuttgart: Motorbuch Verlag, 1979), 118ff.

24. Markus Heiniger, *Dreizehn Gründe warum die Schweiz im Zweiten Weltkrieg nicht erobert wurde* (Zürich: Limmat Verlag, 1989), 42.

25. Robert Urs Vogler, *Die Wirtschaftsverhandlungen zwischen der Schweiz und Deutschland 1940 und 1941*, Dissertation (Zurich: 1983), 51–52; Klaus Urner, "Neutralität und Wirtschaftskrieg: Zur schweizerischen Aussenhandelspolitik 1939–1945," in *Schwedische und schweizerische Neutralität*, 269ff.

26. Also the argument proves untenable that the June 22, 1940, assignment of Reichswirtschaftsminister (Economics Minister) Funk to oversee the organization of the pan-European economy was Hitler's indirect approval of the preservation of Switzerland. With this assignment Hermann Göring intended, as Andreas Hillgruber among others has shown, a safeguarding of his own power base and resulted from the rivalry between the "Four-Year-Plan" and the Office of External Affairs as to the authority to oversee the economic exploitation of the "New Europe." Even four weeks later Funk's greatest problem as to planning consisted in the fact "that the goals and decisions of the 'Führer' were still unknown." Note concerning the "Chefbesprechung" held in the Reichswirtschaftsministerium (Reich Economy Ministry) on 22 July 1940; quotation from Andreas Hillgruber, *Hitlers Strategie. Politik und Kriegsführung 1940–1941* (Frankfurt a. M.: Bernard & Graefe Verlag für Wehrwesen, 1965), 74.

27. Hermann Böhme, *Entstehung und Grundlagen des Waffenstillstandes von 1940* (Stuttgart: Deutsche Verlags-Anstalt, 1966), 366.

28. "Aufzeichnung," St.-S. no. 381, Berlin 24 May, 1940, signed Weizsäcker. Microfilm T-120/ Roll 177, 86112. As to Funk's lacking independent standing and his dependence on Hitler and Göring see Willi A. Boelcke, *Die deutsche Wirtschaft 1930–1945* (Düsseldorf: Interna des Reichsministeriums, 1983), 185ff.; as to the advantage BIZ represented for the *Reichsbank* see Gian Trepp, "BIZ im Zweiten Weltkrieg: Internationaler Arm der Reichsbank," *Basler Zeitung*, 9 June 1990.

Chapter Two

German Hostility toward the Swiss

The attempt to view the question of a possible occupation of Switzerland from the perspective of "below" provides dark insights into the general mood. Secret reports of the security and intelligence service of the SS, published in full by Heinz Boberach in 1984, reveal that the reluctance to "settle accounts" with Switzerland had diminished among the German people, who were enthusiastic about the swift success of the war. Tensions between Germany and Switzerland, primarily in southwest Germany, had already intensified before the start of the war. The hostile atmosphere there was heightened after the general mobilization in Switzerland as well as by travelers' reports about "mean insults and demonstrations" in Zurich against Germany that followed its attacks on Holland and Belgium: "Within the population it is believed that Germany cannot permit the provocative attitude of Switzerland to continue and that this will automatically lead to a settlement of accounts."[1]

At that time, uncertainty about the course of the war in the west still imposed a certain amount of restraint. The German troop movements in the direction of the Swiss borders had provoked numerous rumors in southern and southwestern Germany. In contrast to the alarmed reaction in Switzerland, the worry there concerned speculations regarding a possible French relief offensive towards southwestern Germany through neutral Swiss territory. According to one rumor, the Swiss army had moved the bulk of its troops from the German to the French border.[2]

After the capitulation of Belgium on May 28 and the victory messages from northern France, the enthusiasm of those segments of the German population supporting the regime scarcely knew any limits. All over the Reich those groups considered an accommodation by Switzerland as unavoidable or even demanded a solution by force within the framework of the current reordering

15

of Europe. The SD-report [Sicherheitsdienst, i. e., the Security and Intelligence
Service of the SS] of June 24, 1940, documents this mood as follows:

> The belief still prevails that within this reorganization Switzerland too had to be
> "cashed in" (Munich). The "cheese-state," heavily incriminated by its attitude to-
> wards Germany, should also dissappear (Chemnitz). Common people as well as ac-
> ademic circles have "the impression" "that at the end of the current armed conflict
> all the small countries of Europe would disappear" (Cologne).[3]

Thus no further propagandistic justification would have been necessary for
a "takeover" of Switzerland. This "general interest" in Switzerland continued
until the days after the armistice took effect, as the SD reported on June 27:

> One cannot forgive that this State has become the catch-all for all the unruly ele-
> ments, that from there the most intense hate campaign has been waged against Ger-
> many. The demand repeatedly surfaces that "Switzerland has yet to be swallowed,"
> that "Switzerland may not be overlooked in the reorganization of Europe."[4]

Such an aggressive state of emotions against Switzerland in the second half
of June provided the best precondition to popularize among a people used to
winning the idea to eliminate this small country. The secret "reports from the
Reich" were to provide an unvarnished picture of public opinion—the purpose pursued by those who had ordered them.

The direction the mood at the bottom was taking reflected also the attitude
of those in power who shaped public opinion with their enormous propaganda
machine. As the diary of the German Propaganda Minister Joseph Goebbels
reveals, he had already vigorously heated up emotions against Switzerland.
"Our press," he wrote on February 24, "mightily hits the rotten neutrality of
Switzerland. This is good."[5] He was constantly angry about the "nasty"
voices of the Swiss press. "Now it is necessary to intensify the pressure on
the Swiss," reads the even more determined entry of March 17. Barely two
weeks later follows another attack against "hypocritical" Swiss neutrality:
"Its mendacity is without precedent."[6]

After the attack on Denmark and Norway, when Goebbels considered the
Swiss press "once again super-nasty," unrestrained rage surfaced: "It is either
bought or Jewish. What should be done against it under these circumstances?"[7] If it was a part of psychological warfare to make the Swiss inse-
cure, these diary entries show undoubtedly that for Goebbels, a "settling of
accounts" was only a question of time.

After the leading National Socialist attorney Friedrich Grimm had informed him on May 17 about a "downright poison-spewing mood of hate
against us in Switzerland," Goebbels gave his feelings of revenge free rein:
"Their turn will come all too soon. Then these stunted hotel porters will

have their mouths stuffed."[8] The writer John Knittel won his sympathy in an interview of June 11, but at what a price: "Contemptuous of Switzerland which is his own homeland. It is too confining and small for him. Certainly bids on our victory."[9] As a small state, Switzerland had already been written off.

The above details merely reveal the increasingly emotional potential of aggression as well as the general mood. One may speak of actual danger only if concrete events and developments directed against Switzerland can be observed. In the end, Hitler's own intentions were decisive. There can be no illusion about the position Hitler's views had assigned to Switzerland in the pan-German world empire. This small federal state, a democratic nation based on consent and uniting language regions of varied historical vintage, diametrically contradicted the National Socialist ideology of a "Führerstaat" and its race theories.

However, from Hitler's point of view, the internal conditions of Switzerland were not decisive for its destiny. According to his intentions, quite independent of their internal affairs small states had come into existence due to the weakness of the Empire and should, after the reestablishment of its power, again become fully integrated into it. Goebbels formulated on April 13 how Hitler actually thought when the German invasion of Norway did not turn out as desired: "The Führer rails against the neutrals. The smaller, the nastier. They must not survive this war. They are what the splinter parties were in internal German decisions, they attempt to prevent every great solution, they can be bribed, behave cowardly, and are corrupt."[10]

What he meant by "great solution" Hitler had explained to his propaganda minister a few days earlier: "At the end of the [18]70s war stood the German Reich, at the end of this war will stand the Germanic Reich."[11] The victory over France made him already reach further and, after the attack on the Soviet Union, this "Germanic Reich" became merely a starting point. "Against the uncounted millions of the Eastern world," he stated on February 22, 1942, to a Danish volunteer of the Waffen-SS, the Germanic peoples in Europe must unite. "Once we have Europe firmly in hand, we will create our African continent and, who knows, some day we might find something further."[12] The fate of the Swiss nation, which according to Hitler was "nothing but a wayward branch of our people,"[13] was submerged within these vast dimensions of power-madness.

For the German dictator, then, it was primarily a question of finding the right time. Within the context of the attack against France, he did not think that it had arrived yet; even in May 1940 Switzerland was not on his program, as von Weizsäcker undoubtedly correctly observed. In June, however, because of dramatic developments, it had moved into the field of vision of

Hitler's expansionist policy; the first reference to this was given to me by General Walter Warlimont during an extensive interview in July 1968.[14]

As head of the Department of Defense [*Landesverteidigung*] of the High Command (OKW) [*Wehrmachtsführungsamt*], Warlimont had been a close collaborator of General Alfred Jodl in the High Command of the Armed Forces and occupied an important position in Hitler's war-planning-and-directing establishment. His views are of special interest because he belonged to the inner circle of the "Führer-Headquarters" (FHQ). At the FHQ "Wolfsschlucht," located at Brûly-de-Pesche in southern Belgium from June 6 to 28, 1940, his office was close to that of Hitler.[15]

Transit problems apparently first provoked Hitler. After England had blocked coal deliveries to Italy in March 1940, Germany had to secure almost the whole supply of coal for its Axis partner. Because Italy's entry into the war involved additional German supply obligations, Switzerland was presented with a demand for an enormous expansion of its transit capacity.[16] This could not be met easily as Switzerland had strained all its resources because of its own high degree of mobilization. The crisis which developed after the end of May in trade talks between Germany and Switzerland was only a side show; in Berlin an embargo of already scarce coal was threatened ever more openly.

Without going into detail what Warlimont either did not know or could not recall, merely the assertion that Hitler now began to realize how much he really depended on the Swiss transit routes for his war plans is significant. The Swiss, as guardians of the alpine passes, had already been in the way of his planned detour in Case "Braun," although it had not come to fruition.

During the discussion with Mussolini at the Brenner Pass on March 18 Hitler had proposed that some 20 Italian divisions should be moved to the Upper Rhine to proceed from there jointly along the Swiss border to the Rhône valley. Since troops could not pass through Switzerland, he estimated the time needed for transport at twenty to twenty-five days.[17] He thus became increasingly conscious of the disadvantages of not controlling the Swiss transit routes during the advances of German troops beyond Lyon.

Still more dramatically, the conflict regarding the Swiss and German clashes in the air escalated. On June 4 serious battles between twenty-nine German and twelve Swiss aircraft took place, after earlier violations of Swiss airspace already had led to friction. The history of these incidents has been described repeatedly, most thoroughly in Ernst Wetter's book *Duell der Flieger und der Diplomaten (Duel of Flyers and Diplomats);*[18] therefore the details and controversies these events involve need not be reexamined.

These incidents led to increasing agitation against Switzerland within the German leadership. After two German aircraft had been shot down on June 1 and the following day another was forced to make an emergency landing near Ursins, the highest ranks below Göring in the German air force became involved in the matter. General Hans Jeschonnek, chief of the general staff of the air force, requested on June 2 that the Foreign Ministry file a stern protest with the Swiss Federal Council. As Wetter's book shows, the German air force also wanted to teach a lesson to the Swiss pilots.

As can be learned from the files of Undersecretary of State von Weizsäcker regarding Switzerland, the Foreign Ministry received a message on the evening of June 4 about the air battles that had taken place that day. The message was deemed serious enough to warrant immediate transmission to the headquarters of Foreign Minister Joachim von Ribbentrop who stayed on a special train which was also used as war command post by Reichsführer SS Heinrich Himmler and Lammers, the chief of the Reich's chancellery.

The handling of the matter no longer remained in the hands of von Weizsäcker, but was dealt with by Ribbentrop. One example illustrates the drastic change of tone. Weizsäcker had concluded the now outdated draft for the protest note requested by General Jeschonnek with the statement that if the Federal Council would not comply with the request for an apology and restitution, "the German government would reserve the right to any further action." Based on the new incidents this text was now reworded and in the handwriting of Ribbentrop now ended curtly: "As for the rest, the government of the Reich reserves the right to any further action in order to prevent such acts of aggression."[19]

When on June 5 German Ambassador Köcher handed the note to the President of the Federal Council Pilet-Golaz, the latter remarked with deep concern: "If Germany intends something else with this note, please tell me, but of course, you can't give me an answer to this question." The same evening a report on the implementation of the requested demarche was to be given to Ribbentrop. Goebbels noted in his diary on June 7 that the neutral foreign countries "are eating out of our hands": "Only Switzerland remains incessantly nasty, has downed 2 of our planes, but we took care of 4 of theirs and, in addition, she also has received a sharp note."[20] Goebbels' spiteful glee, however, was based on an erroneous report, as despite of various amounts of damage only one Swiss plane had been shot down.

On June 8, when the Germans again provoked serious air battles between twenty-eight German and fifteen Swiss planes, the correspondents of the most important German papers in Geneva as well as the German News Office received orders to leave Switzerland or to travel to the Ticino. They had orchestrated their recall themselves with their publishers. Switzerland had become too dangerous for them![21]

The German losses must have greatly infuriated Göring, commander in chief of the air force, as Switzerland had received his permission even in 1939–1940 to acquire modern Messerschmitt aircraft. As an act of vengeance, ten saboteurs were sent to Switzerland who were to set off explosions at various airports on June 16 to 17. This act of revenge is directly attributable to Göring. The operation was to occur simultaneously with the arrival of German tank troops at the Jura border of Switzerland and would have caused a tremendous uproar.

The background of this sabotage mission "Adler" [*Eagle*], which was later to be known also as "Unternehmen Wartegau" [Operation *Wartegau*] has still not been fully explained. In the office of Admiral Canaris, where a group around Colonel Oster belonged to the resistance movement, the venture was put into action in such a sloppy manner as though the aim was to initiate an act of revenge ordered from higher up, but with the intent to ensure its failure. The group of saboteurs, assembled on June 6 and subsequently hastily instructed, consisted of two Swiss living abroad and eight Germans—adventurers and fanatics, who came in part from the so-called "Baulehrbataillon z.b.V. 800" in Brandenburg on the Havel, which was in reality a special group of the Intelligence Bureau, Department II.[22] Three of the saboteurs crossed the Swiss border at Martinsbruck while the larger group illegally reached Kreuzlingen with the aid of German customs agents during the night of June 12 to 13. Contrary to all rules of appropriate camouflage, the men had to wear identical, showy civilian clothes—knickerbockers which were also worn at an earlier time by the members of the "Condor Legion" going to fight in Spain. Thus, in different compartments of the train to Winterthur and Zurich were identically clad men with strange and dated shoes, provided with identical capes, berets, and parachutists' backpacks that among other items contained a packet of explosives with suspect labeling. They had all been given tickets which had expired the day before; when they tried to pay the difference to the conductor, none had the necessary change, but only new fifty and hundred franc notes.[23] All the saboteurs were arrested in time. The later statement by Minister Hans Frölicher that Admiral Canaris or Colonel Oster warned Switzerland in a suitable manner is confirmed by further details in the description by Karl Lüond.[24]

The fact that the sabotage action cannot be considered apart from Hitler's own anger about the Swiss air defenses attacking German planes is evident from the internal German assignment of responsibility for continued dealings with these conflicts. At first the command staff in the general staff of the air force dealt with the matter. At the Führer's headquarters it was Nicolaus von Below, as adjutant to Hitler for the air force, who had to keep Hitler informed about important air force matters when Göring and his Chief of the General

Staff Jeschonnek did not participate personally in situation reviews. The command staff of the air force forwarded its reports regarding important incidents first to the Führer's headquarters, so that it must be assumed that FHQ was at least as well informed about the losses caused by the Swiss air incidents as was the Foreign Ministry. The fact that Hitler decided to become involved personally demonstrates the dangerous development of this conflict from the German point of view. The staff of the air force command informed the Foreign Ministry on June 9 that the Führer had taken further measures in this matter into his own hands: "All material received by the air force command staff regarding air fights with Swiss pilots is to be forwarded immediately to the Führer. The Führer has ordered, among other things, the commanding general of the principally involved Air Corps 5 to appear for an oral report."[25]

Although much indicates that the sabotage plans resulted from Hitler's anger about the incident of June 2, it is certain that after the second air battle of June 8 the direct responsibility for further actions was now with the "Führer." There was no reason for either Göring or Ribbentrop to disregard Hitler's intervention in this matter; nor would it have made sense to withhold from him information about an act of sabotage the results and effects of which could not be calculated in advance. That the operation was initiated with Hitler's approval is implied in the instructions given to Canaris. It was possible to entice the admiral to initiate such an action against his will only if ordered to do so with the approval of General Keitel, the chief of the Supreme Command of the Armed Forces, who always took great care to act in accordance with Hitler's plans.

General Warlimont also confirmed that in his presence Hitler was repeatedly incensed about these air incidents. He was indignant that the Swiss fighter planes attacked without any advance warning and that they were directed totally one-sidedly against German aircraft which might have crossed the Swiss border on their flight to or from France. Nothing was known of similar behavior towards French planes.[26] It is not hard to imagine the tone of Hitler's outbursts about Switzerland and its neutrality.

On June 14 Hitler and Ribbentrop discussed further diplomatic steps regarding this conflict, yet no immediate action was taken. After the failure of this "lesson" became clear, the rude text of a verbal note was telephoned to Berlin on June 19 from Ribbentrop's special train. It ended with an undisguised threat directed at the Swiss Federal Council: "In addition, the government of the Reich informs the Swiss government herewith that, should there be a repetition of such incidents, written messages will be omitted and German interests asserted in other ways."[27]

The third, and for Switzerland most dangerous development now began, with Hitler himself standing as a driving force at its center. He no longer cared about the air incidents or other details, rather, he wanted to establish new fundamental conditions in relation to Switzerland on the basis of the exceptionally favorable state of the war. With joint action with Italy, the small country remaining in the center of the Axis powers was to be completely encircled and to be made pliable even without occupation.

NOTES

1. Heinz Boberach, ed., *Meldungen aus dem Reich. Die geheimen Lageberichte des Sicherheitsdienstes der SS 1938–1945*, vol. 4 (Herrsching: Pawlak Verlag, 1984), 1128; report dated May 14, 1940.

2. *Meldungen,* 1176, no. 91, May 27, 1940.

3. *Meldungen,* 1297, no. 99, June 24, 1940.

4. *Meldungen,* 1308, no. 100, June 27, 1940.

5. Elke Fröhlich, ed., *Die Tagebücher von Joseph Goebbels. Sämtliche Fragmente.* Teil I, Bd. 4, *January 1, 1940–August 7, 1941* (Munich: K. G. Saur, 1897), 53.

6. Fröhlich, ed., *Tagebücher,* 91, entry of March 30, 1940.

7. Fröhlich, ed. *Tagebücher,* 111, entry of April 14, 1940.

8. Fröhlich, ed., *Tagebücher,* 164, entry of May 18, 1940; Goebbel's entries usually refer to events the day before the entry's date.

9. Fröhlich, ed., *Tagebücher,* 198.

10. Fröhlich, ed., *Tagebücher,* 110.

11. Fröhlich, ed., *Tagebücher,* 105, entry of April 10, 1940.

12. Werner Jochmann, ed., *Adolph Hitler Monologe im Führer-Hauptquartier, 1941–1944. Die Aufzeichnungen Heinrich Heims* (Hamburg: Albrecht Knaus, 1980), 290.

13. Jochmann, ed., *Monologe,* 217.

14. The interview with General Walter Warlimont was conducted together with Hans Rudolf Humm on July 20, 1968 in Gmund; interview notes.

15. Walter Warlimont, *Im Hauptquartier der deutschen Wehrmacht 1939–1945* (München: Bernard & Graefe Verlag, 1978), 116ff.

16. Eugen Kreidler, *Die Eisenbahnen im Machtbereich der Aschsenmächte während des Zweiten Weltkrieges* (Göttingen: Musterschmidt-Verlag, 1975), 96, 105ff.

17. Andreas Hillgruber, ed., *Staatsmänner und Diplomaten bei Hitler. Vertrauliche Aufzeichnungen über Unterredungen mit Vertretern des Auslands 1939–1941* (Frankfurt a.M.: Bernard & Graefe Verlag, für Wehrwesen, 1967), 102-3.

18. Ernst Wetter, *Duell der Flieger und Diplomaten. Die Fliegerzwischenfälle Deutschland-Schweiz im Mai/Juni 1940 und ihre diplomatischen Folgen.* Frauenfeld: Verlag huber, 1987; see also Gautschi, *General Guisan,* 201ff.

19. See the relevant items of June/July 1940 concerning the fighter plane incidents in folder AA, Büro des Staatssekretärs: Schweiz, Bd. 1, May 14, 1938 to June 30, 1941, in microfilm NA T 120, roll 177, 86 116ff.

20. Fröhlich, ed., *Tagebücher,* 193.

21. Deutsche Gesandtschaft Bern an AA, telegram, Bern, June 8, 1940, signed Köcher; AA an Deutsche Gesandschaft Bern, telegram, Berlin, June 10, 1940, signed Schmidt; microfilm NA T-120, roll 177. Because the events of June 8, 1940, are diffi-

cult to assess, different numbers of planes involved are given; see Gautschi, *Guisan,* 201; Wetter *Duell,* 106.

22. Gert Buchheit, *Der deutsche Geheimdienst. Geschichte der militärischen Abwehr* (München: List Verlag, 1966), 312ff.; diverse newspaper clippings concerning Georg Freiberger, who in mid-1952 was released from prison as the last of the saboteurs, are in folder 18, "Einzelne Strafverfahren," the papers of Heinrich Büeler, Archiv für Zeitgeschichte ETH Zürich.

23. Edgar Bonjour, *Geschichte der schweizerischen Neutralität,* vol. 6 (Basel: Helbing & Lichtenhan, 1970), 104ff.; vol. 7 (1974), 99; Hans Rudolf Fuhrer, *Spionage gegen die Schweiz. Die geheimen deutschen Nachrichtendienste gegen die Schweiz im Zweiten Weltkrieg 1939–1945* (Frauenfeld: Huber, 1982), 28.

24. Karl Lüönd, *Spionage und Landesverrat in der Schweiz,* vol. 2 (Zürich: Ringier, 1977), 87ff.; Hans Fröhlicher, *Meine Aufgabe in Berlin* (Wabern-Bern: Privatdruck, 1962), 31–32.

25. AA Pol. I M g, "Aufzeichnung," Berlin, June 9, 1940, signed Kramarz; microfilm NA T 120/roll 177, 86150. See the complete reproduction below in "Documents."

26. Oral information given by General Warlimont, July 20, 1968.

27. Microfilm NA T 120, roll 177, 86164ff.; Bonjour, *Geschichte,* vol. 7 (1974), 92–93.

Chapter Three

Total Encirclement of Switzerland

Hitler's hasty plan of action against Switzerland began on June 16, 1940, with a dramatic start. On this hot and dry summer day, Guderian's tank group was pushing at breakneck speed in the direction of the Swiss Jura border. Together with Kleist's tank group which advanced against Dijon and on subsequent days further south into the area of Lyon, it had driven a deep wedge into the French armies since crossing the Aisne northeast of Reims. The whole push forward was done at such incredible speed that the supply line for maps had broken down; they had to be satisfied with road maps which were requisitioned from filling stations and automobile assistance services.[1] Guderian was now completing the encirlement of the remnants of the French eastern army which had remained in the Maginot Line and in Lorraine. About midnight of that Sunday its XXXIXth Army Corps with the 2nd Tank Division were positioned near Dole and the 1st Tank Division in the western part of Besançon. The 29th Motorized Division had reached the Saône after pushing across the plateau of Langres and after brief fights crossed the river near the small town of Pontailler; its scouting group had just been able to secure an undamaged bridge across the Doubs near St.-Vit, southwest of Besançon.[2]

On that day, June 16, at 11:22 p.m. a most unusual radio communication arrived at that division which was transmitted to Guderian's group from the command post as very urgent: "Reach Swiss border today still. Immediate message important for political reasons.[3] Three minutes later a radio command also arrived from the immediately superior XXXIXth Army Corps: "Urgently desired still on 6/16 to reach Swiss border with scouting forces. Then immediate radio communication."[4]

From a military point of view, this order didn't make sense. Guderian was already in full advance; reaching the Swiss border was planned for the next day and had, as was noted in the war diary, "only symbolic value."[5] The group's orders for June 17 were unequivocal: "Reach Swiss border, then turn in the direction of Belfort."[6] The sharp turn to the northeast was to take place without any violation of neutral Swiss territory. Although the group could not detect why this special order had to be executed "for political reasons," the 29th Motorized Division immediately gave its scouting section the orders: "After arrival of battle-ready troops at the bridge over the Doubs, scouting to Swiss border."[7] Subsequently a scouting group led by Lieutenant Dietrich started shortly after 1:30 a.m. on a reckless run to the Swiss border, during which it traversed all by itself eighty kilometers of territory occupied by French troops from the bridge near St.Vit to the Swiss border northeast of Pontarlier. They had neither enough time to refuel the three light armored reconnaissance cars, nor did the small group possess the necessary maps. The crazy ride led through Salins, passed enemy troops, broke through all barriers, and moved at high speed between French columns through the center of Pontarlier until it ended in a narrow valley at a tree barricade about five hundred meters from the border. "We still do not know exactly if this is the border," Dietrich reported. "Two of us climb over the tree barricade and continue rapidly on foot. 'There in front is a house!' I look through the binoculars and we are quite happy. 'Douane Suisse,' the Swiss customs house is in front of us. We run back happily. The message: 'border reached!' can feverishly be reported back to the division."[8]

As soon as the message reached the staff of the 29th Motorized Division, the urgently expected message was transmitted to Guderian: "Swiss border reached 8:20 a.m."[9] The risky action by Dietrich's scouting group had saved about four hours. The 29th Motorized Division, whose troops "had to fight great difficulties of terrain in the prealpine landscape of the Swiss Jura," was unable to transfer its command post to Pontarlier before noon.[10] What were the reasons behind this daring operation which had been set in motion "for political reasons?"

As the war diary of Guderian's group reveals, the liaison officer of the Army High Command (OKH) had delivered the order on the evening of June 16. Major Gehlen had at that time returned by plane from the OKH headquarters near Chimay to Guderian at Langres. Communication with the rapidly advancing units created major problems; the normal chain of command from the OKH to Guderian would have run through the Army Group A and from there to the 12th Army under whose command the tank group operated.[11] The special form of delivery alone indicated an order from the highest command and, also, it was not the practice of the OKH to give orders "for political reasons"; it could only originate from the "politician" himself, as Hitler was called ironically by General Halder, the chief of the general staff of the army.[12] That Hitler himself had initiated the whole operation was already confirmed at noon on June 17. At that moment Guderian arrived in Pontarlier where the commander of the 29th Motorized Division, General Baron von Langermann could congratulate him not only for his military success, but also on the occasion of his birthday. Guderian writes in his memoirs: "After receiving our message about reaching the Swiss border near Pontarlier, Hitler reacted with a query: 'Your message is based on an error. You must mean Pontailler-sur-Saône.' Only my response: 'No error. I am myself in Pontarlier at the Swiss border' reassured the mistrusting OKW."[13] With his tactically ingeniously chosen test question Hitler assured himself that German troops were actually at the border of the Swiss Jura, a certainty he needed for his next steps.[14]

The extreme urgency had been necessary because he planned to make use of the message in a particular way in regard to his Axis partner. With the resignation of Reynaud's Cabinet and the formation of a new government under Pétain on June 16, the French requested an armistice, so that the available time for achieving additional secondary military objectives became short. At the Führer's headquarters the working out of a first draft of the German demands for an armistice was already underway by a team under Hermann Böhme, then a lieutenant-colonel.[15] Petain's inquiry regarding the German conditions for terminating the fighting was sent from Bordeaux via Spain and reached Hitler in the morning of June 17. That he continued with his plan to cut off Switzerland during the hectic events of that day shows the determination with which he pursued this matter. At 6:45 p.m. he left his headquarters in Brûly-de-Pesche and flew to Frankfurt. From there he continued by special train to Munich where he met with Mussolini on June 18 to discuss the armistice conditions.[16]

The fact that German troops now stood at the Jura border also fired the fantasy of many small minds who now believed that Switzerland would be easy to deal with. On June 17 Otto Köcher, the German ambassador in Bern, sounded out his colleague Attilio Tamaro as to Italian thinking how a division of Switzerland was to occur. As it became clear, neither of the two diplomats had binding instructions, but each of them was secretly convinced that in case of a division his country would have to be given the key positions in the alpine region.[17]

At that moment, however, Hitler pursued another plan regarding Switzerland during his talks with Mussolini in Munich. The two dictators first talked alone. After Foreign Ministers Ribbentrop and Ciano as well as Generals Keitel and Roatta were called in, Hitler explained, among other things, the occupation demands based on a map and declared, according to the confidential notes of the interpreter that have been edited by Andreas

Hillgruber: "Switzerland too would be fully cut off from France by a cordon of occupied areas and would then have to assume an accommodating stance in the transit question as well as generally in its political attitude and its press." The discussion notes continue: "Also discussed was the area to be occupied by Italy from the Italian border to the Rhone, including Toulon and Marseilles."[18]

It was not Mussolini—as at times has been erroneously assumed—but Hitler who urged that Switzerland be cut off; his relevant remarks were part of an explanation which he gave to the expanded discussion group.[19] Mussolini was able to interrupt Hitler's rhetoric with only two comments that referred to the wishes of General Roatta for the use of the rail connections Paris-Modane-Turin and Ventimiglia-Barcelona. The misinterpretation resulted from the mistaken attribution of the passage to Mussolini about Switzerland when Hitler had continued his explanations. Hermann Böhme first made the error in his 1966 work *Entstehung und Grundlagen des Waffenstillstandes von 1940* [*Origin and Foundations of the Armistice of 1940*].[20]

The fact that Hitler and not Mussolini was the driving force behind the plan to encircle Switzerland is also proven—as will be shown later—by the memoirs of Wilhelm Keitel, chief of the Armed Forces High Command. To decipher the subsequent events, it is important to correct this confusion. During their March 18 meeting at the Brenner Pass Hitler advised Mussolini against an attack on the alpine front between Switzerland and the Mediterranean: "Any frontal attack on this border will only cost blood and bring little success."[21] Now Hitler no longer had such misgivings but rather supported Mussolini by promises of help in his plans to proceed offensively along this difficult front.

While Hitler had already reached his goals—apart from the complete isolation of Switzerland—and restrained himself vis-à-vis France for tactical reasons, Mussolini and Ciano still lacked military success in the Mediterranean region. Ciano started to recognize in Munich that the overblown Italian demands which he had prepared earlier were out of place and that it hardly would be possible to gain quick advantages in the difficult terrain of the Alpine front. At any rate, he declared during a parallel conversation which he held with Ribbentrop alone and recorded later, that it was his personal opinion that Italy would only ask for the Alpine belt without including all of Savoy: "Ho escluso la Savoia, che essando al di fuori della cerchia alpina no viene da noi considerata territorio italiano [I have excluded Savoy which is outside of the Alpine Belt and we do not consider to be Italian territory]."[22] During the subsequent expanded round of discussions it became apparent that the dictators had already decided otherwise.

When on the following day Mussolini wanted to initiate the offensive, it again became clear what among other things Marshal Badoglio had pointed out to him: His forces were not prepared for such an attack and unable to overwhelm even an already beaten enemy. Ciano claims to have warned him on June 20 of the impending clear-cut disaster and noted: "Mussolini listened to me and it appears that he will limit the attack to a small sector near the Swiss border."[23]

Hitler had pressured his ally in Munich to such an extent that the latter, in order to avoid complete embarrassment, wanted to undertake the attack to cut off Switzerland at all cost. The Italian offensive began on June 21 at various places along the western border with France. At the Little St. Bernhard an encircling attempt did not last beyond its start. The "offensive" stalled at the French defense positions and collapsed miserably after only a few kilometers. The capture of Menton changed nothing about this failure.

On June 19, Hitler had returned to the FHQ "Wolfsschlucht." at 2:15 p.m. He immediately gave orders that Lyon was to be occupied as fast as possible by segments of Kleist's group. On the same day the city was ceded to the Germans without resistance and without the blasting of important bridges. According to his orders, within the next few days the offensive into the rear of the French alpine army was to be started from the region of Lyon. Franz Halder, chief of the army's general staff, noted unhappily in his diary on June 20 that he could not understand "what the high political leadership was now still demanding of us and which of its wishes have remained unfulfilled."[24] He had received the instructions for this military advance into Savoy not directly from Hitler but via von Brauchitsch, the commander in chief of the army. It was necessary first to assemble in the area of Lyon a special fighting group under General Wilhelm List, the commander in chief of the 12th Army.

After his return from Munich, Ribbentrop became active again concerning the air incidents. It was now becoming clear why the government of the German Reich, as the historian Edgar Bonjour put it, "had taken very much time" with its note of June 19.[25] They had obviously awaited the results of the talks with Mussolini. After he had agreed to the military goal of a full encirclement of Switzerland, the blunt response to the Swiss Federal Council could be sent with the knowledge that other means of pressure would soon become available.

On June 21 Undersecretary of State von Weizsäcker remarked in his notes not without irony: "In heroic alliance the Italians today also have started their advance on the alpine passes. Perhaps we will shake hands in Grenoble."[26] This (for Switzerland) fateful handshake never took place.

What Hitler initiated in the days of June 19 to 24 as assistance for his Italian friends was nothing less than warfare directed against Switzerland without a direct attack on its territory. A total encirclement by the Axis powers did not happen by itself; it had to be attained as an additional military goal by means of military operations.

Hitler had reserved for himself the right to issue the order of attack to List, where the main task fell to the XVIth Army Corps under General Hoepner. The original idea was to advance not only from the area of Roanne, Lyon, and Bourg-en-Bresse towards Grenoble and the line Chambéry-Annecy, but also toward Valence in order to block—thus the official version—the mountain roads leading from Montgenèvre, from Mont-Cenis and from the Little St. Bernard to the Isère valley.[27] The plan to cut off the retreat route of the French alpine army to the Rhône valley and to join up with the Italians had already turned into fiction on June 21 by the failures of the "Alpini" units. Regardless, Hitler gave orders in the evening of the next day to start the attack on the following day, but "not to advance beyond Grenoble-Chambéry."[28]

Already since June 20-21 the 13th Motorized Infantry Division, under the command of the XVIth Army Corps, together with parts of the 1st Mountain Division, had advanced in two directions from Bourg-en-Bresse towards the Rhône between the Swiss border and Culoz. The bridge near Bellegarde was blown up in time. The courageous garrison of the aged but mighty Fort de l'Ecluse southwest of Geneva successfully resisted the German attacks. The narrow passage of the Rhône valley between the Crêt d'Eau and the Montagne de Vuache remained blocked. Some one hundred men of this garrison with six guns would be captured only on July 3, more than a week after the armistice; they were among those in France who had resisted capitulation the longest.[29]

Although Bellegarde remained in the unoccupied zone in spite of the dividing line imprecisely shown on many maps, the important rail connection from Geneva to France on the line west of the cantonal border near La Plaine to the Rhône was brought under German control; in this manner, the rail line Geneva-Annemasse-Bellegarde was blocked. During the continued push on June 22 the lone bridge that had unfortunately remained intact between Geneva and Lyon, down the Rhône from Culoz, fell into the hands of these troops. When the German offensive against the main targets began on the following day, the French alpine army under General Olry offered bitter resistance.

Towards the evening of June 23, the 13th Infantry Division, using mountain troops, occupied Aix-les-Bains, but failed in their attack near Mont Revard north of Chambéry. The French defense provided fierce resistance on both sides of Lac du Bourget. The German attempt to wheel off one fighting group in the direction of Annecy did not succeed beyond the line Albens-Aix-les-Bains. The key city of Savoy remained undamaged.

The reinforced 3rd Tank Division advanced on June 23 from the area of Lyon towards Grenoble. It failed the next day at the defensive position of Voreppe. In this manner the central traffic junction of the Dauphiné remained out of reach of the German troops. The 4th Tank Division operated southward from Lyon and reached the Isère near Romans and Saint-Nazaire, where it encountered only blown up bridges and, up the valley to Voreppe, a determined defense along the left shore of the Isère.

The overall German plan of operation for this special task reveals that, had it been successful, the total encirclement of Switzerland would have been attained even without Italian participation and without the push into Upper Savoy. It would have cut off even the last remaining approaches to Switzerland by blocking the lower Isère valley and by the continuation of the German line of occupation to the key positions of Grenoble, Chambéry, and Aix-les-Bains, which then approached the Rhône and ran near Geneva to the border between France and Switzerland. It is primarily thanks to the defending troops under General Cartier that Hitler failed in his main objectives in the Dauphiné and Savoy. General Etienne Plan and Eric Lefèvre described in their book *La Bataille des Alpes 10-25 juin 1940* [The Battle in the Alps June 10–25, 1940] the history of this courageous defensive battle, the outcome of which also had implications for the history of Switzerland.[30]

On June 24, Halder realized that Hitler pursued a wholly different goal than the purported assistance with these moves: "The politician wants Switzerland to lose its direct connection to France. This political demand is to be cloaked in a military coat. That will lead to much more unpleasantness." Halder privately opposed the overly hasty offensive and, as he notes in his war diary, pushed forward with only half his strength. A serious attack into the back of the French alpine fortifications would have required careful planning with the use of mountain troops: "It is not possible to improvise this with hastily brought in motorized alpine battalions."[31]

In the meantime, the whole attack, a result of political calculations, had developed into a cynical farce. While the Italian general staff continued to insist on assistance from the German Armed Forces High Command, Mussolini—who had put himself into an untenable position with his unreasonable demands—performed a radical about-face on the evening of June 21. So as not to cause a failure of the armistice he sent word to Hitler on June 22 that he would restrict himself to minimum demands and, among other things, refrain from the occupation of the areas left of the Rhône. He would be satisfied instead with a demilitarized French zone fifty kilometers wide along the border with Italy. However, the French side was unwilling to be humiliated by the dictates of the unsuccessful Italians.[32]

After signing the German-French armistice agreement in Rethondes on June 22 at 6:50 p.m., the French armistice commission under General Huntziger flew early the next morning to Rome. Foreign Minister Ciano opened the short meeting on June 23 at 7:30 p.m. at the Villa Incisa outside the capital. The actual negotiations were conducted by Marshal Badoglio on June 24, analogous to the role that Keitel had assumed earlier on the German side.

As the Italian delegation was now very modest with its demands, an agreement was reached more rapidly than Hitler had expected. He continued to assume that Mussolini would still find a way to complete the encirclement of Switzerland as had been agreed upon in Munich. Although the military occupation of Upper Savoy had failed, the Italians were to link up with the Germans southwest of Geneva at least at the conference table. However, he was not able to present an occupied Chambéry or Grenoble as negotiating trumps. A fiendish plan by Roatta and the Supreme Command of the German Armed Forces to bring Italian troops behind German lines in order to trick the French failed due to Badoglio's correct attitude.[33]

When Hitler learned that his Axis partner had deserted him at the negotiating table in the realization of his plan of encirclement, he tried at the very last moment to avert failure. Enno von Rintelen, the German military attaché in Rome, describes this intervention as follows:

> After the negotiations in Rome had been concluded, I received on June 24 at 7:30 p.m. telephoned instructions from the OKW to prevail upon Badoglio to demand the occupation from Savoy to the southwest point of Switzerland, to connect with the German occupation zone and to cut off Switzerland fully. However, it was too late for that; the agreement had been signed without ceremony at 7:15 p.m.[34]

Hitler had been too late to drop the mask of the altruistic helper to plainly cash in on the promise made by Mussolini in Munich—the purpose of the occupation of Savoy and Upper Savoy was the cutting off of Switzerland! Until now, Hitler's actual intentions had not been fully grasped.

That Hitler's offensive with List's group was really conceived against Switzerland is confirmed by the memoirs of Wilhelm Keitel, the chief of the OKW, who was fully loyal to his master and was executed in Nuremberg as a war criminal. Some of the éclat with which this action ended still lingers in his description: Hitler wanted to induce Mussolini in Munich

> to use the Italian demands for the territory to be occupied by Italy—adjoining ours— to cut off Switzerland from any connection to France. In reality this has not been accomplished in spite of Mussolini's firm promise; the Italians could never get the planned demands accepted, but after their military failures were probably incapable of doing so. Although an armistice was soon concluded, the conditions were modest and culminated in a narrow occupied zone along their alpine front, which, however, had the effect that the French border fortifications fell into the hands of the Italians; they would not have been able to capture them.[35]

Because Walter Görlitz, who was unaware of Keitel's participation in the conference in Munich, omitted this important part in his 1961 deficient edition of *Generalfeldmarschall Keitel, Verbrecher oder Offizier?* [*Field*

Marshal Keitel, Criminal or Officer?], this revealing reference remained unknown.[36]

According to the armistice agreement, the German troops had to withdraw to an agreed-upon demarcation line; among other stipulations, they had to vacate Lyon and their positions in the departments of Isère and Savoy. The course of the demarcation line within France also reveals visually the German intention to encircle Switzerland. The occupied area protruded towards the southeast not far from Dole and approached Lake Geneva by means of a narrowing strip of territory. At its endpoint it included the free zone of Gex and ended at the bridge over the Rhône near the Fort de l'Ecluse next to Bellegarde, southwest of Geneva. Instead of the planned continuation of the German occupation zone by the Italians, Switzerland retained a joint border with the future Vichy state running from the Geneva corner to St.-Gingolph and to the three-country corner east of Chamonix. Switzerland thus kept an initally cumbersome, but certainly usable, transit route, the importance of which will be more closely examined in the second part of this book, dealing with economic warfare.

In the overall view of events, the action designed to cut off Switzerland as a final military goal was merely a quickly improvised side-action during the final phase of the Western offensive. Nevertheless, this failure angered Hitler so deeply that he unscrupulously wanted to order the first breach of the concluded armistice to plug the passage still remaining to Switzerland. Did he consider an attack as a final alternative in his overwrought reaction? Whatever happened on June 23 and 24 within the inner circle of the Führer's headquarters has so far remained hidden. As the ensuing developments will reveal, these were the most dangerous hours which Switzerland had to endure—although unbeknown to it—during World War II.

NOTES

1. "Kriegstagebuch," No. 3, XXXIX. AK, E 63/3, 1–24 June, 1940, 89, BA-MA; significant also is the entry: "South of Geneva and west of Bourges the provisioning with maps ceased completely." I thank Georges Wüthrich for his helpful hints concerning the war diaries used in this chapter.

2. "Kriegstagebuch," 85–93.

3. Group Guderian to 29th Division, Radio Message no. 43, June 16, 1940, sent 9:40 p.m., received 11:22 p.m. in 29. Inf.-Division (motorized), Ia Anlagenheft 2 zum K. T. B. no. 3, Anlagen no. 415–560, June 15, 1940–June 19, 1940, BA-MA, RH 26–29/3. The great urgency is evident from the annotation "so Kr"; the added signs "qwd" mean: "Aushändigung bestätigen [confirm receipt]." "Training Provisions for Communication Troups," Pamphlet 4b, "Radio Operation" 1940, in BA-MA. The telegram is reproduced below, no. 2 in the documentary appendix.

4. XXXIX. AK to 29th Division, radio message no. 255, June 16, 1940, sent 10 p.m., arrived 11:25 p.m. Added notation: "Rot [red]", "Wichtig! [Important]." The Ia officer of the group Guderian had transmitted the radio order to the XXXIX. Army Command as well as directly to the 29th mot. Division; ibid.

5. "Kriegstagebuch Gruppe Guderian," no. 3, May 9, 1940–June 24, 1940, entry of June 16, 1940, 288; BA-MA, RH 21-1/41 D.

6. "Kriegstagebuch" no. 3, XXXIX. AK, E 63/3, 93, BA-MA.

7. Radio Message, 29th Division to AA 29, sent June 17, 1940, at 12:40 a.m.; BA-MA, RH 26-29/3.

8. Aufklärungs-Abteilung 29, Spähtrupp Dietrich, Bericht "Wettlauf zur Schweizer-grenze," o. D, signed Dietrich. BA-MA, RH 26-29/3. As to the date it needs to be noted that the report is in the Anlagenheft 2 zum K. T. B. No. 3 of the 29th mot. Division which ended June 19, 1940. See also Joachim Lemelsen, *29th Division. Das Buch der Falke-Division*, with contributions of J. L. et al. (Bad Nauheim: Podzun Verlag, 1960), 79ff.; Georges Wüthrich, "Höchste Dringlichkeit: Noch heute Schweizer Grenze erreichen!" in *Sonntagszeitung*, no. 25, June 18, 1989. Dietrich's report is reproduced in its entirety in the Appendix.

9. 29th Division to Group Guderian, radio message no. 48, June 17, 1940, 8:45 a.m.; BA-MA, RH 26-29/3. From the notation "qwd" is evident that the acknowledgment of receipt arrived at 11 a.m. at the staff of the 29th mot. Division.

10. "Kriegstagebuch," No. 3, XXXIX. AK, E 63/3, 95; BA-MA.

11. Because Guderian had not received orders for the further deployment of his tank group, Reinhard Gehlen was to get the necessary instructions from the OKH-Headquarters; yet he returned on the evening of June 16 merely with the special order mentioned above, but without the hoped for directives. Gehlen became in 1942 head of the Division "Fremde Heere Ost" in the OKH and supervised after the war the federal information service. Heinz Guderian, *Erinnerungen eines Soldaten*, 11th edition (Stuttgart: Motorbuch Verlag, 1979), 116; "Kriegstagebuch" Group Guderian, no. 3, May 5, 1940–June 24, 1940, entry of June 16, 1940, 9:30 p.m.; BA-MA, RH 21-1/41 D.

12. Halder, *Kriegstagebuch*, vol. 1 (Stuttgart: 1962), 370.

13. Guderian, *Erinnerungen*, 118.

14. Already on the evening of June 16 Halder had noted in his diary: "Guderian has arrived in Besançon." Halder, *Kriegstagebuch*, vol. 1, 359. Generaloberst List extended his congratulations to this event on that very Sunday afternoon so that Hitler could not have been uncertain about the fact that Pontailler-sur-Saône had been passed long before. The chosen form of the question allowed checking without implying a special interest in Switzerland.

15. Hermann Böhme, *Der deutsch-französische Waffenstillstand im Zweiten Weltkrieg*, vol. 1: *Entstehung und Grundlagen des Waffenstillstandes von 1940* (Stuttgart: Deutsche Verlags-Anstalt, 1966),16ff.

16. "Kriegstagebuch Führer-Hauptquartier," no. 3, February 15, 1940–July 31, 1940, microfilm NA T-78, roll 351.

17. Report of Tamaro to Ciano, Bern, June 18, 1940, in *Documenti Diplomatici Italiani*, Nona Serie, vol. 5 (Rome: Liberia dell Stato1965), 40–41.

18. Andreas Hillgruber, ed., *Staatsmänner und Diplomate bei Hitler. Vertrauliche Aufzeichnungen und Unterredungen mit Vertretern des Auslandes 1939–1941*, vol. 1 (Frankfurt a. M.: Deutscher Taschenbuch Verlag, 1969), 141. Entry of June 18, 1940, unsigned; Paul Otto Schmidt was chief translator.

19. Hans Senn, "Die Haltung Italiens zum 'Fall Schweiz' im Jahre 1940," *Neue Zürcher Zeitung*, no. 111, May 14/15, 1988. Compare the rendition in Eberhard Jäckel, *Frankreich in Hitler's Europa* (Stuttgart: Deutsche Verlags-Anstalt, 1966), 36.

20. Böhme, *Entstehung*, 33; Daniel Bourgeois, *Le Troisième Reich et la Suisse 1933–1941* (Neuchâtel: Édition de la Baconnière, 1974), 126ff. Böhme's work about the 1940 armistice is characterized by outstanding expertise which he had acquired in the context of his close collaboration in working out the armistice as well as when he served as chief of staff of the Armistice Commission until 1943.

21. Hillgruber, *Staatsmänner*, vol. 1, 103.

22. *Documenti Diplomatici Italiani*, vol. 5, 51.

23. Galeazzo Ciano, *Tagebücher 1939–1943* (Bern: Alfred Scherz Verlag 1946), 250.

24. Halder, *Kriegstagebuch*, vol. 1, 364.

25. Edgar Bonjour, *Geschichte der schweizerischen Neutralität*, vol. 6 (Basel: Helbing & Lichtenhahn, 1970), 96.

26. Leonidas Hill, ed., *Die Weizsäcker Papiere 1933–1950* (Frankfurt a. M.: Propyläen Verlag, 1974), 207.

27. AOK 12, "Armeebefehl" no. 32, June 21, 1940, signed List; NA, microfilm T-312, roll 427. Rudolf Lehmann, *Die Leibstandarte*, vol. 1 (Osnabrück: Munin, 1977), 302.

28. Halder, *Kriegstagebuch*, vol. 1, 367–68.

29. AOK 12, Abt. "Fremde Heere West, Lagebericht West," No. 397, July 3, 1940; microfilm NA T 311, roll 214, 446. The Germans took the refusal of the defenders of the Fort de l'Ecluse to capitulate as a pretext to continue the illegal removal of valuable goods such as silk for parachutes; Böhme, S. 299f.

30. E. Plan and Eric Lefèvre, *La bataille des Alpes, 10–25 juin 1940. L'armée invaincu* (Paris: Charles Lovauzelle, 1982); Henri Azeau, *La guerre franco-italienne, Juin 1940* (Paris: Charles Lovauzelle, 1967); "Lageberichte West," June 23–25, microfilm NA T 311, roll 214, 455–64.

31. Halder, *Kriegstagebuch*, vol. 1, 370.

32. *Documenti diplomatici Italiani*, vol. 5, 74; Böhme, *Entstehung*, 72ff.

33. Halder, *Kriegstagebuch*, vol. 1, 370; Böhme, *Entstehung*, 69–70.

34. Enno von Rintelen, *Mussolini als Bundesgenosse. Erinnerungen des deutschen Militärattach´s in Rom 1936–1943* (Tübingen: Wunderlich, 1951), 91.

35. Wilhelm Keitel, "Lebenserinnerungen," (typed copy 1946), vol. 5, February 4, 1938–August 10, 1940, BA-MA N 54/5, Papers of Wilhelm Keitel. See also AfZ, papers of Peter Dietz, folder 26.

36. Walter Görlitz, *Generalfeldmarschall Keitel. Verbrecher oder Offizier? Erinnerungen, Briefe, Dokumente des Chefs OKW* (Göttingen: Musterschmidt-Verlag, 1961), 236. The editor gives the following erroneous reason for the omission: "In the original here follow data about the hearsay of a meeting of Hitler's with Mussolini."

Chapter Four

Hitler's Orders of June 23, 1940: A Surprise Occupation of Switzerland

At the June 18, 1940, meeting in Munich Hitler and Mussolini had agreed merely on a complete encirclement of Switzerland from the outside in order to be able all the more easily to extort her in case she failed to be accommodating. The more questionable the success of such an undertaking became, the stronger dimensions of pan-strategic interests emerged which gave the Swiss question new significance. To better understand this one needs to keep in mind that Hitler's restraint in the armistice demands towards France was not inspired by a will to collaborate in partnership in a future Europe, but solely by tactical considerations. He aimed to deprive England of French support beyond continental Europe as well. For him an unoccupied France made sense only as long as Pétain was able to prevent the breaking away of the French colonies, especially those in North Africa.[1] When this overall plan was shattered on November 8, 1942, by the landing of American and British troops in Morocco and Algeria, the German army marched into unoccupied France only three days later to safeguard German interests.

The occupation of France's remnant had thus remained a threatening alternative also after the armistice. Corresponding military plans of the German general staff were therefore kept current and entered an acute phase already in December 1940 with Hitler's directive concerning operation "Attila."[2] The uncertain situation before the armistice derived from opposite considerations. As long as the French had accepted only the German, but not the Italian armistice conditions, the war continued. Even on June 22, the very day the agreement was signed in Rethondes, the French delegation made clear that it would submit to the German victory, but not to an Italian diktat. "L'Italie nous a declaré la guerre, mais elle ne nous la pas faite [Italie has declared war on us, but she has not made it]," General

37

Huntziger declared bitterly.[3] Contrary to the dominant public mood which expected an immediate cessation of fighting, the German leadership took the possibility of the failure of the negotiations into account until they had come into force. While Halder assumed that the French had no alternative than to accept the "humiliating" conditions, General Walther von Brauchitsch, the commander in chief of the army, feared until the last moment that a sudden change could induce Hitler yet to initiate a move beyond the demarcation line.[4] Colonel Hans von Greiffenberg of the General Staff also shared his scepticism. Since September 1, 1939, he had served as head of the division of operations in the army's General Staff; after the departure of General von Stülpnagel as chief quartermaster I at the end of May 1940, he emerged under Halder as a key figure in the area of operations and also became involved in the plans for attacking Switzerland. In the division of operations the situation had been judged with such pessimism that shortly before the signing of the armistice at 6:50 p.m. on June 22 it warned the commander of Army Group C that France was willing to accept the German, but not the Italian armistice conditions. "The war will probably continue," General Ritter von Leeb noted in his diary.[5] That view softened with the arrival of the French delegation in Rome on June 23 but did not prevent von Brauchitsch from continuing his preparatory measures. Yet it remained uncertain until after the armistice whether Pétain's authority would suffice to implement the obligations agreed to in France's capitulation.

It is the main task of this and the following chapters to clarify whether because of Hitler's actions Switzerland had moved into the field of vision of the German planning operations in such a manner that its occupation was finally considered seriously. Did the Führer now tend in the direction of a radical solution, once his attempt to cut off Switzerland by the operation in Savoy had been halted and become futile without the encirclement with the Italians? If an attack under certain conditions was actually under discussion, it presented a totally new situation for the supreme army command which had made no preparations at all for such plans. Therefore a second question needs to be addressed: Was there a demonstrable direct connection between the possible occupation of Switzerland and an eventual continuation of the war in southern France? Subsequent developments, the escalation of which in relation to Switzerland shall now be examined step by step, will provide further clarification.

After June 22 new troop movements in the Jura region occurred which assumed disturbing proportions. The occupation up to the line of demarcation hermetically sealed the border between Basel and Geneva. This repositioning was done so abruptly that the question arises whether the supreme army command pursued additional considerations when it disentangled the units which had become closely enmeshed during the encirclement of the French forces. On June 21 the war diary of the division of operations of the army's general staff noted the intended change as follows: "Group Guderian is to be pulled out and assembled in the area Montbéliard, Besançon, at Swiss border."[6] The sudden withdrawal from their advanced positions near Epinal and Belfort was against the wish of the group. The entry in its war diary for June 21 states: "The group expects to be left in the area it conquered in order to be able to prepare rapidly for desired new assignments."[7] Guderian objected that after the fulfillment of its task his group was "head over heel" being thrown out of its target area; nevertheless, it was granted only a short reprieve in Epinal and Belfort to complete at least the most urgent repair work on the overtaxed armored vehicles. The rapid transfer to the South took place as early as the morning of June 23, while the 16th, 1st, and 7th Armies—the latter with its headquarters in Colmar—now extended their responsibility for the region westward from Basel to Vesoul and Jussey.[8] Even if one could explain the measures taken on the basis of other considerations, the most hasty redeployment of June 23–24 had the result that the German troops northwest and west of the Swiss border had been considerably reinforced. In the evening of June 23 the following new battle formations were near Switzerland: The 29th Motorized Infantry Division had settled in Montbéliard; the 1st Tank Division had been moved to Morteau, not far from Le Locle, while the 2nd Tank Division was stationed in the area of Salins. The general command of the XXXIXth Army Corps settled in Pontarlier; Guderian's staff found quarters in a hotel in Besançon.[9] "Any border crossing into or out of Switzerland must be prevented at all costs" were the orders to the troops stationed on the western border of Switzerland.[10]

Early on June 23 Hitler had visited Paris then returned to the Führer's headquarters. In the afternoon of that Sunday he conducted a situation report which provides the key to the explanation of the subsequent developments. At that time the German armies had achieved practically all their military goals. The only failure came from the recently begun offensive by List's group pursuing the full encirclement of Switzerland. The Italian advance into Savoy had already failed. In this situation Hitler gave the order, misjudged until now, that triggered the planning of an attack against Switzerland. Halder, the chief of the General Staff, noted Hitler's personal instruction during the situation report as follows: "Mental preparation of the tasks of the 12th Army. List: Personnel Kübler, Bergmann, Fahrmbacher, Schörner."[11] Just how threatening this order of June 23 was for Switzerland derives from the fact that Hitler not only initiated the attack planning but also took concrete steps for the preparation of suitable offensive forces. According to his directive, the 12th

Army was to replace Guderian's group and obtain for this purpose two strong mountain divisions under Kübler and Schörner. The alarming meaning of Hitler's order became clear soon after: As part of the 12th Army, all three commanders named by Hitler were, Bergmann excepted, moved with their divisions for a special task to the western border of Switzerland.

Based on sources not previously utilized, it is also possible to perceive how the army's General Staff executed Hitler's orders. On June 23, the "Foreign Armies West" department of the operations division transmitted an exposé with the meaningful title: "The fortifications on the Swiss borders and in the interior of the country." It was needed the next day for writing the first study of an attack on Switzerland.[12] As Halder notes in his war diary, the Supreme Commander of the Army still appeared worried Monday morning about a possible change in the situation: "Supreme Commander of Army flies to 7th Army. His inner unrest pushes him to preparatory measures in case the armistice negotiations with Italy fail and he will still have to execute a first attack into the back of the French alpine fortifications and, simultaneously, push towards the Mediterranean coast."[13] A review of the surprise attack on Switzerland is, as additional source material shows, included in these preparatory measures. As the short study "1st Sketch of Presentation about Attack on Switzerland," cited in the introductory chapter, carries the date of June 25, 1940, but does not indicate the time the order was given, it has been impossible until now to place it precisely as to time and content. Instead, it was only known that the writer of the "Sketch of Presentation" was a Captain von Menges who worked in the Operations Division (I) of the army's General Staff.[14] Thanks to the assistance of Dr. Dietrich Wilhelm von Menges and the private notes of his cousin who had undertaken this study, it is now possible to clear up its uncertain origin; this is also important for the later operational sketches as a continuation of this first sketch concerning an attack that had been made in response to an acute situation.

Otto Wilhelm von Menges (Jan. 9, 1908–Feb. 2, 1943) came from an established family of officers. He spent part of his childhood in East Prussia and then also chose an officer's career. After graduating from high school he entered the military academy and became known as a successful show horseman. On October 20, 1939, he was transferred to the general staff of the army where he served as adjutant to chief quartermaster 1, General von Stülpnagel. When the latter took over the command of the Second Army Corps at the end of May, von Menges rose to the rank of leader of group 1 of the operations division under Hans von Greiffenberg, colonel on the General Staff. There, at the age of thirty-two, he was responsible for all of Army Group C, and his range of tasks extended over six countries in which German troops were stationed. As the OKH had already on June 21 informally planned to subsequently assign the area "Tours-Lake Geneva and northward"[15] to Army Group C in occupied France, von Menges was also in charge of the plans to attack Switzerland. He composed not only the first sketch of operations, but also the more extensive revision of August 8, and four days later, the detailed version which is reproduced in the documentary appendix. His notes contain the following entry concerning the order: "In the morning of June 24 I receive the order to compose a study concerning an attack against a country. My first large independent work!"[16] As the formulation of this order to produce a "short" study regarding the possibilities of a surprise occupation of Switzerland already points to increased urgency, this is also confirmed by the circumstances of its composition. The review had to be done at a time when the operations division already faced a heavy workload. After the armistice the new operational regions of the army's groups, the reorganization of the army for continued warfare against England, and the reduction of the field army as well as other organizational measures required extensive preparations.[17] At 9 p.m. Halder received the orders from the OKW: "Ceasefire starting June 25 at 1:35 a.m."[18] The operations division in the general staff of the army, which included von Menges, had to take care that the troops were informed. However, the question about an occupation of Switzerland was urgent enough that von Menges had to continue working on the study through the night: "Ceasefire after 1:35 a.m. A great moment. We cannot be thankful enough to God and the excellent troops. The related teletype messages are a lot of work; and my study in addition. All the same great joy. Unfortunately no *schampus* [champagne] to celebrate." On June 25, von Menges had completed his attack study and delivered it to his immediate superior, Colonel on the General Staff Hans von Greiffenberg: "Work on my study which completely satisfies the division chief."[19]

This not only negates the old theories about the "unoccupied staff members," but it also shows the allegedly nonexistent concrete background of a threat in two ways. The precautionary measures initiated by the supreme commander of the army in the morning of June 24 were recorded with the following goals: "Obtaining the most important railway and road junctions as well as the numerous bridges and tunnels in an undamaged condition in order to be able to use the country as soon as possible as a transit area for all transports to the south of France."[20] This confirms the results obtained at the beginning of the analysis of the order, which pointed to a larger context for it within the overall military situation. However, this is only one part of the story.

Hitler himself was responsible for the fact that the occupation of Switzerland was even considered. Since June 16 he had secretly and slyly, yet with amazing tenacity, aimed at a complete encirclement of Switzerland. Now, however, the shipwreck of his military action, set in motion by List's group, was apparent. That this forced unpleasant decisions and that Hitler's anger would lead to discord became obvious even to Halder during the morning of June 24: "This is again the same anguished game as when making contact with the Russians during the war against Poland. The politician wants Switzerland to lose its direct contact with France. A military mantle is to be hung around this political demand. Many an unpleasantness will result from this."[21]

In Poland the German troops had overrun the dividing line by up to two hundred kilometers due to their lack of knowledge of the agreements made with Stalin in the secret additional agreement of August 23, 1939. On orders of Hitler, who probably wanted to gain additional territorial advantages against the Russians, the German troops which had marched into Eastern Poland, had to be withdrawn fully behind the agreed-upon demarcation line.[22] In France, to avoid unnecessary sacrifices, a crossing of the demarcation line had been prohibited in time. The only exemption from this was List's group which, as has already been shown, had advanced further from the area of Lyon towards the east and the south. With the conclusion of the Italian-French armistice the situation arose exactly as the leadership of the army had feared: Fully isolated and "for political reasons" pressured into a hastily prepared operation, List's group had no other choice than to retreat unconditionally behind the demarcation line. That Hitler was already irritated about this matter is made clear by Halder, who stated the following to Hans Rudolf Kurz in 1969:

> During this time, when Switzerland was surrounded by German troops, I received repeatedly reports from the OKW—I naturally had my private sources there—about Hitler's fits of rage against Switzerland which, based on his mentality, could possibly lead to sudden military demands on the army. It was not unthinkable that he would suddenly approach the supreme commander of the army von Brauchitsch and request a report on the attack possibilities against Switzerland.

In such a case the necessary documents would have to be prepared for von Brauchitsch by the general staff of the army.[23] From Halder's discussion it cannot be determined how far Hitler's intentions really went and what the background for his "rages" were. After the war Halder made repeated contradictory remarks regarding the plans of attack which were unpleasant to him.[24] Nevertheless, his war diary was of great assistance in this inquiry together with the notes of Otto Wilhelm von Menges, particularly also given the loss of very important OKH files. The consequences to which the "unpleasantness" feared by Halder during the morning of June 24 would lead already became apparent on the evening of that day at the Führer's headquarters.

NOTES

1. In this manner Hitler was able to prevent that the modern French fleet followed de Gaulle; yet it was largely destroyed by the British in the port of Mers el-Kebir on July 3, 1940.

2. OKW/WFSt IV, Chefsachen: Folder "Attila." Directive no. 19 of December 10, 1940, signed Hitler; BA-MA, RW 4/v. 574.

3. Eberhard Jäckel, *Frankreich in Hitler's Europa. Die deutsche Frankreichpolitik im Zweiten Weltkrieg* (Stuttgart: Deutsche Verlags-Anstalt, 1966), 41.

4. Franz Halder, *Kriegstagebuch*, vol. 1 (Stuttgart: W. Kohlhammer Verlag, 1962), 367, 370.

5. Georg Meyer, ed., *Generalfeldmarschall Wilhelm Ritter von Leeb. Tagebuchaufzeichnungen und Lagebeurteilungen aus zwei Weltkriegen* (Stuttgart: Deutsche Verlags-Anstalt, 1976), 244. Leeb judged the situation more positively once the Italian-French negotiations had started. See entry of June 23, 1940.

6. "Kriegstagebuch," Op. Abt. d. GenstdH, May 10–June 25, 1940, BA-MA RH 2/2972.

7. "Kriegstagebuch," (Gruppe Guderian), no. 3, May 9, 1940–June 24, 1940, 323, BA-MA RH 21-141 D.

8. "Kriegstagebuch," (Guderian), 325; Meyer, *von Leeb*, 244–5.

9. The two forts of Pontarlier had been occupied again by the French and capitulated only at 5:10 p.m. on June 24, 1940. BA-MA, "Kriegstagebuch," no. 3, XXXIX, AK, E 63/3, June 1–24, 1940, 133–34.

10. Order Generalkommando XXXIX. AK concerning securing border of June 24, 1940; BA-MA, XXXIX AK/W 6169/43.

11. Halder, *Kriegstagebuch*, vol. 1, 369.

12. Written Communication OKH, GenStdH, Abt. Fremde Heere West to Op. Abt., July 1, 1940, signed Liss, with enclosure. That the stamp of receipt with the paragraphs of von Greiffenberg and von Menges carry the date June 23, 1940, although the communication was post-dated July 1, 1940, indicates the greatest hurry. Also the additional unsigned information "New Formation of the Swiss Army" is from June 23, 1940. BA-MA RH 2/465, Switzerland, vol. A.

13. Halder, *Kriegstagebuch,* vol. 1, 370; Meyer, *von Leeb*, 244-5.Since the papers of Friedrich Dollmann in BA-MA contain only a photo album, it could not be determined if von Brauchitsch also discussed "precautionary measures" with Dollmann besides the awarding of knightly crosses and the transmission of congratulations to the 7th Army. In May the 7th Army conducted the maneuvers of a fake attack against Switzerland; on June 16/17 it broke through the Maginotline and was now stationed in upper Alsace; Meyer, *von Leeb*, 244–45.

14. "1. Vortragsnotiz über Angriff gegen die Schweiz," Op. Abt. (I), June 25, 1940, signed von Menges in :Schweiz," vol. A, BA-MA, RH 2/465 (cited as "Vortragsnotiz").

15. Meyer, *von Leeb,* 243.

16. Private notes of Otto Wilhelm von Menges, October 20, 1939–January 1, 1941, entry for June 24, 1940; clean copy, possession of Dr. Dietrich Wilhelm von Menges whom I thank sincerely for his references and the perusal of the documents of his cousin. Written communication of Dr. Dietrich Wilhelm von Menges to the author, Essen, June 7, 1990. The decisive impetus for this source discovery I owe to Dr. iur. Heinrich Tanner.

17. "Kriegstagebuch," Op. Abt. d. GenStdH, May 10–June 25, 1940, 99, BA-MA RH 2/2972.

18. Halder, *Kriegstagebuch*, vol. 1, 371.

19. Private notes of Otto Wilhelm von Menges, entry of June 24-26, 1940.

20. "1. Vortragsnotiz,", BA-MA RH 2/465, Schweiz, vol. A.

21. Halder, *Kriegstagebuch*, vol. 1, 370.

22. Klaus A. Maier et al., *Das Deutsche Reich und der Zweite Weltkrieg,* vol. 2: *Die Errichtung der Hegemonie auf dem europäischen Kontinent*, (Stuttgart: 1979), 126–27; Halder, *Kriegstagebuch*, vol. 1, 80ff.; Walter Warlimont, *Im Hauptquartier der deutschen Wehrmacht 1939–1945. Grundlagen, Formen Gestalten,* 3rd edition (München: Bernard & Graefe Verlag, 1973), 48–49.

23. Hans Rudolf Kurz, *Operationsplanuing Schweiz. Die Rolle der Schweizer Armee in zwei Weltkriegen* (Thun: Ott Verlag, 1974), 37.

24. Written communication of Halder to H. R. Kurz, in *Operationsplanung*, 37; Werner Roesch, *Bedrohte Schweiz. Die deutschen Operationsplanungen gegen die Schweiz im Sommer/Herbst 1940 und die Abwehrbereitschaft der Armee im Oktober 1940* (Frauenfeld: Verlag Huber, 1986), 11–12; written communication of Halder of November 14, 1952; quoted by Hans Rudolf Fuhrer, *Spionage gegen die Schweiz. Die geheimen deutschen Nachrichtendienste gegen die Schweiz im Zweiten Weltkrieg 1939–1945* (Frauenfeld: Verlag Huber, 1982), 136, note 23; explanation for Dr. Franz Riedweg of August 28, 1960, signed Halder (copy), in the papers of Dr. Heinrich Büeler, folder 17, Dr. med. Franz Riedweg, AFZ.

Chapter Five

Evening of June 24, 1940: Angry Outburst in the Führer's Headquarters

On June 24, 1940, supper at the Führer's Headquarters (FHQ) "Wolfs-schlucht" was scheduled for the late hour of 10:00 p.m. Hitler wanted to spend the last hours before the armistice in the closed circle of his comrades in the staff of his usual escort. He had also invited additional guests: his favorite architects Albert Speer and Hermann Giesler, as well as Arno Breker, the creator of monumental sculptures, with whom he had visited deserted Paris in the early hours of the day before.

Hitler's protégés have described this visit extensively in their published memoirs, yet only Breker tied the visit to Paris to the correct date, June 23. Comparison clearly shows how such retrospectives can be unreliable. The memoirs also describe the experience in Hitler's circle the night before the armistice went into effect. The meal in the mess hall began cheerfully. A thunderstorm was brewing in the distance; towards midnight came the report of enemy airplanes. Breker reports: "We are sitting completely in the dark, at intervals the faces are eerily illuminated by flashes of lightning. Everyone is served a glass of champagne. The thunderstorm departs slowly. An eerie calm ensues."[1] The war diary of the FHQ reports that at 1:35 a.m. German summer time four horn players blow the signal "Company, Halt!"[2]

That evening there had already been another thunderstorm at the Führer's headquarters; Hitler had exploded at about 7:30 p.m. concerning Switzerland. There were several reasons for his rage. His plan for a full encirclement had failed. An ominous "gap" was open near Geneva. In retrospect, the military operations of the List's group made no sense at all. They had continued their fight on June 23 and 24 in vain, hoping at least to strengthen Mussolini's position at the negotiating table.

As it was now established that Switzerland would continue to share a direct border with unoccupied France, the new situation near Geneva was thoroughly scrutinized. Hitler had assumed that List's military operation would secure him a pledge which he still wanted to cash in. By the use of drastic measures, it might be possible to force interruption of the traffic routes for some time before the retreat to the demarcation line.

There was another outburst: Upon review it was revealed that Switzerland still had an uncontrolled rail connection in spite of the German encircling efforts! The Geneva-Annemasse-La Roche-Annecy rail line had remained undamaged and outside of German reach. This discovery was particularly painful for Keitel, the chief of the high command of the armed forces and for von Brauchitsch, the commander in chief of the army, because Hitler had charged both of them with detailed instructions for List's special task. During the six hours between the news of the signing in Rome and the time the armistice took effect, nothing more could be accomplished by military means in the difficult terrain of Upper Savoy. After receiving news of this fait accompli, the only alternatives remaining to Hitler were quietly to write off the operation with the retreat of List behind the line of demarcation or to aim for a direct "settlement" of the problem of Switzerland. During the early evening hours of that day, Hitler made two decisions which show that at the moment of his greatest triumph he was not willing to let this small country get away with anything. On the one hand, the necessary preparations were initiated to trigger a surprise attack on very short notice once Hitler gave the orders. This threatening development will be further discussed in the next chapter. Of interest here is the background of the second decision, the act of sabotage by which he wanted to destroy Switzerland's last uncontrolled rail connection to the West. Had Hitler uncovered a grave error of omission in the OKW that had thwarted his plan of action?

In 1966 Hermann Böhme published the first inadequate references to the remaining "gap at the Swiss border." For him, all this is reduced to merely an oversight. In the haste of June 22, the consequences of Mussolini's relinquishment of occupying the region had been overlooked. The Armed Forces High Command (OKW) was then made aware of the rail line, if too late, possibly by a message from the German consul general in Geneva.[3] Böhme did not know that Hitler himself had systematically pushed for a complete encirclement of Switzerland. There is, however, reason to believe that Hitler pushed the guilt for the failure onto the OKW by making the undamaged rail line the pivotal point of the matter. General Warlimont, head of the home defense department of the armed forces' operational staff in the OKW, remembered the "historically really strange case" as ending in reprimands of the OKW "for serious negligence" for letting the gap stay open: "At any rate, it was suddenly left to me—no doubt just as if there had been in hindsight a case of negligence which would certainly also be connected to an order—to review the possibilities that might still exist for belatedly closing this gap."[4]

Hitler's mistrust was not wholly unreasonable as the chief of the general staff of the army had executed the special order for List's group only reluctantly and without energy. A critical review, however, shows that the failure of the operation, a real stroke of luck for Switzerland, cannot be ascribed to an error made at the OKW or OKH. Rather, Hitler's overall plans had been based on questionable assumptions. When he gave the attack orders for List's group he knew he was taking a high political risk. On that same June 22 he confirmed to Mussolini the receipt of his announcement of relinquishment of Italian claims in Savoy and acted as if he did not care about the Duce's decision.[5] It made no sense to push forward to Grenoble and Chambéry to meet the Axis partner there when Hitler already knew that the Italians would not show up.

However, the limited operation would still fulfill its purpose if it were possible, during the short time remaining to undermine the position of Savoy to such an extent that the French would also have to cede Upper Savoy during the negotiations in Rome to achieve a total encirclement of Switzerland. This calculation, again, did not add up: Grenoble and Chambéry were not reached as planned because Hitler, who assumed that this was an easy matter, underestimated the difficult terrain as well as the required military effort and, not least, the resistance of the French alpine army. He thus lacked the desired means of extortion to be used against the French in the Italian-French negotiations in Rome. His attempted last-minute intervention had been too late.

Hitler, the gambler, had not counted on having to retreat from his offensive operation without success. When this nevertheless happened German troops were in the wrong position to execute successful acts of destruction. A concentrated attack on Annecy in the center of Upper Savoy would have been required to reach those bridges and only their destruction would have seriously impeded the Geneva-Annecy rail line. For such a difficult operation, however, it would have been necessary to prepare an extensive force of specialized mountain troops, and for this Hitler lacked both time and the proper understanding. For this "omission," attributed to General Warlimont in the OKW, Hitler himself was responsible. His hasty attempt to quickly gain a military and political advantage with the occupation of Grenoble and Chambéry and to shut the door on Switzerland's last connection to the outside world with little effort ended in miscalculation.

On the morning of June 25, General von Brauchitsch reported to his chief of the general staff what had transpired the evening before at Hitler's headquarters: "The political leadership," noted Halder, "wanted to have the rail line between Switzerland and France interrupted." For this reason General List received the urgent orders "to destroy the La Roche-Annecy rail line thoroughly." It was not possible to execute this order during the night before the armistice. The German troops were unable to inflict lasting damage during their retreat; near Albens, about ten kilometers before Aix-les-Bains, they merely dismantled some switches and blasted a switch tower.[6] This act of destruction was insignificant, for an undamaged rail line remained available from Annecy via Ugine and Albertville to Grenoble. Only a crippling of the line between La Roche and Annecy, the common "eye of the needle" for all rail connections between Switzerland and Upper Savoy, would have had any effect. Von Brauchitsch stated to Halder "that now, after the armistice has taken effect, a patrol operation of the army should undertake the destruction. I object. When an armistice has been allowed to take effect, such a military order is impossible."[7]

After conferring with Keitel, Halder passed the order to Admiral Canaris: via the intelligence bureau, he should initiate an effective act of sabotage. Halder himself did not witness the scene with Hitler on June 24. At that time he was only called in for conferences with von Brauchitsch at the Führer's headquarters on a case-by-case basis. In a letter of August 10, 1970, he provided me with the following additional explanation:

> I only heard—and this through Admiral Canaris—that during the military encirclement of Switzerland a gap remained open near Geneva, which caused Hitler's nasty interest. Apparently he became a nuisance in his own particular way to those men of his OKW whom he held responsible for this. With this impression Canaris came to me, or rather sent word, that this gap had to be made harmless by the blasting of a bridge which I was to have done in a surprise raid by forces of the army. I sent word to him that I would not accept this type of order: If he really wanted to do such a thing, he as chief of intelligence would have the necessary means at his disposal. I no longer discussed this question. The closing of the offending gap was apparently done by other means in an unobtrusive manner.

Although Halder is mistaken that von Brauchitsch had given him the order according to his notes of June 25, 1940, and that he passed it on to Canaris, he provides at the same time an important documentation in his war diary: The "nasty interest" in the matter clearly originated with Hitler and not with the OKW. An oral communication from General Warlimont of July 20, 1968, also leaves no doubt in this matter. However, since Hitler's personal interest in this encirclement action has already been discussed, this confirmation is no longer a surprise.

On July 1, Bürkner, the chief of the Department of Foreign Offense Defense, reported to the chief of the general staff of the army that the OKW had called off the destruction of the rail line but that it was still to be carried out. To achieve a more lasting interruption, the viaduct of Lavillat near Evires was to be blasted. Hans Rudolf Fuhrer mentions this sabotage operation by the intelligence bureau in his 1982 Zurich dissertation *Spionage gegen die Schweiz* [Espionage against Switzerland] as a single operation initiated by the OKW, without going beyond Böhme's description.[8] A report in the *Neue Zürcher Zeitung* of February 6, 1946, tells in detail how the act of sabotage was undertaken. An attack with explosives was executed by four members of the Belgian Rexist movement on the initiative of the German intelligence officer Major Hoffmann in Annemasse. On September 4, they traveled with a convoy consisting of two passenger vehicles and two trucks, camouflaged as a Red Cross transport, to the rail viaduct of Lavillat near Evires and stopped there for an extended time, allegedly to repair a breakdown. Four hours later the bridge was exploded by means of eight hundred kilograms of Melinit. Two of the stone pillars were destroyed. Rumors were planted that ascribed the attack to the British intelligence service. A Geneva correspondent wrote: "The aim is obviously to cause difficulties for Switzerland which has a free port in Sète and transports goods for the country via Grenoble, Annecy and Annemasse."[9]

Thus, Hitler's orders were still executed after lengthy preparations; the "lasting" destruction, however, did not last. Traffic to unoccupied France would return to service after one and a half months. Incidentally, the saboteurs, together with their leader Cayzeele were discovered and arrested by the French and Belgian police in early 1946.

The history of the "gap" near Geneva, the importance of which has so far been underestimated, has been the subject of only rudimentary research. The subsequent efforts, particularly by the OKW, to close this gap by means of economic warfare will become clear from the inquiry in the second part of this book.

The fact that Hitler was concerned with Switzerland on June 24 also became known to the Swiss Intelligence Service. On June 30, Hans Hausamann who had established his own information network, transmitted a report to it "from a very well informed source" which contained amazing news: On June 24 a Führer conference had taken place at the Reich chancellery in Berlin between Hitler and his close personal staff, at which Switzerland was discussed. In the presence of Göring, Keitel, Ribbentrop, Hess, and Goebbels two views were debated: Ribbentrop especially favored an occupation of Switzerland while the representatives of the armed forces, in particular Keitel, believed that the goal could also be reached by preparatory measures "without risking the lives of several hundred thousand German soldiers." This report, which has been greatly condensed here, ended with the words: "This opinion, presented by General Keitel, found the approval of Hitler himself who repeatedly entered the discussion."[10] In a letter of February 9, 1970, Hausamann explained to me that the report came from a source in the Reich's propaganda ministry: "It was one of my best contacts."

The report of this message has been published repeatedly without realizing that its external form contains a fantasy.[11] No such discussion as described took place either in Berlin or at the FHQ "Wolfsschlucht"; the persons mentioned were at that time at different locations. It was not Hitler's style, furthermore, to arrange heterogeneously composed discussion groups for deciding this type of question and then concur in the debate with a previous speaker like Keitel! Other reports of Hausamann also show that the actual message is fused in an inadmissible manner with interpretations and commentaries to achieve its desired effect. Thus special caution is necessary when using this type of material.

However, if the report is reduced to its substance, it is surprising that Hausamann's source was able to transmit the correct information that Switzerland had been discussed with Hitler in a threatening manner on June 24, the substance of the message. Was an actual event also the basis for the information that the question of a possible attack on Switzerland had been discussed?

In view of these developments it should no longer be surprising that Hitler also included in his considerations the most extreme consequence, attack on Switzerland. Before turning to the actual attitude of the army leadership, a description of a situation review at the FHQ shall be given by way of illustration of the true context, one which General Warlimont had witnessed "probably still during the Western campaign."

On that occasion Hitler indicated by a wide sweep of his hands "that in the course or at the conclusion of the Western campaign the occupation of Switzerland would present only a modest task. And I remember exactly that the late SS Group Leader Dietrich, with whom you are also familiar and who was the leader of the so-called Body Standard of the SS, was also present, and that Hitler stated in a mocking and disparaging manner regarding the military strength of Switzerland: 'That can be done by Dietrich with my Body Standard.'"[12]

Hitler's remarks not only displayed a contempt for Switzerland which to him was in any event merely a phenomenon of degeneration that could not avoid its fate. The reference to Sepp Dietrich (1892–1966), SS group leader and commander of the Body Standard SS "Adolf Hitler," was grounded in actual military conditions. According to the description of Rudolf Lehmann, the Body Standard had been during the final phase of the conquest of France under the command of General Hoepner's XVIth Army Corps. It participated in List's action on June 23, although not in the main push in the direction of

Grenoble-Chambéry, but rather by protecting the flank and advancing under the code "Mittelmeer" (Mediterranean) from Clermont-Ferrand via Feurs in the direction St. Etienne.[13] Thus, Hitler did not pick the mental association Body Standard—"Group List"—Switzerland out of thin air. Even later, the Body Standard was intended to be used in Switzerland, as in the attack plans of mid-August 1940.

Another piece of information is also of interest. A suitable command post would already have been available as the Führer's headquarters in the Black Forest on the Kniebis, west of Freudenstadt. It had been constructed during the winter of 1939-40. Before his triumphant return to Berlin, Hitler stayed from June 28 to July 5 at the Führer's headquarters "Tannenberg" in the northern Black Forest. On June 30 he visited among other places Mulhouse near Basel. General Dollmann explained to him how the 7th Army had broken through the Maginot Line in Alsace; before that, it had feigned attack preparations against Switzerland.[14]

When Goebbels visited the FHQ "Tannenberg" on July 2, Hitler read to him particularly explosive details from the documents seized shortly before from La Charité-sur-Loire.[15] It was not there, but rather in Dijon that the most important documents regarding French general staff discussions with the Swiss were found, which the Germans then kept secret in order to present them during the "general settlement." As Hitler's main interest was directed towards England and the evaluation of the seized documents would need time, these military agreements, which from the German point of view were a breach of neutrality by Switzerland, probably had remained unknown at the time.[16]

How close Switzerland had really come to the abyss of war became clear only after the armistice.

NOTES

1. Arno Breker, in *Strahlungsfeld der Ereignisse 1925–1965* (Preussisch Olendorf: Schütz, 1972), 166ff.; see also Hermann Giesler, *Ein anderer Hitler* (Leoni am Starnbergersee: Druffel Verlag, 1977), 393ff.; Albert Speer, *Erinnerungen* (Frankfurt a. M.: Propyläen Verlag, 1969), 185–86.

2. National Archives, Washington, microfilm NA T 120, roll 351, 6310766 ss.

3. Hermann Böhme, *Der deutsch-französische Waffenstillstand im Zweiten Weltkrieg. Entstehung und Grundlagen des Waffenstillstandes von 1940* (Stuttgart: Deutsche Verlags-Anstalt, 1966), 78–79; 402.

4. Oral communication of General Walter Warlimont, Gmünd, July 20, 1968.

5. I Documenti Diplomatici Italiani, Nona serie, vol. 5 (Roma: Liberia dello Stato, 1965), 74.

6. AOK 12, "Kriegstagebuch der Oberquartiermeister-Abteilung," Qu 2, January 1, 1940–September 6, 1940, 38–39; microfilm NA T-312, roll 433.

7. Franz Halder, *Kriegstagebuch,* vol. 1 (Stuttgart: W. Kohlhammer Verlag, 1962), 371.

8. Hans Rudolf Fuhrer, *Spionage gegen die Schweiz. Die geheimen deutschen Nachrichtendienste gegen die Schweiz im Zweiten Weltkrieg 1939–1945,* (Frauenfeld: Verlag Huber, 1982), 28–29; Halder, *Kriegstagebuch,* vol. 2 (Stuttgart: W. Kohlhammer Verlag, 1963), 4.

9. "Ein Sprengstoffattentat in Hochsavoyen vom Jahr 1940," in *Neue Zürcher Zeitung* February 2, 1946.

10. Archiv für Zeitgeschichte ETH Zürich, Hausamann-Bericht, June 30, 1940, 3.

11. *Schweizerzeit,* no. 17, October 6, 1989; *Appenzeller Zeitung,* June 30, 1989; *Die Weltwoche,* no. 33, August 20, 1971, 5.

12. Oral communication of General Walter Warlimont, June 20, 1968, notes of the interview.

13. Rudolf Lehmann, *Die Leibstandarte,* vol. 1 (Osnabrück: Munin, 1977), 302ff.; Charles Messenger, Hitler's Gladiator (London: Brassey's Defence Publ., 1988), 87.

14. "Kriegstagebuch Führer-Hauptquartier," no. 3, 42ff.; microfilm NA T 78, roll 351; Gerhard Buck, *Das Führer-Hauptquartier 1939–1945,* 3rd edition (Leoni am Starnbergersee: Druffel Verlag, 1983), 62ff.

15. Elke Fröhlich, ed., *Die Tagebücher von Joseph Goebbels. Sämtliche Fragmente,* vol. 4 (München: K. G. Saur, 1987), 225–26.

16. Halder is supposed to have been informed about this already on July 1, that is 21; Ulrich Liss, "Noch einmal: La Charité 1940," *Allgemeine Schweizerische Militärzeitschrift,* no. 12 (December 1967), 729ff.; Halder, *Kriegstagebuch,* vol. 2 (Stuttgart: 1963), 29; the OKW presented Hitler with a first summary on July 29. PAB, F 10 147–49; ADAP, vol. 10, 12–13.

Chapter Six

Readying the 12th Army for "Special Task" Switzerland

While after July 6, 1940, the demobilization of troops from 450,000 to about 150,000 men had made rapid progress in Switzerland, an opposite development occurred on the other side of its western border. During the weeks following the armistice the Germans assembled a threatening military potential which was designed—more specifically than Guderian's tank group—for the topographic conditions of Switzerland. The German troop movements in occupied Burgundy, particularly in the nearby Franche-Comté and Upper Alsace, have remained largely unexamined until recently from a Swiss point of view. Georges Wüthrich, a journalist, who was not satisfied with the statement of a vaguely threatening situation, found alarming information in 1989 derived from an intense research effort.[1] This information was confirmed and reinforced by research done by Michael Müller at the University of Zürich. Until now there has been no explanation why during the first half of July the Germans pursued and actually achieved such a concentration of their forces.

As measures such as these cannot occur without definite goals, the question arises: Had Hitler, while veiling his intentions, already ordered preparation of the necessary offensive units in order to be able to "clean up" this small country by means of a surprise coup? It might have been assumed that further information could be obtained from the files of Army Group C and the 12th Army for the summer of 1940. However, important sources were lost in the fire at the military science department of the General Staff of the Army in February 1942 and by the destruction of the army archives at Potsdam in April 1945. Even in the pertinent documents still available, which the Americans filmed and passed on to the Federal Archives-Military Archives in Freiburg there are numerous signs of fire damage. Among the documents preserved is appendix 23 to the war diary 4 of Army Group Command C from

June 24 to August 2, 1940. This source material reveals the steps that were initiated after the conference of June 24 at the Führer's headquarters.[2]

"Case Switzerland" was the main irritant for Hitler on the evening of June 24, but the discussion involved the whole state of the war at the moment of that triumphant victory. Basic decisions had to be made quickly because of the impending armistice. Although Hitler remained undecided about how to proceed with the war against England, the planned restructuring and reduction of the army as well as the assignment of new tasks could not be postponed. However, definitive orders could only be given after the armistice with France had actually taken effect.

The activities undertaken by General Walther von Brauchitsch, the commander in chief of the army, now move to the center of our interest. Immediately after the conference he informed the commanders in chief of the three army groups A, B, and C in writing about the planned measures. The letter of June 24 provided a preliminary orientation about "the following thoughts which are currently being worked out in the OKH;" according to military thinking this was, as the diary of the chief of Army Group C, General Wilhelm Ritter von Leeb, reveals, a "preliminary order."[3]

According to this "preliminary order," Army Groups A and B would in the future be deployed at the Channel or the Atlantic coast of France. Apart from security functions and training they were assigned to "preparations for the continuation of the war against England." The remaining part of occupied France to the Swiss and German borders was put under the authority of Army Group C. It was not directly involved in the continuation of the war against England. Instead, the letter contained—in analogy to the formulation cited above—the following added order: "Preparation for a special task for which orders will follow."[4]

As Army Group C would subsequently cover all of the western border of Switzerland, the determination of this "special task, for which orders will follow" awakens one's attention. Up to now, almost all relevant historical studies, regardless of their varying evaluation of the threat, have claimed that Hitler never seriously considered an attack on Switzerland. As will be shown, this assumption is wrong.

Two days later, von Brauchitsch issued the definitive "order for the restructuring of the army." The 1st, 2nd, and 12th Armies were assigned to Army Group C for their tasks. No further details concerning Switzerland emerge from this order: "'Orders will be given for special tasks for individual army groups" was the laconic wording.[5] In order better to inform the leading officers of the general staffs of the army groups and the armies regarding the redispositions and new tasks, they were ordered to the headquarters of Army Group B in Versailles for a conference on June 28. During his briefing, the chief of the operations department of the general staff of the army, Colonel on the General Staff Hans von Greiffenberg also referred to Switzerland. With regard to the 12th Army, which was to be moved to the Swiss border in a new configuration, he first stated: "It is necessary that this army must be assembled soon."[6]

As can be learned from an important passage published by Walter Schaufelberger, von Greiffenberg also declared: "Regarding the matter in question, the Führer has so far only stated that under certain conditions an occupation would be considered." These conditions had not yet been met. In view of the armistice now in effect, the orders given by von Greiffenberg sounded much more moderate: "The case is currently not acute. For the time being no deployment and no preparations are to be made. Mental preparation only. If the case in question occurs, forces from the north and northeast will also be used. Army Group C or the 12th Army may present their ideas based on maps at some time, but without any commitment."[7] The air of unconcern displayed at this meeting did, however, not fit in with the measures subsequently pursued by the Army High Command. In spite of the fact that "no deployment" was to take place, the troop movements executed by July 9 in the border area with Switzerland pursued exactly this goal. General Guderian, who on June 23-24 had been suddenly moved to Besançon with his staff and had made reconnaissance drives in the Jura area, was given other orders in early July. The 12th army, under whose command Guderian's tank group had been, was now poised to take up position in the area between Geneva and Basel with added new forces.

The chief of the general staff of the 12th Army also had received a copy of the ominous "advance order" of June 24 with the stamp "Secret command matter! Chief only! [Transmit] only by officer!" In his accompanying letter of June 26 the superior chief of the general staff of Army Group A indicated that this "did concern plans," but that a definitive decision had not yet been made. On these documents, which have been singed by fire, the order "Preparation for a special task, for which orders will be given" had been heavily underlined twice.[8]

It was this same 12th Army whose commander in chief Wilhelm List had shortly before been in charge of the failed special order for cutting off Switzerland in the Dauphiné and Savoy and was now to be deployed along the insufficiently fortified western border of the country. The notes of the meeting in Versailles contained the following remark: "12th Army appears to have a tendency to become sharply engaged."[9] List and his general staff officers were obviously anxious to make up for the previous failures. The headquarters of the 12th Army was moved to Salins-les-Bains, about fifty-five kilometers west of the Swiss Jura border.

In its new composition, the 12th Army comprised nine divisions which covered the border area from northwest of Geneva to Upper Alsace as follows: The 1st Mountain Division under General Ludwig Kübler which had been unable to advance to Chambéry and Annecy was now transferred to the area of Salins-Morez. Added to this was the 6th Mountain Division which had only been assembled in June and had scarcely been able to collect any war laurels on the Upper Rhine. It was now moved to Pontarlier and put under the command of Colonel Ferdinand Schörner; this loyal National Socialist would later be promoted by Hitler, shortly before his suicide on April 5, 1945, to Field Marshal. These two mountain divisions which were moved close to the Swiss border were combined in the XVIIIth Army Corps whose general command established its command post in Malbuisson, near the crossing to Vallorbe.

The 23rd and the 260th Infantry Divisions were moved to the adjoining area near Belfort while the 21st and 73rd Infantry Divisions assumed a favorable position for reaching Basel in the area of Mulhouse and Altkirch. The 15th and 5th Infantry Divisions were placed west and east of Dijon. The 52nd Infantry Division, in readiness northwest of Vesoul, could have been brought rapidly to the Swiss border.[10] To leadership positions were added the General Commands XVIII, XXV, and XXVII and the Superior Command Staffs for Special Assignment XXXIII and XXXVII; "as soon as possible" they will move "to their new quarters and report their arrival to the 12th Army," reads List's army order of June 30, 1940. [11] Together with the sapper units, the bridge building units, and the mixed mobile forces which the general command had to keep ready "for rapid movement to possibly threatened areas," this resulted in an aggressive offensive potential which no longer bore any relationship to general security tasks. On July 24, the strength of the 12th Army was about 245,000 men.[12] The allegedly threatened sites such as Tournus and Lons-le-Saunier which pointed to a pincer maneuver through unoccupied areas, as well as St. Claude, were strategically important avenues for an advance towards Geneva and Lake Geneva.[13]

Army Group C, under whose command the 12th Army now served, made its headquarters in Dijon; relative to its sweeping command area, it was also strikingly close to the Jura region. Under its commander in chief Wilhelm Ritter von Leeb it had feigned deployment maneuvers against Switzerland before the Western offensive. Thus, with Leeb and List who had been promoted to Field Marshals by Hitler on July 19, the two military "Swiss specialists" were joined at the level of high command and selected for the "special task."

The documentary evidence that the "special task" actually referred to the occupation of Switzerland was supplied by Leeb as commander in chief of

Army Group C as well as, in a direct form, by his first officer of the general staff, Vincenz Müller. Leeb had not taken part in the conference in Versailles on June 28. On that day he learned for the first time which composition of forces the high command had planned for the 12th Army. He wrote in his diary when everything still was in flux: "The 12th Army will also get many motorized units and two mountain divisions. Should all this be directed towards Switzerland?"[14]

On July 6 Leeb arrived in the undamaged city of Dijon where he took quarters in the Hôtel de la Cloche. Four days later, accompanied by Colonel Vincenz Müller, he made an intensive reconnaissance of the Swiss border. In the area of Gex he studied the possibilities of an advance towards Geneva as well as to the lake and checked the terrain from Morez to the border crossing at Les Verrières. The finding from his reconnaissance in the area of the two mountain divisions was as terse as it was unmistakable: "No terrain difficulties for invading Switzerland."[15]

Leeb and his escort, however, had discovered some other problems which would constitute impediments for an attack. Representing the chief of the general staff of Army Group Command C, Müller therefore requested on July 11 that the operations department of the general staff of the army eliminate these weak points. On the one hand he demanded a shifting of the demarcation line, as the road between Morez and Gex formed the border with Switzerland for several kilometers and thus provided undesired views: "All troop movements there take place right under the eyes of the Swiss customs agents." On the other hand he drew attention to the situation of the rail line; the destroyed railroad bridges in the border area with Switzerland had not yet been rebuilt. There followed the key sentence: "If the special task for army group C is still under consideration, even if at an undetermined time, it is necessary to take the two points mentioned above into account as soon as possible by corresponding arrangements."[16]

Thus, the "special task for which orders will be given" clearly referred to an invasion of Switzerland. The reconstruction of these bridges was a preparation for it. The fact that this special task continued to be considered emerges from the continued attention to this request, as discussed in the next chapter.

The first officer of the general staff of the 21st Division also conducted a reconnaissance of the "approach routes to the Swiss border" in the Sundgau.[17] The divisional war diary of July 14 states: "The result is that according to the road network an approach in two columns towards the south is possible. It is necessary that the damaged roads and bridges must be repaired first." This resulted the next day in a request to the Supreme Command XXXIII: "Accelerated repair of the roads and bridges on the approach roads to the Swiss border which have been blown up by the French."[18]

Also visiting the Swiss border near Meudon (Les Verrières) on July 15 for a personal inspection was Reichsführer SS Heinrich Himmler with his entourage.[19] Ferdinand Schörner, who was responsible for this section as the commander of the 6th Mountain Division, guided him and answered his questions. As the operational draft of August 12 shows, the Body Standard SS "Adolf Hitler," which had been moved to Metz, as well as the infantry regiment "Grossdeutschland" would have been brought in from farther away as "rapid reinforcements" for the attack forces. The directives of the operation read that "they would be rapidly brought into action after the first breakthrough."[20]

The hasty actions by the commander in chief of the army shows the extent to which Hitler had gone on June 23–24 in planning his attack. At the moment at which he announced the "special task" to the command of Army Group C, usable attack plans regarding Switzerland were not yet even available to the general staff of the army. Neither the Armed Forces High Command (OKW) nor the army high command (OKH) had been prepared for this type of plan from the "political leadership." In order for the attack sketch to be presented the next day, Captain von Menges in the operational section of the general staff of the army had to execute overnight an order which he had received only that morning.

Typical of Hitler's intentions was the fact that he secretly issued the order in duplicate. According to Bernhard von Lossberg, General Jodl, chief of the armed forces operational staff in the Armed Forces High Command, was instructed to investigate without participation of the army high command or other departments how the invasion of Switzerland could be executed. According to Hitler's taste neither von Brauchitsch nor the general staff of the army were daring enough. He felt hampered by them in the realization of his war plans and therefore stirred up rivalry between OKW and OKH. That haste was in order also became clear from the directive of the "rather hurried study" prepared under Lossberg: Participation by the Italian partner, who just had deserted Hitler in his plans for Switzerland's cut off, was not to be considered.[21] All this points to the fact that, as soon as the suitable moment had arrived, Hitler wanted to force a fait accompli by a surprise attack. During the ensuing division of Switzerland, the Italians would have had no choice but to thank Hitler for those areas which he "generously" would have ceded to them.

With the 12th Army under Field Marshal Wilhelm List a unit of high fighting strength was readied for the occupation of Switzerland. At the beginning of the Western offensive it had advanced through Luxembourg; it had broken through the south Belgian fortifications in the Ardennes and pushed forward to the Aisne. In unison with Guderian's tank group that was under its command, it played an important part in the encirclement of the French eastern army, for which List received the Marshal's baton from Hitler on July 19, 1940. In the spring of 1941 the 12th Army was used for the push from Bulgaria towards southern Yugoslavia and Greece. After fights with heavy losses it broke through the heavily fortified Metaxas Line, conquered the Peloponnese, and occupied Athens. In May 1941, List was named "Armed Forces Commander Southeast." He later assumed the command of Army Group A at the eastern front; yet in September 1942 Hitler dismissed him because he had been unable to reach his goals in the Trans-Caucasus. After the war he was sentenced to life imprisonment for crimes in the fight against partisans, but was granted early release in 1952 for reasons of health.[22]

Switzerland could not expect mercy from these troops. An impression of the aggressive mood against Switzerland within the 6th Mountain Division is revealed by a propagandistic commemorative pamphlet published in 1943 by the NSDAP. This elite troop had been formed in great haste only in early June 1940 and had participated with the 7th Army at the Upper Rhine in the penetration of the Maginot Line. Its transfer from the western hills of the Vosges to Pontarlier was achieved by an eight-day march covering over 240 kilometers. The question was raised "where are we now marching to?" after there was hardly anything left to conquer in the west: "The only thought remaining was Switzerland. But all mountain troops were in agreement: One does not attack Switzerland. If anything, Switzerland is only to be occupied. A joker said: 'Simply for a quarter hour we don't even want to get started.' And the others nodded. With roaring laughter."[23] The pamphlet's later derogatory remarks, which deny Switzerland any right to exist, contain the worst Nazi propaganda. In Schörner's 6th Mountain Division, which hosted Reichsführer SS Heinrich Himmler during his visit to the border, it found ready acceptance.

NOTES

1. See Georges Wüthrich, "Vallorbe: Das 'Unterseeboot' an der Schweizer Grenze," and "'Höchste Dringlichkeit: Noch heute Schweizer Grenze erreichen!'" in *Sonntagszeitung*, no. 25 (June 18, 1989), 17–18.

2. Akte: "Heeresgruppen Kommando C," Anlage 23 zum "Kriegstagebuch," IV, June 24–August 2, 1940, microfilm NA T-311, roll 46.

3. Georg Meyer, ed., *Generalfeldmarschall Wilhelm Ritter von Leeb. Tagebuchaufzeichnungen und Lagebeurteilungen aus zwei Weltkriegen* (Stuttgart: Deutsche Verlags-Anstalt, 1976), 245.

4. "Vorbefehl OKH," GenStdH Op. Abt. (Ia) to the commanders of the Army Groups A, B and C, H. Qu. OKH, June 24, 1940, signed von Brauchitsch, von Greiffenberg; microfilm NA T-311, roll 46 (BA-MA, RH 19 III/141). This document is the third issue and has the date of receipt stamped as June 26, 1940; see complete text below in Documentary Appendix.

5. OKH GenStdH Op.Abt. (Ia), "Befehl für die Umgruppierung des Heeres," H Qu. OKH, June 26, 1940, signed Brauchitsch; microfilm NA T-311, roll 46.

6. "Protokoll Besprechung in Versailles, June 26, 1940, Ia No. 1119/40g. K. , 1. version, June 26, 1940, 4; in HGr. Nord, enclosures taken from K. T. B. according to directive OKH Gen. StdH./Op.Abt. (III), no. 9130/40 geh. of October 29, 1940, BA-MA. RH 19 III/128.

7. Enclosure only of Ia no. 1119/40 g. K. of June 26; explanation to page 4; ibid.; see also Walter Schaufelberger, "Militärische Bedrohung der Schweiz 1939/40," in *Kriegsmobilmachung 1939*, ed. Roland Beck ETH (Zürich: 1989), 42–43; thanks to Michael Müller for additional oral references who first discovered this document in BA-MA; it is reproduced in the documentary appendix, no. 12.

8. This refers to the first edition of the document mentioned in endnote 4, in AOK 12, IA. "Aufmarsch E": Umgliederung des Heeres, June 24–26, 1940; microfilm NA T-312, roll 431.

9. See endnote 7.

10. AOK 12, "Armeebefehl," no. 33 of June 30, 1940, signed List, with enclosures; microfilm NA T-312, roll 427. Georg Tessin, *Verbände und Truppen der deutschen Wehrmacht und Waffen im Zweiten Weltkrieg 1939–1945,* vol. 3 (Frankfurt a. M.: Biblio Verlag, 1974), 228.

11. Enclosure 5 for "Armeebefehl" no. 33 of June 30, 1940; microfilm NA T-312, roll 427.

12. AOK 12, Additions of the 12th Army to the "Directives for the Service of Troops in the Occupied Territories after Conclusion of Operations," A. H. Qu., July 16, 1940, signed List; microfilm NA T-312, roll 432. The total strength of the troops to be provisioned was put on July 7, 1940, at 400,000 men.

13. Also 206,000 prisoners had to be provisioned, 75,000 horses of the army and 12,000 captured horses. AOK 12 O. Qu. "Kriegstagebuch," Qu. January 1–September 1, 1940, microfilm NA T-312, roll 431. On July 7, 1940, the total strength of the troops to be provisioned was put even at 400,000 men by including the troops which then were moved back to Germany. Appendix 3, "Kriegstagebuch," AOK 12 O. Qu. January 1–September 1, 1940, microfilm NA T-312, roll 432.

14. Meyer, *Leeb*, 246.

15. Meyer, *Leeb*, 248. After the war Müller made his career in the German Democratic Republic and became in the 1950's lieutenant-general of the stationed people's police; Vincenz Müller, *Ich fand das wahre Vaterland*, Klaus Mummach (Berlin: Deutscher Militärverlag, 1963), 488.

16. "Written Communciation Heeresgruppenkommando C," Ia, OKH GestdH, Op.Abt. H Qu., July 11, 1940, signed Müller; BA-MA, RH 19 III/141. Compare below the parallel demand in Appendix, Document no. 9, digit 6e.

17. Schaufelberger, "Bedrohung," *Kriegsmobilmachung*, 42.

18. "Kriegstagebuch," No. 5 of the 21st Infantry Division, July 3 -September 16, 1940; BA-MA, RH 26-27/9. I owe the additonal referemce to Michael Müller.

19. The picture of Himmler and his entourage at the frontier crossing of Les Verrières is in the Swiss Federal Archive; it was also reproduced, as Geroges Wüthrich discovered, in the propagandistic pamphlet of the 6th Mountain Division: Andreas Weinberger, *Das gelbe Edelweiss. Wege und Werden einer Gebirgsdivision* (München: Zentralverlag der NSDAP, 1943), after 112. Wüthrich, "Dringlichkeit," *Sonntagszeitung*; Willi Gautschi,

General Henri Guisan. Die schweizerische Armeeführung im Zweiten Weltkrieg 3rd edition (Zürich: Verlag Neue Zürcher Zeitung, 1989), illustration XVIII; Schaufelberger, "Bedrohung," *Kriegsmobilmachung,* 42.

20. See below, Documentary Appendix, no. 14, digits 9c, 10d.

21. Bernhard von Lossberg, *Im Wehrmachtsführungsstab. Bericht eines Generalstabsoffiziers* (Hamburg: H. H. Nölke Verlag, 1949), 103.

22. "Einführung zum Verzeichnis des Nachlasses von Wilhelm List;" BA-MA N 527. According to List's directive all his notebooks and personal written documents have been destroyed after his death; what has remained of the relevant sources concerning this subject has not been very rewarding.

23. Weinberger, *Edelweiss,* 91.

Chapter Seven

Status of Swiss Security before the Spring of 1941

That Switzerland had not been used-as planned in the German study of attack—"as a region of transit to southern France as soon as possible"—resulted mainly from the conclusion of the armistice. As long as it remained in effect, there was no real reason to occupy Switzerland for the purpose of transit. The armistice protected it from attack as long as the advantages of a Switzerland in working order retained important weight in the considerably altered overall situation of the war; thus the question of an occupation no longer played any role when Germany finally marched into Vichy France on November 11, 1942.

As Hitler had never considered the armistice agreement to prejudge a final new order, it was part of his tactics to include momentary constellations into his calculation, yet without giving up long-term strategies. At first he hoped still to be able to force England into an agreement, even after it had lost its French ally. His speech to the Reichstag of July 19, 1940, a "call to reason," contained no serious peace proposal and was shortly thereafter decisively rejected by Foreign Minister Lord Halifax. Hitler had the landing Operation "Seelöwe" [Sea Lion] in readiness but concentrated on the air war because a landing appeared to him to be too risky. The failure of the air war had become unmistakably apparent in September. Accordingly, his plans for an attack against the Soviet Union moved into the foreground which he began to consider in July. At that time also an effort was made to win Spain for German plans to conquer Gibraltar.

On the European continent, the object was to set up a most one-sided collaboration which would favorably exploit the potential of economic production in favor of the Axis powers, which in the remaining neutral countries postured as the heirs of the Allies. With the propagated "new Europe," the

63

aim was to form a continental block directed against England on the economic as well as the political front. With the start of planning for an attack on the Soviet Union, the at first divergent concepts for a European supra-regional economy became reduced to maximizing the fulfillment of demands for armaments and military supplies.

However, this development after the armistice, described here only in outline, did not prevent Hitler from keeping all his options open for a future peace accord. He secretly charged Under Secretary of State Stuckart of the Interior Ministry in June 1940 with the preparation of a comprehensive document concerning the future borders of the Reich in the West. For Germany's territorial claims he reached back far earlier than 1648. After the first draft had not satisfied Hitler's notion, the planned border of the Reich ran "about from the mouth of the Somme to the east, along the northern edge of the Paris Basin and the Champagne to the Argonne, there turned southward and proceeded through Burgundy and west of the Franche-Comté to Lake Geneva."[1] This concept of the future territory of the Reich in the west was also important for the pertinent planning about Switzerland.

For the occupation of Switzerland, the German operational drafts of mid-August provided for a line of division with Italy which was precisely aligned with the course of the border in France. The division between Germany and Italy, according to the most minimal version planned by the OKH, ran along the top of the Glarus and Bernese Alps to the area of Martigny. While the course of the border remained open in the Valais, the inclusion of the western part of Switzerland fitted seamlessly into the future Reich, for which divisions based on language no longer had any meaning. Behind the historically blurred claims, which in Burgundy rested on supposedly very old German grounds, hid the desire to reduce France to an inconsequential future size.

The assumption, which in any case was irrelevant in 1940-41, that these questions about frontiers were merely theoretical futuristic play is decisively refuted by the measures Hitler took in France. In approximate accordance with the borders of the Reich planned in Stuckart's study, he determined a so-called "northeast line" in the occupied part of France, which would run from south of Dole to the small corner near Gex and the end point between Geneva and Bellegarde and was identical with the line of demarcation. French citizens who had left their homes due to evacuation or flight from the advancing German troops were not allowed to cross this barrier, even if willing to return. It was also designated as the "Schwarze Linie [black line]" or "Führer Linie" and largely corresponded to borders planned by Hitler, who proposed to reserve these areas for future absorption of Germans. The German land use organization "Ostland" even promoted the takeover of agricultural farms by German "settlers," while their French owners were barred from returning to the restricted zone! Additional surveillance forces were put into place to control this internal border; in spite of gradual loosening, these troops were withdrawn only in December 1941.[2]

While the propaganda to collaborate for a "new Europe" also affected Switzerland, all of the areas immediately adjoining Switzerland between Basel and Geneva were already subjected to special restrictive measures in preparation for later annexation. The planned separation line between the Italian and German spheres of interest in Switzerland also should not be viewed as irrelevant imaginations of an overactive officer of the general staff. Otto Wilhelm von Menges had also worked on Stuckart's study and the question of the borders of the Reich in the West. It was he who, besides the studies for an attack on Switzerland, supplied the relevant maps with the proposed dividing line between the German and Italian zones of occupation. On September 4, 1940 von Menges received, according to his private notes, an order which was particularly interesting in this context: "For the last two days also work on a study for the Ministry of the Interior regarding the future western border in order to bring it into agreement with the border demanded by the OKH." A short time later he made "a presentation before General Halder regarding the proposal about the future western border with its historic justification and our position."[3] If there had still been any disagreements regarding the future frontiers of the Reich in the border area near Geneva, Menges was assigned the central task of bringing the ideas of the OKH in line with those of Stuckart's study.

However, this was not the end of it. The attack plans against Switzerland were continued in the second half of 1940 not with the intent of theoretical planning, but as continued adjustment to reflect the forces available for an attack. In this manner, the options for an invasion were kept alive. As already mentioned, Army Group Command C had sent a request to the OKH on July 11, 1940 to undertake certain actions-moving the line of demarcation and repairing destroyed bridges in the domain of the 12th Army-as preconditions for an attack, in case the "special task" was still under consideration. The OKH initiated the respective measures, but not without first checking with the highest authorities, as the historian Ingeborg Meier, who found a message from the OKH dated July 13, has shown: "Today, a conference with the Führer is taking place, during which the matter in question will also be discussed."[4]

The focus of the conference at the Berghof was Operation "Seelöwe" which was directed against England. No direct response of Hitler regarding Switzerland was recorded. However, subsequent developments show that he considered the question unresolved, even though his interest was totally absorbed in the attack on England. The shifting of the line of demarcation had actually been submitted to the armistice commission, as the operational drafts of the OKH dated August 8 and 12 reveal.

The request to set more favorable conditions for the deployment of German and Italian troops and possibly also to close the gap near Geneva by means of shifting the border involved the armistice agreements and was rejected by the Armistice Commission.[5] Thus, the draft of attack of August 12 contained the renewed demand: "As the advantages of a German and Italian deployment of forces south of Lake Geneva are great, it should be demanded by the German political leadership that it permit the march of German and Italian troops through unoccupied territory and the 50-km zone (on the Italian/French border), or create the preconditions for it."[6] As long as the question of an occupation of Switzerland remained tied to the overall situation in France, there was from Hitler's point of view no need for a decision; this problem would resolve itself with the occupation of Vichy France. Here one discovers again the protective effect of the armistice for Switzerland.

It is particularly impressive to what extent the availability of German forces was basic to the attack planning. The deployment of the 12th Army at the Swiss border, which had followed in response to the events of June 24, required a concentration of forces which in view of the preparatory measures for Operation "Seelöwe" could not be maintained for long. As the originally announced order for the special task did not arrive, the 1st Mountain Division was withdrawn on July 24, 1940; it was now assigned to the 16th Army and moved to the area Amiens-Abbeville. The 6th Mountain Division also left the area of the Jura and was put under the command of the 9th Army. In order to secure the continued full attack strength on the Swiss border, the general staff of the army safeguarded that goal in that the troops needed for the operation could be brought back within a few days.

On August 3, 1940, Otto Wilhelm von Menges had returned from his vacation to the headquarters of the general staff of the army, now located at Fontainebleau. Four days earlier von Brauchitsch and Halder had attended an important Führer conference at the Berghof which after several weeks of wait and see led to the active continuation of warfare. This included the planned air offensive against England, but also Hitler's following decision: "In the course of this conflict, Russia has to be finished. Spring 1941. The more rapidly we smash Russia, the better."[7] During this phase of intensive examination of all possibilities for weakening England, including an increased engagement in the Mediterranean, it was advisable to modify all plans in accordance with the new situation. Also on August 3, von Menges received an order to begin immediately revising his attack sketch. Both the partial demobilization as well as the re-disposition of military forces in Switzerland and, on the German side, the regroupings in Army Group C, had created a new basis for planning. He first reported to Hans von Greiffenberg, Chief of the Operations Division who in the meantime had been promoted to Major General, about the principal assumptions which should underlie the plan. One result of the discussion was that as many tank troops as possible instead of the motorized divisions should be employed.[8] For August 8, the following significant entry is found in his private notes:

> Work on the Swiss study after the picture there has changed due to the beginning of partial demobilization and changed Swiss regrouping. Switzerland knows that it is in our hands after we have found in France the yet unpublished documents about the cooperation between the general staffs of France and Switzerland. But they still revile us in the press. I don't believe that Switzerland would defend itself with weapons. This would be crazy. On the other hand, our invasion could be a welcome pretext for Roosevelt to intervene.[9]

This note clarifies why von Menges remarks in all three attack studies that "with the current political situation in Switzerland" it could be possible that "it might accede to ultimatum demands in a peaceful manner, so that after a warlike border crossing a rapid transition to a peaceful invasion must be assured."[10] The private notes make it clear that von Menges considered an armed resistance of Switzerland as unrealistic and an "Anschluss" without fighting as probable. No less interesting is his remark regarding the secret Swiss-French military agreements. Although the presenting of the discovery of these explosive documents was to be reserved for the moment of revenge, keeping them secret was also advantageous to the German strategy of creating uncertainty. Both Hitler and the OKH viewed the leadership of the Swiss army as compromised. Franz Halder, the former Chief of the General Staff of the Army, expressed this view as late as 1970 and considered General Guisan more as a politician than as a soldier: "The machinations of your—in my opinion considerably overrated—General are not the 'scratching or violating' of the principle of neutrality, but quite simply, according to my military education, an irresponsibly high-handed act of military leadership."[11] Von Menges also included insights gained from these documents in his attack study.[12] An additional nuance is added by his expressed fear that the United States might actively enter the war because of an attack on Switzerland.

On August 8 von Menges had provisionally completed elaborating the operational concept. Apart from the information about the Swiss defenses which was based on incomplete and partly wrong data, he presented a quite detailed attack scenario for the German forces. However, the examination of the Italian attack possibilities remained in the range of "mental preparation." In this context, his next steps are of interest. For August 10 and 11 von Menges notes: "Again working on the Swiss study in order to determine individual orders and forces." Over the weekend—interrupted only by a swim in the Seine on Sunday—followed the detailed tie-in of the attack plan with the movement of individual troops considered for this operation. For them the specific orders were pre-formulated to assure that they would be passed on rapidly; the means and time required for transporting the troops were also calculated. The 1st Mountain Division then stationed at the Pas de Calais against England would according to the revised attack plan of August 12 be brought back to the Swiss border by means of trucks and camouflaged trains. The dispositions in the operations department were made in such a manner that those fighting units which formerly had already been more or less closely connected with "Case Switzerland" would be brought back as much as possible. Thus, the 29th Motorized Division which had been the first to reach the Swiss Jura border with Guderian's tank group and was now part of the 2nd Army, would be part of the second attack group. Its 4th Tank Division from the area of Auxerre was also planned for use in Switzerland; they had already worked for Hitler's "special task" with List's group before the armistice. Also participating at the time had been the SS Body Standard "Adolf Hitler" which was now stationed in Metz. According to the orders they would have to be "brought rapidly into the action after the first invasion" together with the infantry regiment "Grossdeutschland." New was the addition of the SS motorized division "Totenkopf [Skull]." The dispositions in the general staff of the army were such that the complete deployment for an intended attack could be achieved within one week. The troops destined for the invasion were specified as well as the needed time of transport: "On day 7 before the attack it is necessary at least to give the railroad an advance warning."[13]

Although the detailed draft of operations carries the date of August 12, Menges still worked on it the following day. His last commentary on the matter reads: "Switzerland, Turkey, and Yugoslavia continue to be more or less enemies. It looks as if Germany, Italy, and Russia will have to clear this up."[14] Within the general staff of the army, von Menges was considered a technically highly qualified collaborator. In October 1940, at the special request of Field Marshal von Brauchitsch, he was promoted in spite of his youth to Ia-officer in the 1st Cavalry Division which he later helped to convert to the 24th Tank Division. He fell on February 2, 1943 at Stalingrad.[15]

As Werner Roesch has pointed out in his examination of the Swiss aspects of the operational drafts, this last version was used as the basis for all further plans.[16] Soon, however, extensive changes occurred in the forces considered for the attack, so that new troop dispositions became necessary. On August 26, 1940, Franz Halder ordered Army Group C to prepare an operational draft against Switzerland, among other things based on the premise that "Switzerland is determined to resist an invasion with all its might."[17] As to this order, Halder explained in 1969 to the military historian Hans Rudolf Kurz that he had made it personally clear to his friend, the Chief of Army Group C, Field Marshal Ritter von Leeb "that, if need be, this study intended to deter Hitler."[18] This shows again that even after the war Halder did not address the real reasons for giving the order.

On the one hand, a conflict had arisen in the Armistice Commission concerning Alsace-Lorraine as well as the occupation costs; General Huntziger accused the Germans of breach of contract. Halder noted on August 22, 1940 in his war diary: "It may be necessary to take military action if France creates problems. However, we are not prepared for this with our current structure."[19] At that time major redispositions were just ahead. In the evening of August 26, Halder was informed by Field Marshal von Brauchitsch about the results of the conference with Hitler. As the latter was afraid that the Soviet Union could use the sharpening of the Hungarian-Romanian conflict to grab the Romanian oil fields ahead of him, he ordered the immediate movement of German troops to the East. As von Menges noted on August 29: "For the last two days great activity with the dispatch of 10 infantry divisions and 3 tank corps to the East and preparation of the rapid occupation of the oil fields in Romania, in case an invasion becomes necessary due to the failure of an agreement between Romania and Hungary."[20] Subsequently, in spite of the rapid settlement of the conflict Army Group B as well as Army High Command 12 were moved from France to the *Generalgouvernement* (parts of the former Poland) and to East Prussia. Field Marshal List arrived in Krakow on September 25, 1940.[21]

In this course of events it is surprising how promptly Halder reacted with his order to Leeb to a possible conflict in France as well as to the impending troop movements to the East. Army High Command 12, which should have been leading the attack against Switzerland, for the foreseeable future was now unavailable for this purpose. For this reason the center of planning shifted now to Army Group C, in which until its transfer Army High Command 12 was still a participant. Leeb noted on August 27, 1940 in his agenda: "Operations draft against Switzerland completed."[22] On September 2, Colonel Vincenz Müller, the Ia officer of Army Group C, brought more detailed information from the OKH regarding the redispositions. The handwritten notes of General Hans Felber, the Chief of the General Staff of Army Group C, contain the following revealing entry: "Müller of the OKH brings considerable news this evening. Becoming rich people, but unfortunately stay in the West. But this appears better to me than new regulations for HGr B (*Army Group B*). Living conditions better here."[23] Regarding this rich loot,

Felber already had on the following day a "conference with army chiefs about new tasks (Switzerland) 'Tannenbaum.'" On September 9, Leeb again reconnoitered the area of attack with his entourage, among it Assistant Adjutant Prince Adalbert von Bayern: "Reconnoitering Swiss border from Pontarlier eastward to St. Hippolyte. Roads everywhere very good. All two-lane roads usable for troop movements. Use of three divisions in the direction of both sides of Bielersee possible."[24]

The planning for an occupation of France with which von Menges had been newly entrusted on September 21 as well as the preparation of the draft of operations requested from Army Group C were continued against the background of concrete political and military considerations.[25] The "Operations Draft Switzerland (Tannenbaum)" of Army Group C of October 4, 1940 again planned for a very short time of deployment, but claimed that double the forces, that is 21 divisions, were needed. Halder reduced this estimate to 11 divisions on October 17, in agreement with the proposal of Colonel Adolf Heusinger, the successor to von Greiffenberg as Chief of the Operations Department. With this contingent of forces it would again be possible to have the necessary troops ready for the special task without significant problems.[26]

On October 26, the new Army Group Command D under General Field Marshal Erwin von Witzleben assumed von Leeb's former domain of command. Under General Hilpert, Chief of the General Staff of Army Group D, another study for the occupation of Switzerland had been ordered from Army High Command 1 in September, so that even after the change the new leadership was already well informed about the plans for an attack on Switzerland. Like that of Army Group C, this operational draft was also dated October 4, 1940; it had been prepared by Bodo Zimmermann, Major on the General Staff, who was now as Ia officer in the General Staff of Army Group D Hilpert's most important collaborator. On November 11 the OKH declared that operation "Tannenbaum" was no longer relevant.[27]

At that time German troops were moved again along the Jura border. On October 26, General Hubert Lanz, the recently appointed commander of the 1st Mountain Division, had received orders to prepare for the attack on the fortification of Gibraltar. To be able to train in suitable terrain, the division was moved back to the Jura region. Together with the infantry regiment "Grossdeutschland" as well as with other special troops they did their operational training at Valdahon, not far from the border of La Chaux-de-Fonds. Operation "Felix," for which these troops had trained and to which Hitler had assigned great importance, failed on December 7, 1940 because of Franco's refusal to enter the war on the side of Germany.

On the following day, afraid that General Weygand would establish an opposition government in North Africa, Hitler began to plan for operation "Attila" against Vichy, France: "If something happens in North Africa, we have to occupy immediately the rest of France."[28] In this constellation of forces it was to Switzerland's advantage that the 12th Army was in the middle of preparations for Operation "Marita"; it had already transferred many of its troops to the region around Vienna for the planned attack on Greece. Hitler did not have to make the political decision whether the special task Switzerland should became relevant once again. As the feared breaking-away of the French regions of North Africa did not happen and the sharpening critical situation that involved Pétain's unexpected dismissal of Laval could be overcome, the armistice remained in effect.

The moving away of the last forces of the 12th Army around the New Year and, finally, the shifting of the 1st Mountain Division to the East in early April 1941 meant that the military threat to Switzerland had been sharply reduced.[29] Instead, in February 1941 the Armed Forces High Command began to intensify economic warfare against Switzerland with the aim to close finally the gap between Geneva and St. Gingolph. The second part of this book examines this continuation of war carried out with different means; it contains the history of the strategy then attempted to conquer Switzerland not by occupation but by complete encirclement.

NOTES

1. *Der Prozess gegen die Hauptkriegsverbrecher vor dem Internationalen Militär-gerichtshof Nürnberg, November 14, 1945–Oktober 1, 1946*, vol. 6 (Nürnberg: 1947), 470; Hermann Boehme, *Entstehung und Grundlagen des Waffenstillstandes von 1940* Stuttgart: Deutsche Verlags-Anstalt, 1960), 258ff.; Eberhard Jäckel, *Frankreich in Hitler's Europa. Die deutsche Frankreichpolitik im Zweiten Weltkrieg* (Stuttgart: 1966), 46ff.

2. See Jäckel, *Frankreich*, 89–90; Böhme, *Entstehung*, 260ff.

3. Private notes of Otto Wilhelm von Menges, September 6 and 9, 1940; papers in possession of Dr. Dietrich Wilhelm von Menges, Essen.

4. "Schreiben Hgr. Kdo. C, Ia," to OKH GenStdH, Op Abt., H. Qu., July 11, 1940, signed Müller; BA-MA, RH 19 III/141; note of July 13, 1940, RH 19 III/129.

5. "Der deutsche Angriff gegen die Schweiz. Neufassung infolge neuer Nachrichten über die Schweiz," OKH, Op. Abt. (I), August 12, 1940, signed von Menges, digit 16, e., in "Schweiz," vol. A, BA-MA, RH 2/465.

6. "Deutsche Angriff;" see also below, Documentary Appendix, No. 15.

7. Franz Halder, *Kriegstagebuch. Tägliche Aufzeichnungen des Chefs des Generalstabes des Heeres 1939–1942*, vol. 2 (Stuttgart: W. Kohlhammer Verlag, 1963), 46ff.

8. "Vortrag vor Ia über Studie," August 3, 1940. The handwritten and unsigned copy in Dossier "Schweiz," Vol. A, BA-MA RH 2/465; Dr. Dietrich von Menges as well as M. Bachmann, who transcribed the private notes, identified the author as Otto Wilhelm von Menges. Since June 1940 von Greiffenberg had also taken on the tasks of the major quartermaster 1.

9. Notes, Otto Wilhelm von Menges, entry of August 8, 1940; in private possesion of Dietrich Wilhelm von Menges, Essen.

10. See digit 6, f of the "1st. Sketch of Presentation," June 25, 1940; also digit 11, h of the new version of August 8, 1940 and digit 17 of the new version, August 12, 1940, in Dossier "Schweiz," BA-MA RH 2/465.

11. Letter of Franz Halder to author, dated Aschau, September 21, 1970.

12. "Rückschlüsse aus einem Schriftwechsel französischer Komandobehörden über die Beziehung Frankreich-Schweiz vom Oktober 1939 bis Februar 1940," unsigned exposé o. O., o. D., with a listing and the conclusion: "Daraus geht hervor, dass die Schweiz bis zum Ende des Jahres 1939 für den Ausbau der Grenze nach Frankreich nur wenig oder gar nichts getan hat, sondern nur die Grenze gegen Deutschland in Verteidigungszustand versetzt hat."

13. See the particulars below in Documentary Appendix, No. 15.

14. Private notes of Otto Wilhelm von Menges, August 13, 1940. At that time von Menges still hoped for a German-Russian coexistence: "I cannot see why there one cannot keep peace [Ruhe] with Russia," he noted August 17, 1940.

15. Reinhard Hauschild, *Der springende Reiter. 1. Kavallerie-Division-24. Panzerdivision im Bild* (Gross-Umstadt: Dohany, 1984), 11; notes to Otto Wilhelm von Menges, July 14, 1990 for which I thank Dr. Dietrich Wilhelm von Menges, Essen.

16. Werner Roesch, *Bedrohte Schweiz. Die deutschen Operationsplanungen gegen die Schweiz im Sommer/Herbst 1940 und die Abwehrbereitschaft der Armee im Oktober 1940* (Frauenfeld: Verlag Huber, 1986), 16.

17. Befehl OKH, GenStdH Op. Abt. (I) Heeresgruppe C, H. Qu. OKH, August 26, 1940, signed Halder; BA-MA RH 2/465.

18. Hans Rudolf Kurz, *Operationsplanung Schweiz. Die Rolle der Schweizer Armee in zwei Weltkriegen* (Thun: Ott Verlag, 1974), 45.

19. Halder, *Kriegstagebuch,* Vol. II, 73.

20. Private notes of Otto Wilhlem von Menges, August 28, 1940.

21. "Schreiben der Kommandatur Krakau," September 24, 1940; MA-BA, microfilm T-312, roll 431. Halder, *Kriegstagebuch,* Vol. II, 78; Georg Meyer, *Generalfeldmarschall Wilhelm Ritter von Leeb. Tagebuchaufzeichnungen und Lagebeurteilungen aus zwei Weltkriegen* (Stuttgart: Deutsche Verlags-Anstalt, 1976), 253.

22. Meyer, *von Leeb*, 253.

23. Handwritten notes of Lietenant General Hans Felber about the events of April 16, 1939-September 3, 1940: "Vorbereitung und Einsatz im Polenfeldzug 1939 und Westfeldzug 1940," BA-MA N 67/2.

24. Meyer, *von Leeb*, 254. The accompanying transport officer Major Lieutenant Bernhard von Watzdorf also made his later career in the Nationale Volksarmee [National Peoples Army] of the German Democratic Republic as did the Ia officer Vincenz Müller.

25. Details of the plans of attack elaborated in the fall of 1940 are not given here; see Hans Senn, *Der schweizerische Generalstab*, Vol. VII. Basel: Helbing & Lichtenhahn, 1995.

26. "Schweiz," Vol. B, "Op. Entwurf H. Gr. C "Tannenbaum,'" BA-MA RH 2/465; see also Roesch, *Bedrohte Schweiz*, 24- .

27. KTB, RH 19IV/2: Hgr. D. See also a study for an invasion of Switzerland from the domain of the 1. Armeeoberkommando 1, A. H. Qu., October 4, 1940, signed Zimmermann as well as other documents in "Studie Schweiz," AOK I, microfilm NA T 312, roll

25. Meyer, *Von Leeb*, 221. See also Halder's typical entry of October 27, 1940: "Hilpert (Chef), Zimmermann (Ia) der Hgr. D announce themselves. Hilpert desires political orientation; I decline. Shall concern himself with his troops."

28. Halder, *Kriegstagebuch*, Vol. II, 218. "Chefsachen," General Dossier "Attila," BA-MA, RW 4/v. 574. Hitler's directive No. 19, "Operation Attila" is dated December 10, 1940.

29. Charles B. Burdick, *Hubert lanz. General der Gebirgstruppe 1896-1982* (Osnabrück: Biblio Verlag, 1988), 90ff. The troops for "Undertaking Felix" numbered some 17,000 officers and soldiers.

Part II

GERMAN ECONOMIC WARFARE TO CLOSE THE GAP BETWEEN GENEVA AND ST. GINGOLPH

Chapter Eight

Last Escape Hatch between Switzerland and the Allies

At the start of World War II, Switzerland had learned painfully that it would not be kept out of conflict. Besides facing the risk of total warfare of the belligerents the country faced unrelenting hostility in the form of economic blockades and propaganda. It was particularly in these noncombat areas that the neutral countries were in an exposed position. To the strategists of the politics of blockade and counterblockade neutral countries were porous entities which, if necessary, had to be effectively sealed by using considerable pressure at the expense of the enemy.[1] As the blockade agreement of April 25, 1940, shows, at the beginning of the war the Allies were stronger for waging economic warfare. As soon as the defeat of France and with it Switzerland's encirclement became apparent, the Axis powers began to relentlessly enforce their interests against this small neutral state.

The gap which had remained open in the encirclement of Switzerland after the German victory over France threatened to endanger seriously the success of the counterblockade. Under the new hegemonic conditions in continental Europe, Switzerland represented an island deep within the domain of the Axis powers. It had an independent connection all the way to Lisbon, thus could provide valuable services to Great Britain not only for effective espionage, but also for a continued supply of war-related precision goods. The importance of this gaping hole in the counterblockade becomes readily apparent in view of the far-reaching German strategy to seal off and occupy the whole Atlantic coast all the way to Spain.

The disputed gap extended from the Rhône bridge southwest of the Canton Geneva to St. Gingolph and along the Valais border to the Three-Country Point near Mont Dolent east of Chamonix. Yet Switzerland had retained only one continuous rail line that ran from St. Maurice in Canton Valais via the customs house at Boveret to the border town of St. Gingolph on Lake Geneva and on via Thonon-les-Bains to Annemasse. As its continuation from Belle-garde had been blocked by the German occupying forces, this line connected via La Roche-sur-Foron and Annecy to the rail network of unoccupied France. Whoever was able with the necessary visa to get from the local Geneva station of Eaux-Vives to Annemasse was also able to reach far-away destinations by using the Annemasse-Annecy rail line that led out of the Axis Powers' jurisdiction. In addition, another regional connection joined the line near La Roche which, given the cutting-off strategy, could have been used for a limited purpose; it started in Martigny in Valais as a one-meter gauge cog wheel rail line and ran to Chamonix and Le Fayet, from where a standard gauge rail line continued.[2] It was thus no coincidence that the German act of sabotage in September 1940 targeted the viaduct of Lavillat near Evires; at that point the whole rail traffic from Annecy to Switzerland could be crippled in one stroke. Referring to this important rail segment, the term "gap near Geneva" is appropriately chosen. In view of the blocked or limited rail capacity, trucks became an important alternative means for the transport of people and goods. Certain smuggling paths that were hard to monitor led through the alpine passes of Upper Savoy into Switzerland.[3]

Though it was no longer possible to close this gap by military means without a breach of the armistice agreements, the offices of the Armed Forces High Command (OKW) pursuing economic warfare still aimed to achieve complete surveillance of the Swiss border by negotiation. To prevent uncontrolled traffic from the start, Switzerland and the government in Vichy were pressured to cooperate in appropriate preventive measures. However, such an undertaking met with considerable difficulties because of the complicated system of jurisdiction in unoccupied Upper Savoy. From the German point of view the simplest solution of the problem would have been to compel Switzerland to block the remaining gap itself. During the trade negotiations which led to the agreement of August 9, 1940, Germany actually demanded that exports to England de jure would be totally blocked. Even direct traffic to France would be prohibited. What Germany demanded was no less than a relinquishment of neutrality and the submission to the dictates of the Axis Powers. The Swiss negotiating team sidetracked this demand by the clever argument that under the current situation the exports in question were actually insignificant; the requested formal ban would endanger the import of supplies to Switzerland and thus also the capacity to provide Germany with goods.[4] It was also important for the further disputes about the gap that, after a transitional nonneutral course, Switzerland at least in principle upheld neutrality by insisting that the implementation of the control measures outside the Swiss borders was a matter for the blockading powers.

There is still no comprehensive study of the history of this gap to the West; that history pertains not only to questions concerning the traffic of goods but also provides insight into connections to the outside world available for intelligence services and the Résistance. Connected with the gap is also the history of the last legal emigration path which led out of the central Axis domain and promised freedom as long as—at least on paper—all preconditions for the journey were fulfilled. If Lisbon could be reached and the prebooked ocean journey begin, there was of course still the risk of being hit by a torpedo during the crossing. This escape hatch is also connected to the dark chapters of Swiss refugee policy. In order to relieve its burden, the Federal Immigration Office made every attempt to persuade even those asylum seekers who wanted to stay in Switzerland to travel on and, if other possibilities of settlement emerged, to urge them to seek by this route a destination overseas. In the opposite direction, the gap allowed certain difficult paths of flight to remain open. Unless rejected at the last moment at the Swiss border, the paths helped the persecuted to be saved before the ring was completely closed by the German invasion of Vichy, France, on November 11, 1942.

In the context of this study it is not possible to offer the results of a comprehensive research effort which would include materials from the archives of the Allies. Neither will the history of the British sea blockade be explored nor the activities of the Swiss Federal War Transport Office which used rail cars and trucks on land routes to secure the country's food supply by using chartered as well as its own ships and had to overcome numerous obstacles at sea. In particular the services of private transport companies that collaborated with the Swiss Federal Transport Office through wartime-economy syndicates have been little researched to date. They attempted to exploit any possibility for importing and exporting; the freight bookings on foreign liners and tramp steamers were centralized only in July 1942.[5] In the various studies of the trade negotiations between Germany and Switzerland, which up to July 1941 Robert U. Vogler has explored most extensively, the question of the gap has been treated only marginally.[6]

Of prime importance to this study is the attempt within the German armed forces high command to close the gap by means of economic warfare after the military operation to cut off Switzerland had failed. There were considerable discrepancies between the actual conditions and the German demand of totally monitoring this border section. Detailed information can be gained from sources gleaned primarily from the Armed Forces High Command that illustrate the activity of the German customs frontier service and of other agencies charged with border surveillance at the gap.

NOTES

1. For the unique situation of Switzerland and Sweden in relation to the belligerents see Klaus Urner, "Neutralität und Wirtschaftskrieg: Zur schweizerischen Aussenhandelspolitik 1939–1945," in *Schwedische und schweizerische Neutralität im Zweiten Weltkrieg,* ed. Rudolf L. Bindschedler et al. (Basel: Helbing & Lichtenhahn, 1985), 250–92.

2. For several references concerning the rail system in Upper Savoy I thank Attorney Werner Gloor, Geneva (letters of June 24, and July 16, 1990) and Walter Trüb-Reiser (1991).

3. Although after the armistice the establishment of an air route to Portugal or even England failed due to German pressure, after April 1, 1940, a limited air service existed from Locarno to Barçelona; see Robert Urs Vogler, *Die Wirtschaftsverhandlungen zwischen der Schweiz und Deutschland 1940 und 1941,* new edition (Basel: Helbing & Lichtenhahn, 1997), 160, note 5.

4. Telegram Seyboth to AA, Bern, July 13, 1940, as well as further sources in folder AA, HaPol, Handel 13-Schweiz, as well as materials concerning the trade negotiations with Germany, vol. 9, July–December 1940. MF NA T120, roll 3672, E 694127ff.

5. E. Matter and E. Ballinari, "Eidgenössisches Kriegs-Transport-Amt," in *Die schweizerische Kriegswirtschaft 1939/1948. Bericht des Eidgenössischen Volkswirtschaftsdepartementes* (Bern: 1950), 109ff., esp. 122–3.

6. Vogler, *Wirtschaftsverhandlungen,* 145ff.; Daniel Bourgeois, *Le Troisième Reich et la Suisse 1933–1941* (Neuchâtel: Éditions de la Baconnière, 1974), 169ff.; Edgar Bonjour, *Geschichte der schweizerischen Neutralität. Vier Jahrhunderte eidgenössischer Aussenpolitik,* vol. 6: *1939–1945* (Basel: Helbing & Lichtenhahn, 1970), 213ff., 314ff. For the British measures of blockade concerning Switzerland see W. N. Medlicott, *The Economic Blockade,* reprint, vol. 1 (London: Kraus Reprint, 1978), 223ff.; 585ff.; vol. 2, 206ff. First published in 1952/1959, the study has been enriched by Swiss studies. See Oswald Inglin, *Der stille Krieg. Der Wirtschaftskrieg zwischen Grossbritannien und der Schweiz im Zweiten Weltkrieg* (Zürich: Verlag Neue Zürcher Zeitung, 1991).

Chapter Nine

After the Armistice

Even before the agreement of August 9, 1940, between Germany and Switzerland became effective, Switzerland made feverish efforts to get at least those goods through the gap into the country that had remained blocked in French ports due to the course of the war. On July 10, 1940, two weeks after the armistice had taken effect, it was possible despite technical obstacles to re-establish continuous rail traffic from the ports of Marseilles and Sète via Grenoble-Albertville-Annecy-Annemasse to St. Gingolph and St. Maurice or to the Geneva station of Eaux-Vives. Primarily shipments intended for the cantons of Geneva and Vaud were unloaded there and shipped by truck to their destinations. Although the detour through Upper Savoy was arduous and less efficient than the blocked main line from Geneva through Bellegarde, the gap proved to be a special blessing, particularly in the early phase. In Marseille alone some 65,000 tons of goods were awaiting transport to Switzerland, which could take months given a daily capacity of only 700 tons.[1] In the opposite direction through St. Gingolph, only a few carriages with assorted goods were shipped each day. These export attempts through unoccupied France, whose ports could no longer be used according to the armistice agreement, went to the Spanish border at Cerbère/Port-Bou where they had to be unloaded because of a change in rail gauge. Also at the border of the Pyrenees, the traffic now converged on the transit point along the Mediterranean to unoccupied France since the transport route via Hendaye/Irun that was more important for the Atlantic ports was under direct control of the German occupation forces.

After the armistice private Swiss businesses still hoped to circumvent the counterblockade by an extensive use of the gap's escape hatches to be supplemented, if possible, by suitable air connections. The German Embassy in Bern duly noted the pertinent hints and newspaper advertisements. In July the transport company Welti-Furrer AG offered its services even to German export companies for the transport of important goods such as medicines from Basel via St. Gingolph to Spain, although the prohibition against the transit of German merchandise through France had not yet been lifted. Similarly, Danzas & Co. made varied shipments to Port-Bou, although without a similar offer to German firms.[2] From the German government's point of view the announcement of the Geneva Chamber of Commerce that it had decided on July 18 to resume as soon as possible the transit exports with sealed cars through unoccupied France not only to North and South America, but also to England was especially alarming. To conceal war-related materials, the shipments would be sent to fictitious addresses in Lisbon. As the export capacity of the Swiss armament industry, which also included suppliers from the watch industry, had been fully exhausted by the Allies, the counterblockade caused an emergency in available supplies because except for the gap the encirclement was then complete. Department Wi IV in the OKW's office for war industry and armaments that was responsible for economic warfare had obtained order forms issued by Swiss shipping companies which were to arrange this kind of circumventing transports. "The open border between Switzerland and unoccupied France," the Department claimed in early August 1940, "at present gives England sufficient opportunity to obtain from Switzerland high quality war materials of small size."[3] The intelligence service was ordered, therefore, carefully to observe the rail traffic from Geneva and St. Gingolph via Annemasse as well as the truck traffic to Upper Savoy. The nearby border traffic also supposedly continued without control.[4]

The resumption of these exports came to a standstill primarily because of the increased blockade by the Allies who also held back important supply ships destined for Switzerland. The difficulties in the ports of departure could be overcome only with great delays and were connected with significant risk.[5] The transport company Chs. Natural AG in Basel, which on July 27 already had been able to ship 470,000 kilograms of Swiss export goods from Genoa, announced a further transport from Lisbon every three weeks by Japanese steamers; these would stop in South African and East Asian ports, thus also in English colonies.[6] Based on confidential figures concerning statistics of Swiss foreign trade, in July 1940 the German Embassy in Bern estimated exports of finished movements and other components of pocket watches to the United States, Canada, Great Britain, and Australia at a total value of 11.3 million francs. These exports of small weight and size were then not considered in violation of agreements, although the goods exported contained precision parts usable for the making of fuses. Still, in July 1940 less than ten percent of this value was supplied to victorious Germany which, however, the month before had already sharply demanded a reversal of this state of affairs.[7]

NOTES

1. "Schweizerische Verkehrsprobleme während der Kriegszeit," in *Neue Zürcher Zeitung*, July 29, 1940.

2. "Bericht Deutsche Gesandtschaft Bern" to AA, July 31, 1940, signed von Selzam in OKW, Wehrwirtschafts- und Rüstungsamt, Wehrwirtschaftsoffizier Bern, Wi/IF September 1, 1938–1941. Microfilm NA T-77, roll 707. Also in September the French blockade of larger German transit goods via the Swiss gap to Spain and Portugal remained in force. Telegram Köcher to AA, Bern September 20, 1940, microfilm NA T-77, roll 706.

3. Note in folder Wi IV concerning continuation of Swiss exports of parts for war instruments through unoccupied France and Portugal to England, Berlin, August 1, 1940, microfilm NA T-77, roll 706.

4. Written communication Wi IV to Abwehr-Wi, Berlin, August 2, 1940 in OKW, Wehrwirtschafts- und Rüstungsamt, Wi/IF, 1.8, microfilm NA T-77, roll 706.

5. "Report A.," Ausl./Abw to WiRüstungsamt/Wi IV, Berlin, September 6, 1940, microfilm NA T-77, roll 707. "Transportsorgen und Handelsverkehr," in *Schweizer Handelsbörse*, August 2, 1940. The rigorous blockade controls primarily concerned imports which were subject to the system of navicerts. After an interruption, after August 1, 1940, navicerts could again be obtained for goods from overseas. The earliest exports after the armistice occurred with foreign shipping lines. The first ship under Swiss jurisdiction could leave Genua with export goods on August 25, 1940. See E. Matter and E. Ballinari, "Eidgenössisches Kriegs-Transport-Amt," in *Die schweizerische Kriegswirtschaft 1939/1948. Bericht des Eidgenössischen Volkswirtschaftsdepartementes 1950* (Bern: 1950), 90, 123–24. For a criticism of the Swiss Kriegstransportamt [Office of War Transport] that it had procured too late sufficient shipping space as well as the needed means of transport in Portugal and Spain see "Schwierigkeiten der Landtransporte," in *Schweizer Handelsbörse*, April 25, 1941.

6. "Bericht Deutsche Gesandtschaft Bern," to AA, August 15, 1940, signed von Selzam.

7. "Bericht Deutsche Gesandtschaft Bern," to AA, August 20, 1940, signed Selzam, in OKW, Wehrwirtschaft- und Rüstungsamt, Wi/IF 1.6, "Schweiz, Geleitscheinfragen," microfilm NA T-77, roll 706.

Chapter Ten

Loopholes in German Export Prohibitions

Through the agreement of August 9, 1940, Germany abruptly sought to end attempts at circumventing the counterblockade. The system of documentation agreed upon with Switzerland was supposed to assure that only actually authorized types of goods would be exported. For exports that were not destined for Germany or Italy, there were now three types of categories: Apart from a list of "free" and one of quota-limited exports, there was a category of important blocked goods subject to specific accompanying documents. On August 29, 1940, the Finance Ministry of the Reich issued regulations implementing the transit prohibition for Swiss goods. There was a general transit prohibition for unquestionable war materials which were not even included in the list of goods subject to escort documents.[1]

As Germany had to enforce its export prohibitions at the frontiers outside of Swiss territory, it did not want to issue the needed documents before having the chance to set up a comprehensive customs belt. In addition, it still had to negotiate the processing of escort documents with Italy. In order to prevent the complete blocking of all exports, Minister Jean Hotz had made a most problematic concession to the German negotiating delegation on August 6: "As the establishment of the system of escort documents will take some time and as the Swiss-French border can not yet be monitored, the Swiss are prepared for the time being not to issue any export permits for goods subject to escort documents."[2] Although this temporary measure was based on rational considerations, it nevertheless violated the obligation of treating belligerents equally as set down in Article 9 of the Fifth Hague Convention of October 18, 1907. Thus Switzerland became temporarily involved in directly supporting the counterblockade, as it would cooperate closely with the office of the German Embassy in Bern that was entrusted with issuing the necessary documents.[3] As a consequence the Swiss Federal Council guaranteed that temporarily no goods subject to escort documents would be exported through the border section of Upper Savoy.

Switzerland's refusal to cooperate directly and permanently in the counterblockade made Germany's negotiating position difficult regarding the enforcement of the final agreement in the region of the gap. In order for the barrier not to be breached near St. Gingolph or near Geneva, Vichy, France, would have to be induced by negotiations with the German Armistice Commission in Wiesbaden not to allow the transfer of any goods without permits issued by the Axis powers. On October 15, 1940, therefore, the General Customs Office of the French Ministry of Finance issued a prohibition against the import, export, or transit of war materials. Exceptions were subject to special permits, yet the transit between Germany and Italy was exempt from this rule. Only later did the Germans become aware of the extensive and time-consuming problems that resulted from this arrangement.

As the French border and customs controls satisfied neither the high command of the German armed forces nor the agencies responsible for economic warfare, they began to press for the involvement of German agents at the outer French border posts. However, along the border between Switzerland and unoccupied France, Italian interests also had to be taken into account. According to the June 18, 1940, agreement between Hitler and Mussolini, the region left of the Rhône was considered in Italy's sphere of influence, although its occupation planned by Italy before the armistice had not occurred.[4] According to Hermann Böhme, the chief of staff of the German Armistice Commission, the arrangement failed because the Italians wished to participate rather than to grant the Germans complete control at the French side of the border with Switzerland and concerning Spain: "Nothing came from these negotiations, they came to naught in 1941. The question was only resolved when German troops occupied southern France in November 1942."[5] A compromise solution which became effective in May 1941 will be discussed later.

Although according to the agreement of August 9 the transitional phase was supposed to last only a few weeks, the blockage of exports to the West for goods subject to permits remained under the auspices of the Swiss Federal Council also in September. Vichy had no reason to hurry in adopting the German control measures. Instead, another spectacular event now endangered Swiss imports going through Annecy.

On September 3, 1940, an act of sabotage against the Lavillat viaduct near Evires was committed, causing the interruption of the rail line, the destruction of which Hitler had ordered on June 24, 1940. The German consul in Geneva, Wolfgang Krauel, telegraphed Berlin the following day at noon: "Rail bridge Annecy-Geneva near La Roche-sur-Foron blown up by act of sabotage last night after passage of a freight train with foodstuffs for Switzerland. By blowing up this bridge, the last existing rail connection France-Switzerland has been interrupted which will make provisioning Switzerland with foodstuffs through France extraordinarily difficult."[6]

Although the initial consequences of this attack were sharply felt by Switzerland, immediately every effort was made to maintain the traffic in goods from Annecy by means of trucks. Between Geneva and Annecy the road was used for transports while some of the goods were trucked from Annecy to La Roche-sur-Foron from where they reached Valais via St. Gingolph and Boveret in Swiss railway cars. Only a week after the attack, Krauel had to inform the Foreign Ministry: "Exports from Switzerland to occupied France suffered no substantial interruption due to the destruction of the rail connection. As to Switzerland's goods, the export of which is to be prevented by Germany, they must be highly priced industrial products for which transport by truck is suitable."[7]

Before long-distance travel by rail had become possible for people, the Blenk & Fert Company had installed the "Train Routier" which went with one truck and two buses in a twenty-nine-hour trek from Geneva to Cerbère; from there, the passengers continued by rail to Lisbon and overseas. For this trip, passengers needed transit visas for France, Spain, and Portugal, as well as an entry visa for a destination country; in an emergency, a steamship ticket would suffice.[8] Other transport companies also offered this kind of service.[9]

On October 23, 1940, Switzerland concluded a provisional trade agreement with Vichy, France, that included the mutual obligation to accommodate as much as possible each other's interests in the granting of import and export permits.[10] This improved Switzerland's transit situation. Germany, however, was put into the uncomfortable position of having to leave the monitoring of traffic along the gap exclusively to the French after the Germans had been unable to place their own customs officers along the unoccupied territory of France bordering on Switzerland after the permit system had been initiated in October.[11]

For this reason, the German consul in Geneva urged that the Geneva-Bellegarde rail line be reopened as soon as possible. The approach Krauel recommended sounded promising. It was based on the premise that this connection would bring considerable relief in the traffic of goods. If German controls were dispensed with, it would be only a question of time for the main traffic to run again through Bellegarde and then would have to cross terrain occupied by German troops. Such a solution concerning the French customs controls in Bellegarde would at least provide certain opportunities for control. As the Annecy-Annemasse line damaged by sabotage would also be ready for traffic within a few weeks, Krauel urged haste.[12] The responsible office at the OKW interpreted this suggestion in its own way and attempted, although with little success, to dispatch a number of German customs officers to monitor the French customs controls in Bellegarde.[13]

On November 20, passenger rail traffic through Bellegarde at a standstill since June started up again, but it was blocked once more less than a week later. What had happened? Freight cars had been attached to the passenger trains in Geneva in order to traverse the occupied region without stops and controls. The inspector general of the German Customs Office Hossfeld opposed, therefore, the continuation of this route.[14] On December 15 two passenger and two freight trains daily nevertheless began to run in each direction. A report of the German customs office at Pougny of January 18, 1941, reveals that the passenger trains were also used by French persons from occupied areas who had passes for crossing the line of demarcation but then traveled on unhindered to Switzerland, contrary to the German demarcation policy. The office at Pougny did not forego the control of freight either and in early 1941 discovered four crates of merchandise in a passenger train that had been sent express and contained magnetic detonators. The Swiss Federal Ministry of Foreign Affairs found itself obligated to give assurance that in the future only accompanied luggage would be transported on the Geneva-Bellegarde passenger trains.[15] The admissible freight traffic remained "remarkably light" according to the observations of the German customs officials in Pougny. They also made another sobering discovery: "The disproportionately strong traffic in empty cars from Switzerland to unoccupied France could only be explained by the fact that all the goods Switzerland wanted to import outside of German control is routed via the Annemasse-Geneva line. Thus, there is a circular traffic." Between December 15, 1940, and January 14, 1941, 2684 freight cars were sent from Switzerland through Bellegarde, of which only 187 were loaded; 1897 returned via Bellegarde with imported goods.[16]

Under these circumstances Intelligence Department III, which was in charge of counter espionage in the economic sector, considered monitoring the goods transported through Geneva-Bellegarde as useless because Switzerland, if it wanted to withhold them from German control, "was able at all times to transport goods unchecked to unoccupied France via the Annemasse-Annecy line."[17] The German military intelligence service received numerous reports from agents about the supply of war materials sent to England by Swiss companies.[18] Although there were plenty of groundless rumors, they were based on fact in that Great Britain was deeply interested in maximizing the evasion of the counterblockade, primarily in order to obtain Swiss precision products that were important to the war effort.[19] From the German perspective it was unconscionable that despite of its overwhelming might it was unable to bring this border segment under its control.[20]

One extensively used detour was discovered only at the end of November 1940 by the economics and armament branch of the OKW due to a careless notice in the *Schweizerische Handelsamtsblatt* [Official Swiss Commercial Gazette] of October 12: Small precision parts important for military use could pass the counterblockade without problem by using letter mail, which accepted shipments up to two kilos. That such small packages could be sent even through Germany without permits points to a grotesque error by the German customs administration. In addition, the counterblockade was breached by courier luggage. Further investigations supplied alarming information: "According to reliable information, British diplomatic representatives carry jewel bearings from Switzerland in their courier luggage for the use in time fuses and optical war devices." Major Sommer, who played an important role in the office for escort documents of the German Embassy in Bern and who belonged to the economics and armament branch of the OKW had found out more from a manufacturer of Swiss watch bearings; "shipments of jewel bearings were continuously sent as air mail shipments to the United States in sealed Swiss postal bags through the airport in Stuttgart. The same is to be assumed for fuse springs." Therefore the Department of Economic Defense suggested that disregarding existing agreements the postal bags passing through Stuttgart were to be opened. Such an intervention was not yet possible for the path through the gap, but there were already suggestions within the OKW "that the courier luggage should be examined in principle as soon as the shores of Lake Geneva had come fully under German control."[21]

After discovering the export of goods by letter mail one would have assumed that at least in Germany such mail would be immediately stopped. But an investigation about how the Swiss transit mail could best be monitored revealed that the problem of such measures was in their detail. At first, the Reich Postal Ministry declared that because of the upcoming Christmas mail it would not be able to make any changes before January 10, 1941. During a conference at the Economics Ministry of the Reich and in the OKW in early 1941 it was finally determined that the real obstacle was caused by a genuine internal German conflict of interest. The final reason would rest on the decision about which goal had primacy for German warfare: "The detection and prevention of shipments from Switzerland of certain small industrial products important to the enemy, or keeping the ways open for sending their own German letters abroad without being censored." Major Sommer, who favored comprehensive monitoring, pointed to the importance of the jewel bearings, spiral springs, and ejector prongs. Because of their precision, they were produced almost exclusively in Switzerland; they were urgently needed in England and the United States for the production of ignition devices, aircraft engines, and rapid fire flak guns. However, Sommer was not able to dispel the doubts of the intelligence service as he, too, had to admit that these tiny products could get through the counterblockade by means other than letter mail and that "the measure would have conditional value only, that is if also Italy and unoccupied France instituted similar measures."[22]

NOTES

1. "Durchfuhrverbot für schweizerische Waren," Erlass des Reichsministers der finanzen zu Handen der Oberfinanzpräsidenten, Berlin, August 29, 1940, signed Siegert, in *Deutscher Reichsanzeiger*, No. 203, August 30, 1940.

2. "Vermerk: Überwachung der schweizerischen Ausfuhr," Berlin, August 7, 1940; microfilm NA T-120, roll 3672, E 694156.

3. Written communication concerning permits for transit goods of the German Embassy in Bern to the OKW, WiRü-Amt, Wi IV, September 30, 1940, microfilm NA T-77, roll 706. The Italian office for issuing permits was to be housed at the same place as the one of the German Embassy in Bern. "They do not have a technical expert, thus will probably work most closely with the German office." Dr. Sommer to the Head of Wi, "Bericht über Stand und Organisation des Geleitscheinwesens in der Schweiz," Bern, September 18, 1940, microfilm NA T77, roll 706.

4. Even on August 14, 1940, Reichsmarschal Göring declared: "We want to keep our hands off the French-Italian border." Hitler had initially decided "that the controls at the Mediterranean should also be left exclusively to the Italians." See Georg Thomas, *Geschichte der deutschen Wehr- und Rüstungswirtschaft (1918–1943/45)*, ed. Wolfgang Birkenfeld (Boppard am Rhein: Harald Boldt Verlag, 1966), 512–13. Complaints about the lacking efficiency of Italian control activities led to a gradual change of this view.

5. Interview with General Hermann Böhme, Munich, August 10, 1968 (taperecording made together with Rudolf Humm). Since Böhme died in 1968, the continuation of his study *Der deutsch-französische Waffenstillstand im Zweiten Weltkrieg* (Stuttgart: Deutsche Verlags-Anstalt, 1966) which would have been relevant for this work, remained incomplete. In the context of the control of the French production of armaments the Germans had already viewed the cooperation of the Italians as bothersome. See Karl-Volker Neugebauer, *Die deutsche Militärkontrolle im unbesetzten Frankreich und in Französisch-Nordwestafrika 1940–1942. Zum Problem der Sicherung der Südwestflanke von Hitler's Kontinentalimperium* (Boppard am Rhein: Harald Boldt Verlag, 1980), 34–35, 40–48, and note 24.

6. Telegram Krauel to AA, Geneva, September 4, 1940, microfilm NA NA T-77, roll 707.

7. Reports of the German Consulate in Geneva to AA, September 6 and 10, 1940, signed Krauel; microfilm NA T-77, roll 706. Krauel estimated that this export was "less than extensive."

8. "Die einzige Verbindung von Genf zum Atlantik und nach Übersee," in *Schweizer Illustrierte Zeitung*, No. 31, July 31, 1940.

9. For detailed explanations and documentary evidence I thank René Nordmann who, after his military service as a Swiss living abroad, journeyed on July 24–27, 1940, from Geneva to Lisbon and from there by boat to the United States; see illustration XV.

10. "Bericht des schweizerischen Bundesrates an die Bundesversammlung über seine Geschäftsführung im Jahre 1940," April 17, 1941, 216.

11. Dr. Sommer to Chef Wi, "Bericht über Stand und Organisation des Geleitschein-wesens in der Schweiz," Bern, September 19, 1940; microfilm NA T-77, roll 706. For the German-French negotiations concerning questions of the control at the frontiers see ADAP, ser. d, vol. 10, documents nos. 184, 331, 337–38, 360; vol. 11, 1, no. 206.

12. Krauel to German Embassy in Bern, Geneva, October 12, 1940; microfilm NA T-77, roll 706.

13. WiRü Amt/Wi Ivb to AA, October 30, 1940; microfilm NA T-77, roll 706.

14. Written communication of Hossfeld to OKH, Berlin, December 28, 1940; micro-film NA T-77, roll 706.

15. "Bericht deutsche Gesandtschaft Bern an Auswärtiges Amt," Bern, February 18, 1941, signed Selzam. Note EPD to German Embassy in Bern, February 14, 1941; micro-film NA T-77, roll 706.

16. "Bericht Deutsches Zollamt Pougny an Kommandostelle des Zollgrenzschutzes Frankreich," January 1, 1941, signed Hentschke (copy); microfilm NA T-77, roll 706.

17. Written communication Amt Ausl/Abw/Abt. Abw III an Gen. St. d. H./Gen Qu. Berlin, January 27, 1941; microfilm NA T-77, roll 706.

18. See Robert Urs Vogler, *Die Wirtschaftsverhandlungen zwischen der Schweiz und Deutschland 1940 und 1941* (Basel: Helbing & Lichtenhahn, 1983), "Exkurs," 158ff.

19. See the memoir of John G. Lomax, *The Diplomatic Smuggler* (London: A. Barker, 1965) for a view of the economic warfare from the British perspective; until shortly before the closing of the gap in July 1941 H. L. Setchell served as Trade Counselor in Bern who had a greater understanding of Switzerland's predicament; see Heinrich Homberger, *Schweizerische Handelspolitik im Zweiten Weltkrieg. Ein Überblick auf Grund persön-licher Erlebnisse* (Erlenbach-Zürich: Eugen Rentsch Verlag, 1970), 77.

20. See the summary of the insights gained from the news received in the second half of 1940 in the "Abwehr-Bericht" of February 4, 1941: "Zur Lieferung von Waffen und an-deren kriegswichtigen Erzeugnissen aus der Schweiz nach dem feindlichen Ausland seit dem Abschluss des Waffenstillstandes mit Frankreich," unsigned, in Wi/IF, 1.6 "Schweiz;" microfilm NA T-77, roll 706.

21. Wi IVb to Chef Wi, "Vortragsnotiz für HPA," Berlin November 28, 1940; micro-film NA T-77, roll 707; the document served Major Becker for his intervention in the com-mittee dealing with trade policy [Handelsausschuss].

22. "Besprechung über Warenkontrolle in Schweizer Transitpost," January 27, 1941, Aktenvermerk Abw III, Berlin, January 27, 1941, with relevant correspondence; microfilm NA T-77, roll 707.

Chapter Eleven

Extortion against Switzerland

In February 1941, the German special staff of the division called "Handelskrieg und wirtschaftliche Kampfmassnahmen" (HWK) [Trade War and Measures of Economic Warfare], for short, began its aggressive activities. It was an internal coordinating group of the Armed Forces High Command for Conducting Economic Warfare and also protected the interests of Reichsmarshal Göring. He viewed the monitoring of transit mail as quite ineffective, "as it was in any case unable to produce genuine results." The chief of the HWK's special staff in the OKW was Admiral Dr. h.c. Otto Groos, the former head of the naval command office in the Reich's War Ministry. He was no longer willing to be restrained by concern for diverse interests and by other various obstacles. As he was dissatisfied with the current fight against British economic warfare in Switzerland, he wanted to end British efforts to thwart the counterblockade by taking a comprehensive aggressive step. To work out a uniform strategy of the OKW against Switzerland he called a meeting for February 27, 1941, at which the relevant intelligence departments as well as HWK participated. The agenda contained eight questions, the first of which revealed an unscrupulous determination: "How can the British Ambassador in Bern be eliminated?"[1] At the beginning of the discussion Groos stated that the available information as well as "a kind of secondary government of the British Ambassador in Bern" required a change in the measures then in place for economic warfare. "From messages received and from intercepted reports of the British Ambassador in Bern it emerges without doubt that Swiss companies, especially those which have subsidiaries in the United States and England, keep working for the enemy and pursue exports with all the means at their disposal."[2]

Through Göring's research office, which had decoded the relevant transmittals between the mission in Bern and London, the HWK's special staff learned that British Ambassador David Kelly was directly involved in the acquisition of urgently needed armaments from Switzerland.[3] For future action only a single alternative was presented for discussion, the murder or expulsion of Kelly! Intelligence Department 2, however, which was responsible for subversive actions, rejected the idea of murder outright. Thus it was to be determined how Kelly could be removed from Switzerland. As an immediate measure, the group decided to put pressure on the Swiss Federal Council through the Foreign Ministry, informing its members that in the future all exports from Switzerland would be checked on German, Italian, and French soil, including goods which until then had not been subject to permits. If those measures did not succeed, "Germany would demand an end to all Swiss exports." The group also decided to test a plan that would bring Swiss watch manufacturing under German control through the formation of a syndicate of the industry producing the needed raw material. Yet experts sent by the OKW determined that this plan was not feasible because the production involved a large number of establishments operating from homes that were beyond control. The monitoring of letter mail, the continued emigration of Swiss experts to "enemy-dependent countries or to England" despite preventive measures of the Swiss Federal Council, and the removal of British officers accepting Swiss-made goods from Switzerland led the conference to adopt further measures.[4]

As part of this offensive against Switzerland, simultaneously a new round of economic negotiations between Germany and Switzerland was opened with the surprising declaration that it had to increase its credit massively and that future orders from Germany had to receive flexible payment options. This request made by Ambassador Hemmen was all the more astonishing as in the provisional protocol of February 7, 1941, Switzerland had more than doubled the credits granted the previous August; it had hoped that the 317 million francs would provide a satisfactory basis for further negotiations regarding deliveries of German coal and iron.[5] Without further dealing with the details of these well known trade negotiations, the background for this escalation is of particular interest, as it was connected to drastic changes in the conditions guiding the German monitoring of Swiss trade passing through the gap. The great extent to which Germany fueled a real economic war against Switzerland in March and April 1941 to enforce its demands is fully recognizable only if the OKW's intentions, that far exceeded the credit demands, are considered.[6]

Even within the OKW Admiral Groos encountered opposition to his extreme requests. Leopold Bürkner, chief of the Foreign Intelligence Division, objected vehemently to the original intent of the HWK's special staff to control all Swiss exports. He considered it impossible to implement the plan because of the gap. Bürkner believed that for reasons of German prestige and credibility Switzerland should be threatened with the complete control of its exports only if the required measures could actually be implemented: "All such measures only *fulfill a purpose* if the *gap through France can be sealed or France can be forced into cooperation.* Thus it should be *the first goal* of economic warfare against Switzerland *to force France into blocking the Swiss transit and to reopen it only under the conditions which we consider necessary.* If that is not possible, none of the proposed measures under consideration will truly make an impression on Switzerland." Given the state of French-German relations Bürkner found it "very doubtful" that such a goal was in reach. He also pointed out that expelling Kelly from Switzerland would be almost impossible and that such an act would only set an undesirable precedent. It would also endanger the position of those diplomats who had cooperated with Germany in "breaking the blockade" and who worked in countries subject to British pressure.[7]

On March 8, the Foreign Office nevertheless transmitted instructions to the German Ambassador Köcher if not to announce, at least to threaten the full control of Swiss exports. To the dismay of Minister Jean Hotz, head of the Swiss Federal Department of Commerce, Köcher declared that according to German findings goods subject to permits were being exported illegally in great quantities. For this reason the Swiss government would in the future be required to cooperate with the permit system. "If our demand is rejected, we would consider ourselves forced to monitor all Swiss exports, regardless of the transport disruptions that this would cause. Italy and France would do the same."[8] Because the Swiss Federal Council stuck to the principle of autonomy despite this threat given its concern for vital imports from overseas, the Germans had to find another solution.[9]

Groos, who had no intention to give in, again "considered the murder of the ambassador." If it were possible to get Great Britain to break relations with Switzerland, it would become totally isolated and would be driven into the arms of the Axis powers. As the execution of such a proposal had already been rejected by the intelligence agencies, he ordered his subordinates to contact the Gestapo in this matter. This became known to Helmuth James Graf von Moltke at section VI d that was concerned with matters of war-related international law in the Division of Foreign Affairs; he sharply vetoed "an office of the armed forces to approach the Gestapo with such a request."[10] That the office in question had its own point of view in matters of economic warfare against Switzerland must be attributed gratefully to this known opponent of the regime who in 1944 became a victim of Hitler's "justice of revenge." Although Admiral Groos had overstepped his bounds with his murder plot, as Bürkner wanted to make clear to him orally, the closing of the gap along the

Swiss border now gained utter priority for the HWK's special staff.[11] All military as well as civilian agencies that had been annoyed by this gap were in full agreement on this point. To attain the desired result it was necessary, besides concentrated blackmail against Switzerland, to take steps against Vichy, France, to finally obtain German control over the outside borders of the unoccupied areas.

The Trade Policy Committee [Handelspolitischer Ausschuss], the internal body of interested German ministries that determined the guidelines for trade negotiations, which in turn was influenced by the HWK's special staff, decided on March 5 on a series of delaying and blocking maneuvers. This included dilatory treatment of requests for permits, obstruction of transit, Italian blockage of the port of Genoa, crippling transports of mineral oil from Romania, and prevention of exports via France.[12] While the government of Switzerland was told of "delays," the WWi IV section in the OKW that pursued economic warfare now left no doubt about its determination:

> The application of the measures of pressure entails a sensitive disruption of the orders of the German armed forces in Switzerland, particularly of new orders by the RLM[13] which, however, was tolerated by the various segments of the armed forces. On April 30 the contract between Germany and Switzerland for the German delivery of coal and iron expires. As the Swiss economy will become paralyzed without these supplies, it is to be expected that the Swiss government will request the resumption of the previously broken off negotiations quite soon.

The quartermaster general in the General Staff of the army was thus also asked to interrupt the transit of goods through unoccupied France, yet only the Geneva-Bellegarde line could be crippled by the occupation force. "It has to be accepted that the entire traffic on this line will come to a halt or that other transport difficulties will arise. The Reich Transport Ministry will tolerate such difficulties to a still greater extent on other relevant lines."[14]

In the OKW this blackmail was clearly designated as "economic warfare" against Switzerland[15] and the OKW stressed that the government of the Reich had decided on this maneuver of extortion at its suggestion.[16] It was undertaken with a double aim: On the one hand, the Office of War Economy and Armament wanted to press for a credit in the amount of 1.2 billion francs instead of the previously rejected demand of 700 to 800 million; on the other, Admiral Groos of the HWK special staff was determined to end permanently all attempts overcoming the counterblockade.

On March 28, 1941, the Bellegarde-Geneva line was blocked in both directions and demonstratively damaged by the removal of a pair of rails.[17] The special controls to which the permit-bound exports of the Swiss watch industry to the West were subjected by mid-March were not considered as a war measure but instead as a permanent regulation. These important exports were to be routed for checking through the German customs office in Basel and only then be transferred to Geneva. This cumbersome procedure as well as the lack of trained personnel—at first only a single master watchmaker was to be provided for checking all the pertinent freight, parcel post, and letter mail—had the effect of paralyzing these exports to the United States and South America.[18] Because of the increased counterblockade, furthermore, shipments that had been checked and sealed in Basel for transport to Geneva could not be exported at all.

NOTES

1. Concerning the Session at SdST HKW, February 27, 1941, 11:30 a.m., "Schweiz, Frageliste," Berlin February 27, 1941, in OKW/1095, Amtsgruppe Ausland, "Wirtschaftliche Kriegsmassnahmen in der Schweiz, 1940–1943"; microfilm NA T-77, roll 902.

2. "Bericht über die Sitzung am 27. 2. 1941 11:30 Uhr, beim Sonderstab HKW betreffend die Änderung der bisherigen Massnahmen der Wirtschaftskriegsführung in der Schweiz, Berlin 28. 2. 1941," signed Groos; microfilm NA T-77, roll 902.

3. Pertinent materials were used for the summary "Abwehr-Bericht" of February 4, 1941; they contain exactly dated details which documented Kelly's dealings, but could not be presented to the Swiss without jeopardizing the deciphering success; microfilm NA T-77, roll 706. Although forewarned by Max Prinz von Hohenlohe, Kelly had not recognized the danger; see David Kelly, *The Ruling Few, or The Human Background to Diplomacy* (London: Hollis and Carter, 1952), 273.

4. "Sitzungsbericht," February 27, 1941, Berlin, January 28, 1941, signed Groos; microfilm NA T-77, roll 902. "Aufzeichnung, Verhinderung der schweizerischen Ausfuhr kriegswichtiger Waren," Berlin, June 12, 1941, signed Wiehl. PAB, AA, Ha.-Pol.Wiehl, "Akten, betr.: Schweiz," vol. 8, January 1940–August 1942.

5. Robert Urs Vogler, *Die Wirtschaftsverhandlungen zwischen der Schweiz und Deutschland 1940 und 1941* (Zürich: Helbing & Lichtenhahn, 1983), 183, 191.

6. Daniel Bourgeois first used the documents of the Wehrwirtschafts- und Rüstungsamtes in a summary fashion. They would have substantially added to the clarification of the dangerous sharpening of the conflict in the chapters "Erhöhter deutscher Wirtschaftsdruck" and "Die entscheidende Phase" in Vogler, *Wirtschaftsverhandlungen*, 191, 199; Daniel Bourgeois, *Le Toisième Reich et la Suisse 1933–1941* (Neuchâtel: Éditiobs de la Baconnière, 1974), 172–73; without this background material Edgar Bonjour, *Geschichte der schweizerischen Neutralität*, vol. 6: *1939–1945* (Basel: Helbing & Lichtenhahn, 1972), 229, chapter titled "Deutscher Wirtschaftsdruck."

7. Written communication Amt Ausl/Abw. to Chef Sonderstab HKW, Berlin, March 8, 1941, signed Bürkner; microfilm NA T-77, roll 902.

8. Telegram AA, HaPol, to German Embassy in Bern, Berlin, March 8, 1941, signed Clodius ("Bereinigter Entwurf mit Verbalnote"), in PAB, AA HaPol, "Schweiz," vol. 8, January 1940 to August 1942.

9. Telegram Köcher to AA, Bern, March 12, 1941, signed Köcher, "Schweiz," vol. 8.

10. "Vermerk," Abt. Ausland, VId, to Chef Ausland, Berlin, March 29, 1941, signed Moltke, in OKW/1095, microfilm NA T-77, roll 902.

11. Bürkner had asked Moltke in reaction to his message of March 29, 1941: "Please make sure that the Gestapo is not being approached before the head of the Foreign Affairs Division had time first to consult the head of the HKW"; see OKW/1095, microfilm NA T-77, roll 902.

12. Vogler, *Wirtschaftsverhandlungen*, 194; Rome was hesitant to create too great difficulties concerning the transit trade by rail "because Italy was quite interested in a smooth transit of coal via Switzerland and could not risk the danger that the Swiss might somehow create obstacles for that transit." Telegram Mackensen to AA, Rome, March 12, 1941, in AA. HaPol., "Schweiz," vol. 8.

13. RLM refers to "Reichsluftfahrtministerium," the Department of the Reich dealing with air traffic.

14. Written communication OKW, WiRüAmt/Wi Ivb to the Quartermaster General, Genst. d.H, March 24, 1941, "Revised Draft," microfilm NA T-77, roll 902.

15. On March 7, 1941, the Wehrwirtschafts- und Rüstungsamt informed the special committee of the HKW that all conditions had been met "so that no further obstacles existed as to initiating economic warfare on the basis of the decisions taken"; "Aktenvermerk," HKW, W in matters Switzerland, Berlin, March 7, 1941, in OKW/1095, microfilm NA T-77, roll 902.

16. HKW, W in matters Switzerland; the OKW, the Reichswirtschaftsministerium, and the AA [Division of Foreign Affairs] pursued certain divergent interests; the AA viewed concerns about smuggling as "overblown"; note, AA, HaPol IIa, Berlin, May 27, 1941, unsigned; microfilm T-120 I, roll 1990, E 064989.

17. Feldtransportabteilung [Division of Transports in the Field] of the head of the transport system of the army's General Staff to OKW WiRüAmt/W, communication of April 1, 1941, to Abw.I, Referat I/wi, April 3, 1941; microfilm NA T-77, roll 706.

18. Communication of AA, HaPol to OKW, WiRüAmt Berlin, March 18, 1941, signed Schüller; microfilm NA T-77, roll 706. Some 10 percent of the about 10,000 packages sent via the main customs office in Basel for transit to Germany needed permits; some 5 percent contained prohibited or permit-needing products of the watch industry. Now special controls were added which, however, the Swiss watch industry was able largely to avoid or circumvent. Circular of the Reichsfinanzministeriums, Berlin, May 13, 1941; enclosure "Inspektionsbericht Dr. Wallenfels."

Hitler himself takes charge of responding to the air incidents (left to right: Hitler; Supreme Commander of the Air Force, Göring; Jodl; Chief of the General Staff of the Air Force, Jeschonnek)

On June 18, 1940, in Munich, Hitler and Mussolini plan the full encirclement
of Switzerland

Even the Supreme Commander of the Army acted only on Hitler's orders.—
review of the situation at the Führer's headquarters "Wolfsschlucht": (left to
right) Major Deyhle; Chief of the Command Office of the Armed Forces
[Wehrmachtführungsamt], Jodl; Hitler; von Brauchitsch, Chief of the Supreme
Command of the Army [Oberkommando des Heeres]; Fleet Admiral Raeder.

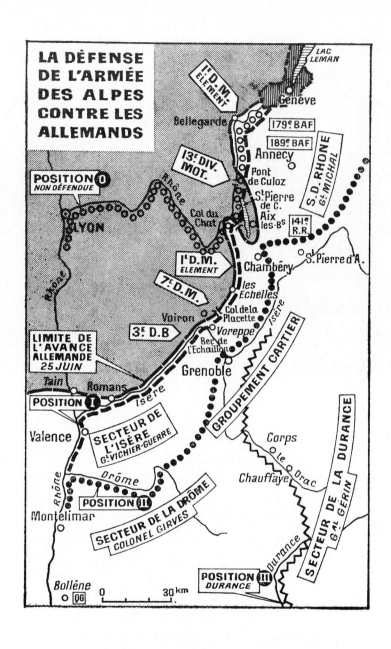

LA DÉFENSE
DE L'ARMÉE
DES ALPES
CONTRE LES
ALLEMANDS

I⁰ D.M. ÉLÉMENT

LAC LÉMAN

Genève

Bellegarde

179⁰ BAF

189⁰ BAF

Annecy

S.D. RHÔNE Gⁱ MICHAL

13⁰ DIV. MOT.

Pont de Culoz

POSITION 0 NON DÉFENDUE

St Pierre de C.

Rhône

Col du Chat

Aix les Bˢ

141⁰ R.R.

LYON

St Pierre d'A.

I⁰ D.M. ÉLÉMENT

Chambéry

7⁰ D.M.

les Échelles

Voiron

Col de la Placette

Isère

GROUPEMENT CARTIER

3⁰ D.B

Voreppe

Bec de l'Échaillon

LIMITE DE L'AVANCE ALLEMANDE 25 JUIN

Grenoble

SECTEUR DE LA DURANCE

Rhône

Tain

Romans

Corps

POSITION I

Isère

le Drac

Valence

SECTEUR DE L'ISÈRE Gⁱ VICHIER-GUERRE

Chauffaye

SECTEUR DE LA DURANCE Gⁱ GÉRIN

Rhône

Drôme

POSITION II

SECTEUR DE LA DRÔME COLONEL GIRVES

Montélimar

Durance

Bollène

OG

POSITION III DURANCE

0   30 km

(above) Swiss border reached—Brigadier General von Langermann and Erlenkamp (front right), Commander of the 29th Motorized Division at the guardpost at Goumois, June 1940. (private possession of Georges Wüthrich) (left) Advance by "Gruppe List" against "L'Armée des Alpes" on June 23–24, 1940. The Attempt to cut off Switzerland fails. (From Henri Azeau, *La guerre franco-italienne, juin 1940*. Paris 1967)

(above) After the outburst at the Führer's headquarters during the night of June 24–25, 1940, Hitler awaits with his entourage the start of the Armistice. Albert Speer, second from left; Hitler, center; Martin Bormann, front row, second from right. (AfZ)

(right) Armistice, June 25, 1940, 1:35 a.m.: Guderian is again at the Swiss Jura border. Between Geneva and St. Gingolph, a gap exists in the encirclement of Switzerland. (From *World War II in Pictures*, Vol. I, Munich 1963).

(pages H and I) Ready to attack within seven days—German troops set for deployment against Switzerland according to the Operational Draft of August 12, 1940. [BA-MA, RH 2/v.465 K-17].

(page J) Proposal for an Italian attack with two variants of dividing up Switzerland between Italy and Germany according to the study of August 12, 1940. [BA-MA, RH 2/v.465 K-18].

(page K) The scheme of attack worked out by Otto Wilhelm von Menges of the OKH for the German invasion of Switzerland, operational draft of August 12, 1940. [RH 2/465 K1-19].

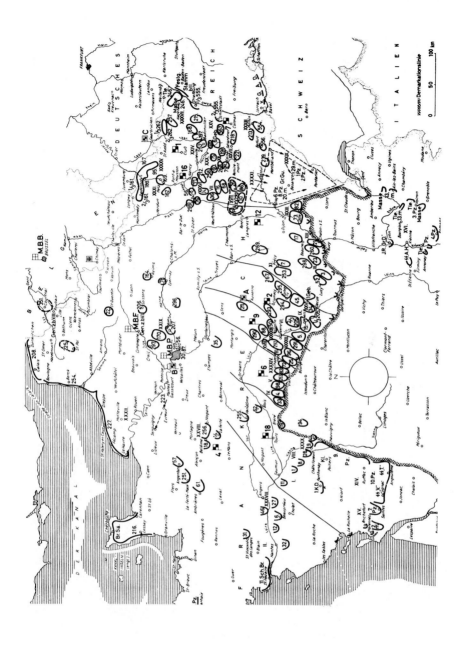

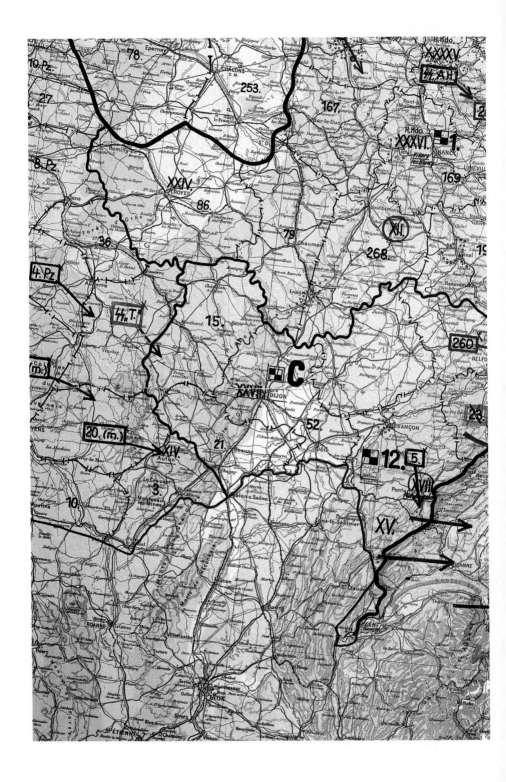

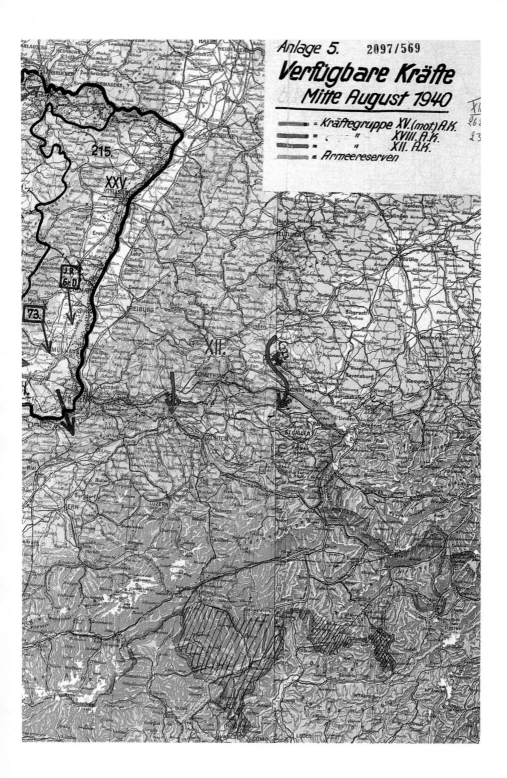

Anlage 5.   2097/569

Verfügbare Kräfte
Mitte August 1940

≡ = Kräftegruppe XV.(mot.)A.K.
≡ = " XVIII.A.K.
= = " XII.A.K.
= = Armeereserven

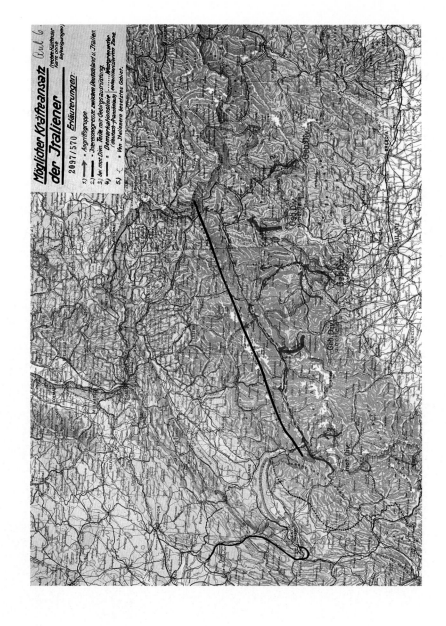

Möglicher Kräfteansatz
der Italiener

Anl. 6.

(rote Häftmeyer
Karte ohne
Bezeichnungen)

2097/570 Erläuterungen:

1.) ⟶ = Angriffsgruppe
2.) ⟶ = Interessengrenze zwischen Deutschland u. Italien.
3.) bei mot.Div. Teile mit Gebirgsausrüstung.
4.) ――― = Demarkationslinie
     (deutsch französisch) ┈┈┈ = Westgrenze
     = Von Italienern besetztes Gebiet.
5.) ◡ = Von Italienern besetztes Gebiet.

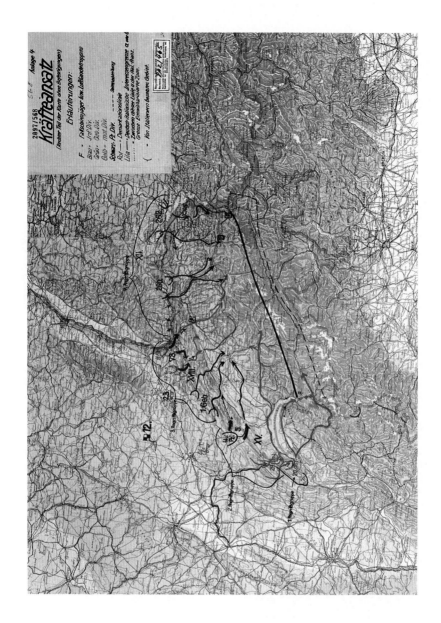

(left)
Upper left: Wilhelm Ritter von Leeb, Chief Army Group C (BA-MA)
Upper right: Walter Warlimont, Chief of Section Domestic Defense in OKW
(BA-MA)
Lower left: Wilhelm List, Supreme Commander 12th Army (BA-MA)
Lower right: Heinz Guderian, Commanding General Tank Group Guderian.
(AfZ)
(above)
Upper left: Hans von Greiffenberg, Chief Operations Division in General Staff
of the Army (BA-MA)
Upper right: Otto Wilhelm von Menges, author of the attack study, worked out
for the General Staff of the Army. (private possession of Dr. D. W. von
Menges)

(above) From his headquarters in the Black Forest, Hitler visits Upper Alsace on June 30, 1940; General Dollmann describes from the Vosges Mountains the breakthrough of the 7th Army through the Maginot Line. Dollmann, Hitler, Keitel, Meissner. (AfZ)

(right) Travel through the Loophole from Geneva to Lisbon (July 24–27, 1940). Necessary visas from the Spanish Consular Section, Bern (upper left); the Portuguese Consulate, Zurich (upper right); the French Consulate, Geneva (lower left); stamp by border controls at Annemasse, Cerebère, Port-Bou (lower right). (private possession of René Nordmann).

VISTO EN ESTE CONSULADO DE ESPAÑA.

BUENO PARA *atravesar el territorio*

Nacional, sin facultad de dete-

nerse en el mismo, en viaje

de tránsito a Portugal

BERNA, 13 DE *Julio* DE 19 40.

Secretario de la Legación de
España en Berna,
con funciones de Cónsul

válido para un solo viaje hasta el 9 de Agosto 1940.

Derechos percibidos N.º
Art. Arancel
Ptas.

En España está terminantemente prohibida
la importación y exportación de moneda española
quedando los infractores sujetos a las responsa-
bilidades establecidas en las Leyes.

Visto de tránsito n.º 454 - Utilisável até

11 de Agosto de 1940.

Visto, bom a fim de seguir viagem

para Portugal –

Consulado de Portugal em Zurich,

aos 11 de *Julho* de 1940

Consul

25$00 SERVIÇO CONSULAR
25$00 SERVIÇO CONSULAR
25$00 SERVIÇO CONSULAR

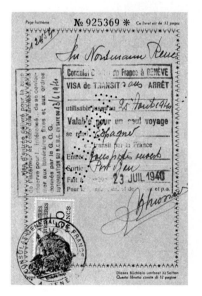

M. Nordmann René

Consulat Général de France à GENÈVE

VISA de TRANSIT avec ARRÊT

utilisable jusqu'au 25 Août 1940

Valable pour un seul voyage

se rend à Espagne

en transit par la France

Entrée *Canfranc* inscrit

Sortie Port Bou

Fait à 23 JUIL 1940

Pour le et p.o.

CONSULAT GÉNÉRAL DE FRANCE GENÈVE

MINISTÈRE DE L'INTÉRIEUR
Poste de GAILLARD
24 JUIL 1940
ENTRÉE
Commissariat Spécial d'ANNEMASSE

SUISSE
E 28 JUIN 1947
AÉROPORT-GENÈVE

COMMISSARIAT SPÉCIAL CERBÈRE
25 JUIL 1940
SORTIE

Ruta: Madrid - Badajoz

PORT-BOU
ENTRADA 25-7-40
Procedencia
PORT-BOU

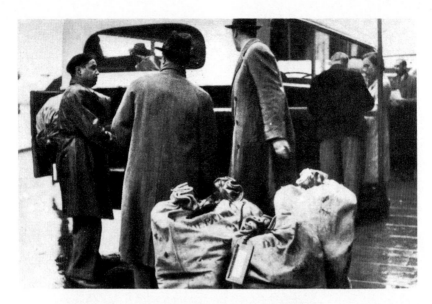

(top) Diplomatic courier luggage, prepared in Geneva for overseas transport, July 1940. (This luggage was also used to smuggle industrial diamonds and tiny precision products for construction of explosion devices through the counter-blockade.

(bottom) The first passenger long distance travel through the gap: Train-Routier with two buses and one truck for luggage at departure point in front of the Hôtel des Bergues in July 1940. The trip from Geneva to the Spanish border lasted 29 hours. (AfZ)

Chapter Twelve

Partial German Success Due to French and Swiss Concessions

Germany achieved the decisive breakthrough of closing the gap not in its negotiations with Switzerland, but in the context of a wider agreement with France negotiated in Paris on May 7–8, 1941. The Pétain regime had been continuously successful in evading the long requested establishment of German controls along its exterior borders. Shortly before the removal of Laval as deputy prime minister on December 13, 1940, the government of the Reich had even considered using force in the surveillance of the borders as retaliation for delays in French payments.[1] The military occupation called Operation "Attila"[2] which was under consideration at that time would by itself have taken care of the matter. However, the German leadership always recoiled from the use of ultimate force in this context; at one time Ribbentrop explained to Mussolini "that it was not possible to use pressure tactics against France because of the danger that North Africa might break away, and that the French were very well aware of this."[3] It was particularly detrimental for Switzerland that during this phase of increased pressure Admiral Darlan endeavored to intensify collaboration with Germany in order to improve the position of France in the "new Europe." The respective negotiations within the German armistice delegation dealing with economic matters were conducted by Ambassador Hans Richard Hemmen who had also been vocal during the trade negotiations in Bern and had shown himself as a hard-liner.[4] Even in April 1941 the German delegation had to be satisfied with only modest success in that the French Customs Office merely reminded its agents once again of the import, export, and transit prohibition for war materials that had been agreed to on October 15, 1940.[5] In the second phase of collaboration with Germany initiated by Laval's successor, the previous autonomy concerning border controls of the traffic in goods was sacrificed in exchange for relief relating to the line of demarcation and to the costs of occupation; the latter had been designated primarily for the support of German assistance to Iraq. In recognition, Hitler received Darlan at the Berghof on May 11, 1941.[6]

On May 20, 1941, the HWK special staff sent the following message to the ministries responsible for the war economy and armaments as well as to other agencies:

> The Foreign Ministry has just reported that the French government has signed the agreement regarding external border controls. Accordingly, the contractually planned 200 customs officers will be dispatched for border controls in [sic] Switzerland, at the Mediterranean and Pyrenees borders. Twelve customs officers will be dispatched immediately to Annemasse as an advance patrol.[7]

The German-French agreement was limited to the "monitoring of French border controls as to traffic in goods and currency operations at the external borders and at airports under customs control" and permitted neither permanently placed German agents of control nor a surveillance of the "green" border. Germany wanted to counter these defects using a "flying squad" of customs agents in rapid succession. In case of a "threatened violation of existing regulations" the German monitoring officials could cause delays as well as institute a checking procedure by the responsible German and French agencies. The French government also obligated itself to "restrict the number of border crossings to a minimum."[8]

From the German perspective the ideal solution consisted of keeping just one border crossing open to unoccupied France. Admiral Groos, the head of the HWK special staff, was now in a position to initiate the necessary measures to close the gap. On June 4 he met the Minister of Finance Lottner at the "Chicago" hotel in Divonne-les-Bains. In the command post entrusted with the protection of the German border with France, Minister Lottner was responsible for all customs surveillance at the external French borders. In accordance with the newly acquired rights and together with Consul General Krauel and Major Kayser, Groos first inspected the German customs office at Pougny outside Geneva, and then the unoccupied border section. Groos wanted to ascertain that the crossings near Chamonix, St. Gingolph, and Annemasse could be blocked so that long-distance rail traffic could be limited to the Geneva-Pougny-Bellegarde line, which was shortly to be reopened.[9]

The German negotiating team confronted the Swiss delegation with the totally new situation that had resulted from the border agreement with unoccupied France. Unable to take any action against this fait accompli, Switzerland had lost the last transit route by rail for its imports and exports that was not subject to direct German control. Its former stalling tactics now had a negative effect. As Switzerland's situation threatened only to get worse, in return for concessions to be made, the delegation of Hotz, Homberger, and Kohli now mainly sought to reopen the blocked supply lines as soon as possible and to secure the delivery of German coal and iron for as long as possible. At the same time more flexible regulations were to supplant special controls and the transit blockage in the West was to be overcome.

On June 13, 1941, the Swiss Federal Council issued a decree prohibiting the export of goods by letter mail, a step long sought by the OKW's Office for Military Economics and Armaments.[10] This decree, which became effective on June 19, disadvantaged mainly Great Britain and the United States which therefore considered it an insult. The Swiss government's ordinance made it impossible for these countries to overcome the counterblockade by means of letter parcels up to two kilograms which till then had been legal and which they had enabled them to secure, if precariously, the watch bearings and precision parts needed for the conduct of war. The threatened alternative to this concession was the prospect of having all letter mail going to the West checked on French soil. However, there are indications, to be discussed later, that the Swiss negotiating team had been deceived by German pretenses.

The economic warfare unleashed by the HWK special staff provided Germany with considerable success, particularly because the negotiating position of Switzerland, in comparison to that at the war's start, had greatly worsened not only in regard to the Axis powers, but also to Great Britain. This loss weighed much heavier than the financial concessions made in the agreement of July 18, 1941, which were, although not to the extent hoped for, counterbalanced by the saving of time and the securing of vital imports from Germany. The debt limit granted Germany for financing its orders primarily of war supplies was increased to 850 million francs, a sum not to be exceeded until December 31, 1942; however, the German breach of contract already became obvious in mid-1942. Switzerland obligated itself to run its exports and transit shipments through France only via Basel or via the Geneva-Bellegarde rail line. This was a severe blow to the traffic via St. Gingolph which had increased enormously. As the border station at Pougny in occupied France was unsuitable for efficient traffic, the activity of the German customs service was moved to the border station at La Plaine on Genevan territory. Switzerland had nevertheless been able to keep a back door open. It had been able to keep the "little border traffic" beyond the free zone safe from German control. The agreements also did not include road traffic at the various border crossings. Only the traffic on the reopened Geneva-Bellegarde road was checked by German customs officers in the occupied territory.[11]

On July 25, 1941, exactly one year after the armistice, the Swiss-German agreement became effective. From the Swiss perspective it had remained a puzzle why this "escape hatch to the west'" had come into existence.[12] Neither Hitler's failed plan for complete encirclement through military means nor the consequently pursued economic warfare by the HWK special staff could be fully understood. Summarizing the results of this first phase in the history of the gap, it should be noted that its importance cannot be assessed solely by the quantity and value of the goods which Switzerland managed to import and export through it. Much more significant is the relevance which the belligerents assigned to economic warfare that in turn shaped Switzerland's negotiating position.

NOTES

1. Eberhard Jäckel, *Frankreich in Hitler's Europa. Die deutsche Frankreichpolitik im Zweiten Weltkrieg* (Stuttgart: Deutsche Verlagsanstalt, 1966), 147.

2. Hitler was afraid that under General Weygand the breaking-away of North Africa was imminent. The tense situation was aggravated shortly thereafter when on December 13, 1940, Pétain dismissed the Deputy Prime Minister Laval; see *Kriegstagebuch des Oberkommandos der Wehrmacht 1940–1945*, ed. Percy E. Schramm, vol. 1 (Frankfurt a. M.: Bernard & Graefe Verlag für Wehrwesen, 1965), 223, 225–26, 230.

3. Andreas Hillgruber, ed., *Staatsmänner und Diplomaten bei Hitler. Vertrauliche Aufzeichnungen über Unterredungen mit Vertretern des Auslandes 1939–1941* (Frankfurt a. M.: Bernard & Graefe Verlag für Wehrwesen, 1967), 561; the meeting between Hitler and Mussolini occurred on June 6, 1941, on the Brenner pass). See also ADAP, Series D, vol. 11, 2, documents nos. 518, 574.

4. Hans Umbreit, *Der Militärbefehlshaber in Frankreich 1940–1944* (Boppard am Rhein: Harald Boldt Verlag, 1968), 70.

5. *Bulletin Douanier*, No. 1798 (April 1/4, 1941), 76 (copy), in Wi/IF, August 1, 1941, "Schweiz, Grenzkontrollen," microfilm NA T-77, roll 706.

6. Jäckel, *Frankreich*, 90–91, 160ff.

7. "Rundschreiben," OKW, Sonderstab HWK, Berlin, May 20, 1941, signed Kayser; microfilm NA T-77, roll 706; see also ADAP, Series D, vol. 12, 2, document no. 475.

8. Written communication, Deutsche Waffenstillstandskommission to OKW Wi/RüAmt/Wi, Wiesbaden, July 4, 1941; also copy of the German-French agreement concerning the control of the frontiers, concluded on May 8 and finalized by the exchange of notes on May 17, 1941.

9. "Rundschreiben," OKW, May 20, 1941.

10. For the Swiss public the prohibition was justified by reference to the increasing scarcity of vital foodstuffs which "also led to further rationing"; see "Ausfuhrverbot im Briefpostverkehr verboten," *Der Bund*, June 17, 1941.

11. Notation "Verhinderung der schweizerischen Ausfuhr kriegswichtiger Waren," Berlin, June 6, 1941, signed Wiehl; PAB, AA, HaPol. Wiehl, "Akten betr. Schweiz," vol. 8, January 1940–August 1942. Robert Urs Vogler, *Die Wirtschaftsverhandlungen zwischen*

der Schweiz und Deutschland 1940 und 1941 (Basel: Helbing & Lichtenhahn, 1983), 213; Edgar Bonjour, *Geschichte der schweizerischen Neutralität. Vier Jahrhunderte eidgenös-sischer Aussenpolitik*, vol. 6 (Basel: Helbing & Lichtenhahn, 1972), 173.

12. Paul Keller, delegate for commercial issues in the Swiss Foreign Office, remarked on the agreement of July 18, 1941: "Thereby the 'hole in the West' has been filled in, which by now has existed a full year for reasons never clearly understood"; see Edgar Bonjour, *Neutralität*, vol. 8 (1976), 173–84: "Eidgenössisches Volkswirtschaftsdeparte-ment an schweizerische Gesandtschaft in London," dated Bern, June 15, 1941; quotation, 182–83.

Chapter Thirteen

Importance of the Gap until the Agreement of July 18, 1941

For the Germans, the uncontrolled border section represented a continuous hindrance for pressuring Switzerland successfully, and the mere existence of this gap was a serious obstacle to a more merciless approach. It was decisive that within the OKW the organizations responsible for economic warfare were convinced that their counterblockade could not be truly effective because of the gap in the southwest. Hitler had based his offensive of June 1940 in Savoy on the same assessment and had assumed that it would be easier to blackmail Switzerland after its full enclosure. That its implementation was delayed by a year emerges in hindsight as an enormously lucky event, particularly when considering the situation in the summer and fall of 1940. After the Germans had finally achieved full control of all imports and exports, the attack on the Soviet Union began on June 22, 1941, and directed the power of German military aggression against the East.

The importance of this last direct connection through unoccupied France for Swiss-British trade relations can be gauged by the disappointment and total rejection with which the British authorities, particularly the Ministry of Economic Warfare, reacted to the Swiss government's prohibition of export goods by letter mail and to the agreement of July 18, 1941. Since after the collapse of France England had nearly written off Switzerland and detained its supply ships, it was not insignificant to be able to stress during the difficult negotiations that in spite of the permit system during the summer and fall of 1940 a trade route for goods without direct customs control by the Axis powers had remained open. As soon as the Allies had become aware of the possibility of bypassing Axis control, they used this gap to acquire precision items for weapons which in turn eased the passage of important supplies for Switzerland through the British blockade. Yet Britain had been disinterested already in early 1941 in the traffic of goods through German-occupied territories and thus via Geneva-Bellegarde. The forced agreement of July 18 had led to a turning point in the relations with Great Britain, that is to a painful setback which could never be reversed during the subsequent often stalled and complex efforts to overcome the Allied blockade. General Hermann Böhme pointed to another, still unexplored aspect. He claimed that from a German perspective more important than this traffic in goods had been "that the French were unable to obtain replacement material for their secret camouflaged arms depots which they maintained contrary to the conditions of the armistice."[1]

One must stress, furthermore, Switzerland's considerable interest in evading German surveillance as much as possible of those imports that loomed large in its strategy of survival. It had deliberately steered this traffic in such a manner that the officers of the German customs office at Pougny mostly saw only "harmless" imports and exports. These legal ways of circumventing German control were used exhaustively within the many restrictions to which the rail and road traffic through Upper Savoy had been subjected. A report of the Swiss Federal Council declared that

> while the Bouveret customs office had served only insignificant local traffic during normal times, it had to be converted to extraordinary activity particularly during the temporary closing of the Geneva-Bellegarde line; its customs revenue increased from 2 million francs in the previous year to 8.6 million. Similar conditions also existed at the Genevan customs office of Eaux-Vives where the revenue increased from 1.9 million to 4.8 million francs.[2]

Until mid-July 1941 the Bouveret-St. Gingolph-Annemasse line had provided outstanding service.

No actual deceptive maneuvers by the official agencies can be detected. The Germans accused neither the Swiss Federal Council nor its executive agencies of deliberately violating their obligations as established by the agreements. On the contrary, they helped ensure that, apart from the blockade and counterblockade, any illegal traffic in goods had to overcome a third effective obstacle, the economic control measures of wartime Switzerland. In particular, the Central Office for the Surveillance of Imports and Exports, established on October 24, 1939, within the Commercial Section, was charged with monitoring the agreements made with the blockade powers which regulated the processing and final destination of the imported goods. Ministerial Counsel Gottfried Seyboth of the Reich's Economics Ministry who, in contrast to the OKW, was solely guided by economic considerations, considered the contractual fidelity of Switzerland so reliable that he viewed the permits and Swiss customs controls sufficient as long-term guarantees.[3] Although the

Swiss Federal Council declined to participate directly and continuously in the counterblockade, the obligations Switzerland had assumed towards the Third Reich were fulfilled with such loyalty that it obstructed the full exploitation of the chances offered by the gap.

NOTES

1. Oral communication of General Hermann Böhme, Munich, August 10, 1968.

2. "Bericht des schweizerischen Bundesrates an die Bundesversammlung über seine Geschäftsführung im Jahre 1941," April 21, 1942, 212–13.

3. "Bericht über Stand und Organisation des Geleitscheinwesens in der Schweiz," Bern, September 18, 1940, signed Dr. Sommer, in microfilm NA T-77, roll 706.

Chapter Fourteen

Semilegal and Illegal Attempts to Break through the Counterblockade

For an overall evaluation of the situation, it is important also to consider the underground economic war for which the gap provided valuable opportunities for semilegal and illegal transit of goods. To explore this difficult to analyze subject intensive further research is needed which in this context can only be suggested. The OKW's principal concern at that time was not the integrity of the Swiss authorities, but rather attempts of British and other trade representatives to break through the counterblockade by working with those segments of the Swiss economy that wanted to keep their traditional business connections with the West. The documents of the intelligence services and the German border control reveal that the practical execution of the counterblockade was deficient for an unexpectedly long time; its circumvention would have been considerably easier for the specialists in the shipping industry had they been aware of these weaknesses. Based on its activity in Pougny the German customs office stated in early 1941 "that the office issuing the permits does not even see the items for which a permit is issued."[1] In May 1941 supervisory personnel on an inspection tour discovered that adequately trained examiners were not available even at the main customs office in Basel or in Lindau where all postal packages except those destined for France were to be checked: "Due to the difficulty of recognizing watch movements, watch parts etc. and to distinguish them from war material, it appears advisable to train the examiners for about three weeks in a watch and fuse factory (Junghans Company in Schramberg)." There were also problems with checking merchandise from the chemical industry: "The passage of such goods could be speeded up by adding certificates from official Swiss authorities."[2] The requested special training of about twenty German customs officials was initiated only after the gap had lost its importance for exports.

The customs officials in Upper Savoy then had neither the technical means nor the motivation to conduct costly and demanding inspections of goods. After German surveillance units had begun their work in the unoccupied regions, their leadership stated arrogantly that they had "brought the French customs officials who generally in regard to thorough checking tend to perform their work only superficially to a correct behavior. This becomes apparent particularly in the checking of export goods which before our intervention was done only on paper."[3] If the issuance of permits by the Axis powers as well as controls at the entry point in Upper Savoy was primarily or by certain agents "done on paper only," numerous possibilities for circumvention emerged. The methods to evade controls at customs involved a wide spectrum of deceptive measures such as various forms of false declarations or smuggling and included crafty cheating maneuvers on a large scale undertaken in cooperation with companies in France, Spain, or Portugal. Even after mid-July 1941 smuggling paths to the Allies persisted; precision items important for the war effort that had been transported through the gap into unoccupied France could be shipped without leaving French customs territory to regions belonging to France in northern and western Africa. As the leading officials of the surveillance unit in Marseilles reported: "Thus the possibility remains that goods which are prohibited for export get to their destinations via the French colonies or from there to third or enemy countries. This gap must become particularly sensitive for the war effort of the Axis powers where goods are involved that are of special importance to the enemy powers."[4]

There is no lack of reports from agents and hints from business circles which mix fantastic stories of adventure, half-true rumors, and genuine insight. The first category included, for instance, an agent's report of the German intelligence of March 22, 1941, that every week one thousand (!) pieces of 20-mm aircraft cannons were being shipped from Oerlikon to England. According to the agent, the parts of the weapons and ammunition drums "were first transported by overland buses of the Clipper Service from Geneva to Marseille, from there by boat to Lisbon and then by planes of Pan American Airways to New York. In New York trans-shipment to England."[5] That the route to England often led via the United States or Canada, however, was not pure imagination. More reliable were reports of the German and Italian consulates in Geneva which contained precise information about eleven Swiss companies that shipped by registered mail parcels containing watch components weighing up to two kilos via Spain or Portugal to England and the United States: "These packages number in the hundreds. Given the small and very tiny objects involved, this represents considerable quantities."[6] According to Italian observations, many trucks with goods for England allegedly still drove in May 1941 through Annemasse into unoccupied France.[7] Based on a comparison of Swiss export statistics with those of German and Italian offices issuing permits, an analysis of the German embassy in Bern concluded "that in disregard of permit procedures great quantities of goods subject to permits were exported from Switzerland to enemy countries and the United States without the required transit permits."[8]

Finally an illustrative and—until the closing of the gap—successful evasion of the blockade shall be mentioned by means of which the Swiss, German, and French systems of surveillance were outwitted in a semilegal way until July 1941 when the German intelligence section responsible for economic espionage became aware of it. The investigations rest on information that a co-owner of a watch factory in Bienne wanted to provide; the watch samples analyzed by experts came from a French customs agent who dealt with goods in transit subject to customs along the Geneva border in places such as St. Julien, Collonges, Monnetier, and Annemasse.[9] As to the production and delivery of electrical ignition timers via France to England the investigative report observes: "Swiss watch production is currently very tightly monitored by Swiss authorities. Fully assembled ignition timers may neither be produced nor exported." To circumvent theses obstacles electric watches were exported via France that exactly resembled peacetime products and which could be sent without permits. But that was not all: "In a subsequent shipment ignition settings and contact springs were provided as harmless replacement parts. As all components are standardized, it is easy within minutes to convert a regular electric clockwork mechanism into an ignition timer." Ten companies from the Jura region and Geneva were named in this report as manufacturing these electric ignition timers or components such as ignition settings and contact springs. Concerning the volume of these shipments which the interviewed shipping agent helped move through customs the following detail emerged: "The production of electric ignition timers for England varied between 6000 and 7000 pieces per month. There were various models of a more or less difficult kind." This transit traffic occurred without obstacles. If in exceptional cases fully assembled ignition timers had to be produced in Switzerland due to the required precision, it was still possible to do this: "The customs agent estimated the actual shipments through France at about 200 pieces per month. These fully constructed and mounted instruments are easily exported from Switzerland without control by customs agents through the auxiliary customs stations at Collonges-sous-Salève, Juvigny and Veigy; on the French side there is practically no control." In German documents these auxiliary customs stations are barely mentioned, which clearly shows that local people knew how to use these escape hatches.

The trick of sending double shipments was used in various forms and quite extensively. The exports of spring-loaded ignition timers were also subject to precise Swiss controls. Simple contact timers, however, were considered peacetime merchandise and used in great quantities as switching timers for monitors of electricity. Depending on requirements, they provided one or several electrical contacts within twenty-four hours and were exported fully assembled. "At the same time, however, the additional transposing gear wheels and contacts are being supplied. In this manner it is possible to convert such a contact watch (representing peacetime material) into a contact watch that can be set as an explosion timer from half an hour to 30 days. The timer is a precision instrument and for 30 days a setting of between about 5–8 minutes is possible." These timers were produced in various formats and technical models and the firm Landis & Gyr played a leading role. According to the available information, the shipments designated for England were organized by the Zug-based company in the following manner: It shipped the contact timers legally to French companies with which it regularly conducted business in Cluses in Upper Savoy or in Montbrison in the Loire region. The French companies ordered other components such as wheels and anchors that were produced by smaller companies in Switzerland. "These components were then assembled in France under the guidance of specialists from Landis & Gyr." In this manner complete timers for explosions were constructed: "The total number of ignition timers supplied to England is about 3000 pieces per month; the average factory price per ignition timer with its wheels and contacts is about 120 Swiss francs." For special ignition timers produced in England, components were purchased from Switzerland in great quantities.[10] Swiss expert workers were therefore in high demand in foreign countries that were setting up their own industry of ignition timers. The German embassy in Bern was successful in having the Swiss Federal Council take measures to prevent the travel of these experts to the United States, Canada, and England.[11]

Such reports are more impressive than statistics in demonstrating the great importance that the belligerents assigned to the gap in the Swiss border. Although Germany had now largely succeeded in making it impossible for Great Britain and the United States to obtain these precision items so important for their armament industry, it soon became clear that the German success was only partial and that resistance against the German encirclement continued in secret.

NOTES

1. "Bericht deutsches Zollamt Pougny an Kommandostelle des Zollgrenzschutzes Frankreich," January 18, 1941, signed Hentschke, copy; in microfilm NA T-77, roll 706.

2. "Reisebericht Dr. Wallner, o. D. Beilage zum Rundschreiben des Reichsfinanzministeriums," May 13, 1941, in microfilm NA T-77, roll 706.

3. "Tätigkeitsbericht vom 9. Juni 1941 des Leiters der Überwachungsabteilung des Zollgrenzschutzes im unbesetzten Frankreich," Marseille, 11. August, 1941, signed i. V. Schulze; excerpts, copy, in microfilm NA T-77, roll 706.

4. "Tätigkeitsbericht."

5. "Meldung vom 22. März, 1941, Anlage 1 zu Ast. Wiesbaden," in microfilm NA T-77, roll 706. In the folder Wi/IF 1.8, "Verschiedenes," are further reports of agents.

6. "Rundschreiben Abwehrabteilung III," Berlin, April 17, 1941; "Anlage: Bericht Boris," in microfilm NA T-77, roll 706.

7. See Edgar Bonjour, *Geschichte der schweizerischen Neutralität. Vier Jahrhunderte schweizerischer Aussenpolitik*, vol. 6 (Basel: Helbing & Lichtenhahn, 1972), 322–23 for the reference to the note of Woermann, AA, Berlin May 16, 1941.

8. "Bericht Deutsche Gesandtschaft Bern" to AA, May 21, 1941, signed Selzam; Wi/IF 1. 8., in microfilm NA T-77, roll 706.

9. Excerpted copy, "Schweiz. Feinmechanik. . . . Lieferung von Zünduhren aus der Schweiz über Frankreich nach Grossbritannien," A Ausl/Abw. No. 284/7/41g Abw I (Iwi), July 17, 1941, in microfim NA T-77, roll 706. The excerpt seems to derive from a court case and contains only that passage which was of special interest for the OKW's groups concerned with economic warfare.

10. This form of evasion indicates why afterwards such steps are nearly impossible to retrace. Major Sommer instructed the customs offices at Basel, La Plaine, and Lindau to stop immediately the transit of electric counters, contact- and low voltage watches, and watches running for several days [Mehrtageuhren]. "Schreiben Reichsfinanzministerium an OKW," Wi/RüAmt Berlin, July 26, 1941. This led to a corresponding expansion of the list of items needing permits. "Schreiben OKW, WiRüAmt/Wi IVa to RFM, October 1, 1941, signed Sommer (draft); microfilm NA T-77, roll 706.

11. "Bericht Deutsche Gesandtschaft," signed Köcher, February 7, 1941.

Chapter Fifteen

The "Little Border Traffic": Hidden Door to the West

As yet little attention has been paid to the second phase in the history of the gap which lasted until the German invasion of Vichy, France, on November 11, 1942. Although it no longer had the tension of former times, its history is still of considerable importance. Its subsequent development shall be sketched at least in outline to demonstrate this fact. As the reports of the customs authorities show, the border segment with Upper Savoy still left open important avenues of escape in unoccupied France that were largely outside of German control.

Although Germany attained its goal to control the transit of goods, it did not happen in the way the Reich had hoped. After a delay that violated the terms of the agreement, the Geneva-Bellegarde line was finally reopened August 1, 1941.[1] The securing of complete German control still gave no assurance that customs agents and intelligence personnel would be able to see those export goods which they were most anxious to check. During the following months the trend, already evident at the first reopening of that line in mid-December 1940, was to become more evident. Under British pressure Switzerland more than ever preferred the transit routes through Italy. Thus the already important transshipment port of Genoa gained in significance. A large part of those shipments which had evaded the sea blockade were brought from Iberian to Italian ports after a complicated reloading onto primarily Spanish and Portuguese ships.[2] The HWK special staff had warned in October 1941 that Germany's position of power in regard to Switzerland would be weakened if the granting of permits should shift to the Italians. Now, in mid-January 1942, the Department for Trade Policy of the Foreign Office had to admit that this had actually happened:

> Till now we negotiated with the Swiss regarding the permits and asked the Italians merely to participate. Thus we had all the pressure means against Switzerland in our

hands. This has now changed due to the fact that Switzerland no longer exports its goods through Bellegarde due to the blockade, but rather through Italy. To a certain extent Switzerland was forced to do this, as the British no longer issue any navicerts for goods leaving Switzerland through Bellegarde. Thus, what we always wanted to prevent has indeed occurred, which is that the Italians occupy a preferred position in regard to Switzerland.[3]

Germany, therefore, had aimed for some time to have the permits issued in Bern and signed jointly, thereby to secure for itself the right to veto a too generous treatment by its Axis partner. Yet, as the German embassy in Rome reported to Berlin in December 1941, the Italian government rejected such a proposal: "At the current time it did not wish to burden Switzerland with controls exceeding the current level since it had assumed the representation of the interests of the Axis powers in enemy countries."[4]

The urge to gain absolute control had not strengthened the position of the German monitors but rather weakened it. Although they now controlled the only transit connection from Switzerland to the West, important goods were sent through Genoa. In 1941 some 7,800 empty railroad cars were sent to France for the importation of goods, but in 1942 this number had shrunk to only 405. However, compared to the previous year, 1941, more than 8,000 additional empty cars were sent to Italy. When in September 1943 Germany also established its occupation regime in Italy, the Italian ports could no longer be used, so that Switzerland was forced to reorient its trade to the French transit routes.[5]

The German hope of controlling all automobile and truck traffic to unoccupied France also suffered a setback. The blocked route Geneva-Chancy-Pougny-Bellegarde was reopened in the hope that road traffic would again prefer this direct and important main route to the Rhône valley. Yet the determination to gain absolute control stood in the way of these plans as well. Strong security measures ensured that during the crossing of the corner near Gex no access to the occupied area was possible. In Pougny, where all passenger trains had to stop, the occupation forces undertook a thorough border control. This had the effect that the detours through Upper Savoy's network of roads continued to be preferred. As the scathing report of the border authorities of mid-October 1941 stated: "The road traffic overland through the occupied territory has totally failed to take off."[6]

As the German monitoring activity indicates, the attempt to interfere with traffic beyond the strict customs operations was subject to greater limits than one might assume. The controversy regarding traffic via letter mail presents an illustrative example. In this matter the Vichy government resisted German impositions more deftly than the Swiss Federal Council. On September 9–10, 1941, German inspectors at the Centre de Contrôle in Lyon discovered eleven letters from Switzerland which contained parts of watches between two pieces of cardboard. Each envelope contained 1,044 watch jewels or 1,008 screws measuring about one half millimeter each, which gives an idea of the tiny parts involved.[7] The German customs authorities used this incident to demand that the transit of goods by letter mail even through unoccupied France be prohibited. However, the French postal authorities referred to the freedom of transit set down in the Universal Postal Agreement. The German armistice delegation in Paris concerned with economic issues put pressure on the French delegation by pointing to the concessions already granted by Switzerland: "As the transit of goods from Switzerland through France by letter mail has been essentially cut off by the decision of the Swiss Federal Council of June 13, 1941, it is to be expected that the opposition of the French postal authorities can also soon be eliminated."[8] The French government referred instead to Article 26 of the Universal Postal Agreement of Buenos Aires: "The freedom of passage is guaranteed throughout the territory of the Association." The term "freedom of passage" had been interpreted by the meeting in Buenos Aires to mean that mailings in open or closed packages were neither to be checked nor confiscated. According to Article 46 only explosives, other dangerous materials, and indecent items were exempt. In a declaration also the Postal Ministry of the Reich came to this most significant conclusion: "If the view of the French government is such that it is prevented by the regulations of the Universal Postal Agreement from the practical execution of prohibiting the transit of a certain kind of letter mail, such a view cannot be challenged."[9]

The more decisive position of the Vichy government as well as the unambiguous opinion of the Postal Ministry of the Reich require a reevaluation of the decision the Swiss Federal Council had made on June 13, 1941. It had been taken too hastily and for a considerable time was to burden heavily the relationship with Great Britain. The Reich's Finance Ministry also considered it hopeless to refute the French government's point of view: "Under these circumstances we have no other choice than to be satisfied with the measures by the Swiss Federal Council against the export of goods by letter mail and to file protests in Switzerland regarding violations that are detected by our supervisory personnel in France."[10] In mid-October watch jewels, watch springs, and tiny screws in letters coming from Switzerland were again found during postal checks in Lyon. Yet in November the French postal authority took the offensive and instructed its agents, by referring to the international convention of Cairo of March 20, 1934, to deny the customs administration the right to check transit as well as export mail. The French customs authority then instructed the postal customs offices no longer to execute such checks. This chess move was directed against the

German supervisors who attempted everywhere to interfere with the control rights of the French customs authorities.[11] The prohibition against export of goods by mail through the gap was effective primarily because of Switzerland's voluntary self-control.

Even for those who for various reasons wished or were forced to circumvent direct control by the Axis powers, the agreement of July 18, 1941, had significant effects. In Article 7, item 5 contained the following ruling: "The border crossing for persons to and through France by rail is limited to the Geneva-Bellegarde line. Permissions for exceptions must be individually granted in advance. A precondition for the granting of exceptions is to guarantee the control of luggage by German customs agencies." In item 6, the local and nearby border traffic was exempted from this ruling.[12] Already during the negotiations, the Swiss delegation had made it clear that it was neither willing nor able to enforce these restrictions; Switzerland only consented to comply with possible German-French agreements that might be negotiated.[13] Nevertheless, it proved to be a grave error that any such discussion even took place. The French government was rightfully shocked that without being informed in advance agreements were being made between Germany and Switzerland concerning the use of its railroads. It therefore filed a protest with the Armistice Commission against the relevant regulations in the agreement of July 18, 1941.[14] There are many indications that the Swiss delegation was the victim of a deception. For intelligence reasons the OKW was particularly interested in gaining control over the passenger traffic in the gap. Accordingly, the Swiss were put under pressure in this matter. They were "informed" by the Germans of the new negotiating situation resulting from the May concessions of Vichy, France, in a manner that gave the erroneous impression German surveillance would also extend to passenger controls: "German control agents are already now in Annemasse. France has thus enabled Germany to monitor all traffic of passengers and goods from Switzerland to and through France."[15]

However, it was the occupation force itself which made the planned restriction of transit traffic of passengers to the Geneva-Bellegarde line ineffective. According to instructions by the military commanders in France of June 28, 1941, with the exception of French nationals, residents of "enemy countries" as well as of the occupied territories were not permitted on this line. The prohibition was for reasons of defense against espionage and only reinforced the intentions of many travelers not to use the direct line through occupied territory, but instead to reach their distant destinations by using the more cumbersome route via the regional lines.[16] Based on discussions within the HWK special staff, which was dissatisfied with the latest developments, the command section of the border customs service for France in early October 1941 undertook a thorough analysis of the situation regarding long distance passenger traffic from Switzerland to the West. The use of passenger trains through Pougny, which was substantial in the beginning, had constantly decreased and was by now insignificant:

> While the daily number of passengers on this line in August numbered 120 to 180, among them several diplomats and couriers, by the end of September the number of passengers had dropped to only 10 to 20 per day, mostly women and children. Due to the drop in traffic, the sleeping cars to Cerbère, which were initially running on the line via Pougny, since September 2, 1941, have been routed from Geneva (Eaux-Vives) via Annemasse. According to the traffic on the rail line via Pougny, the passenger traffic from Switzerland directly to unoccupied France has constantly increased.[17]

The reason for the massive defection and return to the regional lines was based on the peculiarity of the German surveillance authority in unoccupied France. Monitoring by the surveillance unit at Annemasse was restricted to passengers arriving by train in Annemasse from Geneva, in particular to those persons encountered during French customs and currency control. The German monitors were not granted a continuous presence. The lists of passengers maintained by the French police which was responsible for passport control were unavailable to German officials. Those passengers who arrived by car in Annemasse from Geneva via the road customs stations at Moillesulaz or St. Julien in order to board the train to southern France were not registered. The annoyance of the French government at the agreement of July 18, 1941, between Germany and Switzerland resulted in the great advantage that Vichy was not inclined to complement those arrangements by corresponding measures. As the line from the Geneva station of Cornavin through Bellegarde was little used, the French railroad administration made the sleeping car to Port-Bou run from Evian and Annemasse despite German objections.

As no further concessions could be obtained in this matter in unoccupied France, the German efforts were now directed at attempting to install permanent German customs control in the Geneva station of Eaux-Vives. However, the agreement made between Switzerland and France on June 14, 1881, concerning the "connection of the rail line Geneva-Annemasse to the Savoy rail network at Annemasse" preempted an opportunity to reach this goal. Under this agreement, French customs agents had not been given control rights at Eaux Vives. This now forestalled the plan to have German personnel in the local Geneva station monitor the French customs agents put there for this purpose.[18]

The German surveillance intended to put pressure on the French customs officers, yet provoked resistance instead. Obstructive maneuvers even at the periphery of Geneva made the forced surveillance ineffective. Thus when checking the customs office at St. Julien two German customs inspectors discovered "that the list concerning traffic in goods listed the entering and leaving of diplomatic representatives only of neutral countries or countries allied with Germany. The representatives of enemy countries were listed only when forced to do so by the presence of surveillance officers." The far closer traditional association with Geneva, particularly expressed in the special usage of the free zone, as well as the personal contacts between border personnel, encouraged another type of collaboration along the gap. Both Switzerland and the Vichy state shared the interest in helping young Alsatians, who had fled compulsory work service by flight into Switzerland, to reach unoccupied France via Annemasse by avoiding any type of customs inspections. When two German monitors at the customs office at Moillesulaz observed that Swiss soldiers brought fourteen Alsatians to the passport control post of the French police, they requested the French customs officer to conduct a customs inspection in order to enable them to get involved. The official rejected this request with the justification that he lacked the power to give orders to the police. The surveillance authorities suspected that there were other forms of French collaboration with the Swiss that were totally beyond German control: "It has been observed that officers of the Sûreté have brought people from Switzerland to France day and night without satisfying the required customs formalities. These people were Alsatians and escaped prisoners of war. The customs officials tolerate this circumvention because it is executed by officers of the Sûreté. They appear to be totally unconcerned about this activity. This activity is supported by the Swiss gendarmes. There is a cordial understanding between the officers of the Sûreté and those of the Swiss gendarmes."[19]

NOTES

1. "Fernschreiben OKH," Gen.Std H/Gen.Qu to Mil. Bef. in France, Chef GenStab Ic/4 July 20, 1941; "Schnellbrief," AA, HaPol to OKW, WiRüAmt, Berlin, July 31, 1941, signed Sabath; microfilm NA T-77, roll 706.

2. Concerning the issue of ships chartered and purchased by the Confederacy, the question of transit in Spain and Portugal, and the tasks of the truck-syndicate "Autotransit" founded in May 1941, see E. Matter and E. Ballinari, "Eidgenössisches Kriegs-Transport-Amt," in *Die schweizerische Kriegswirtschaft 1939/1948. Bericht des Eidgenössischen Volkswirtschaftsdepartementes* (Bern: 1950), 109–46.

3. "Vermerk" for the Director HaPol, Berlin, January 15, 1942, V. L. R. Sabath; PAB, AA, HaPol, Wiehl, "Akten betr. Schweiz," vol. 8, January 1940–August 1942. The "navicerts" were needed for imports, the "Certificates of Interest and Origin" for exports.

4. "Schnellbrief," AA, HaPol, to RWM and others, Berlin, December 18, 1941; microfilm NA T-77, roll 706.

5. In 1943 the number of empty cars sent to France rose again dramatically to 16,579; see *Kriegswirtschaft*, 133–34.

6. "Bericht der Kommandostelle des Zollgrenzschutzes Frankreich" to the Finance Minister of the Reich, Paris, October 16, 1941; microfilm NA T-77, roll 706.

7. "Meldung der Zollinspektoren Treuber und Evers an Bezirkszollkommissar," Annemasse, September 11, 1941, with enclosure; microfilm NA T-77, roll 706. The firm Jaeger-Le Coultre of Geneva mentioned as sender on eight of the letters already had been on the list of suspects of the German Embassy in Bern because of delivery of ignition devices to England.

8. "Telegramm Deutsche Waffenstillstandsdelegation für Wirtschaft" to AA, Paris, September 29, 1941, signed Coenen; microfilm NA T-77, roll 706.

9. "Schnellbrief," the Minister of the Reichspost to AA, Berlin, November 6, 1941, unsigned copy; microfilm NA T-77, roll 706.

10. "Schreiben Reichsfinanzministerium," to AA, Berlin, November 19, 1941, signed Wucher; microfilm NA T-77, roll 706.

11. "Erfahrungsbericht für die Zeit vom 1. September bis zum 10. November, 1941. Der Leiter der Überwachungsabteilungen des Zollgrenzschutzes im unbesetzten Frankreich," Marseille, November 20, 1941; microfilm NA T-77, roll 706.

12. Article 7, no. 6 of the Special Agreement of July 18, 1941 stated: "The border- and local traffic to France remains untouched at all frontier crossings as well as the traffic between countries on the line Le Bouveret-EauxVives. Switzerland will issue export permits for goods subject to permits in the border- and local traffic to France that are valid only via La Plaine, special arrangements excepted that have been made with the German Embassy in Bern. The Swiss Government will continuously inform the German Embassy in Bern about export licenses granted for goods that are not subject to permits for the border- and local traffic. Switzerland will not allow the traffic in persons by means of cars or buses on any other road than Chancy-Pougny except if the destination is clearly in the domain of the local or border traffic. Exceptions require a separate agreement. A precondition for exceptions is the guarantee of baggage control by German customs agents. In case of a misuse the German government reserves the right to demand a change in this arrangement." See "Fernschreiben," AA, HaPOl IIa Hemmen, July 22, 1941, signed Sabath; microfilm T 120/roll 1990, E 06491 f. The text reveals that Germany hoped by the control of exports to control also the traffic in persons.

13. "Bericht Deutsche Gesandtschaft Bern," to AA, November 3, 1941, signed Selzam, microfilm T 120/roll 1990, E 06491 f.

14. "Telegramm Waffenstillstandsdelegation für Wirtschaft," to AA, Paris, October 7, 1941, signed Hemmen. "Bericht der Kommandostelle des Zollgrenzschutzes Frankreich an Reichsminister der Finanzen," Paris, October 16, 1941, microfilm T 120/roll 1990, E 06491.

15. "Eidgenössisches Volkswirtschaftsdepartement an Schweizerische Gesandtschaft London," Bern, July 15, 1941, signed Keller; printed in Edgar Bonjour, *Geschichte der schweizerischen Neutralität. Vier Jahrhunderte schweizerischer Aussenpolitik*, 6, Auflage, vol. 8 (Basel: Helbing & Lichtenhahn, 1976), 182–83.

16. "Bericht über die Tätigkeit des Zollgrenzschutzes im unbesetzten Frankreich, Kommandostelle des Zollgrenzschutzes Frankreich," Paris, August 8, 1941, signed Lottner;

"Schreiben Reichsfinanzministerium" to AA, Berlin, October 11, 1941, signed Wucher, with enclosure; microfilm NA T-77, roll 706.

17. "Bericht der Kommandostelle des Zollgrenzschutzes Frankreich," to the Reichsminister of Finances, Paris, October 16, 1941; microfilm NA T-77, roll 706.

18. "Schnellbrief," AA, HaPol, IIA, to Reichswirtschaftsministerium and others, Berlin, November 12, 1941, signed Sabath. "Übereinkunft zwischen der Schweiz und Frankreich betreffend den Anschluss der Eisenbahn Genf-Annemasse and das savoyische Bahnnetz bei Annemasse," June 14, 1881, signed Kern, Jagerschmidt, copy; microfilm, NA T-77, roll 706.

19. "Erfahrungsbericht für die Zeit vom 1. September bis zum 10. November 1941. Der Leiter der Überwachungsabteilungen des Zollgrenzschutzes im unbesetzten Frankreich," Marseille, November 20, 1941; microfilm NA T-77, roll 706.

Chapter Sixteen

The Special Emigrant Railroad Car of the Swiss Alien Police

While this type of assistance mainly benefited French refugees, the Swiss Federal Immigration Office cooperated with the German Embassy in Bern regarding the departure of emigrants through the gap:

> The embassy has so far not approved any long distance trains on the line Geneva (Eaux-Vives)-Annemasse. Approval was only given immediately after the conclusion of the agreement of July 18 of this year that on each Wednesday certain emigrants, traveling long distance, may use a certain train which operates daily as border or local traffic from Geneva (Eaux-Vives) in the direction of Annemasse. The luggage of these persons, which will be listed by the Federal Immigration Office, is regularly inspected by officers of the customs service in La Plaine at the Eaux-Vives station.

This arrangement indicates the direction negotiations regarding long distance passenger traffic had taken before the conclusion of the agreement of July 18, 1941. Although Switzerland had rejected a general obligation to stop that traffic, it soon became clear that special oral understandings had been reached with regard to "emigrant trains."[1] This led to the untenable situation that Swiss authorities forced the emigrants of the weekly trains to undergo German luggage controls which occurred without legal justification in an endstation for regional trains going to unoccupied France. As this station as well as the trains were operated by the French railroad administration, Germany had no right either to permit or forbid anything to the Swiss concerning trains running out of Eaux-Vives. Even the Office for War Economy and Armaments admitted this in an internal investigation.[2]

The special agreements concerned the "Swiss collective transport from Geneva Eaux-Vives to Barcelona-Lisbon" which according to an information sheet of August 4, 1941, consisted of one special railroad car that operated every Wednesday between Geneva Eaux-Vives and Port-Bou. Authorized to use it were: "1. Any traveler from the Swiss Federal Immigration Service. 2. Any traveler residing in Switzerland or in transit through Switzerland, irrespective of nationality, traveling to a Spanish or Portuguese port of embarkation." A representative of the Swiss Immigration Service and of the organizing travel agency accompanied the travelers to Port-Bou. The luggage had to be delivered clearly labeled to Geneva the day before: "In our office the luggage is weighed and registered on a special list which we have to submit to the control agency of the customs office."[3] It was left unsaid that German customs agents from La Plaine went there to check the last remaining possessions of these harried and persecuted people. As an intelligence report of late October 1941 indicates, circumvention of this arrangement was at least not made impossible: "Within the last weeks, however, no persons departed on the Wednesdays agreed upon. Rather, the departure took place before or after, without anything being done by the Swiss or French authorities to ensure that the luggage was checked by German authorities."[4]

The more the influence of the surveillance officers increased at the official border crossings, the more the pressure grew to use detours along smuggling paths. In spite of the German controls, John Lomax, who was assigned to the British Embassy in Bern and worked for the Ministry of Economic Warfare, was still able to maintain a smuggling enterprise via Vichy, France, Barcelona, Madrid, and Lisbon. "Operation Viking" not only acquired industrial diamonds and micromechanical goods, but supposedly also managed to get larger precision items through the counterblockade. The information given by Lomax has not yet been verified. An investigation of Allied attempts to break the blockade would also have to include the question to what extent these attempts were tolerated or even supported in Switzerland by the police and the espionage service. According to Lomax, Swiss authorities lived by the motto that the right hand did not always know what the left hand was doing.[5]

In December 1941, Major Sommer appeared to be disturbed by the smuggling of weapons and money along the Swiss-French border near St. Gingolph. The answer of the Inspector General of the German Customs Office Hossfeld sounded resigned: "I have stated repeatedly for more than a year, orally and in writing, that it was high time really to close the 'Swiss gap' between Geneva and Chamonix." No matter how frequently and rapidly controls were made at the French customs offices, the illegal traffic across the "green border" could not be prevented in that manner: "On the contrary, they would lead to a total shift of the illegal traffic across the 'green border.'"[6]

NOTES

1. "Schreiben Deutsche Gesandtschaft Bern" to AA, November 3, 1941, signed Selzam. "Rundschreiben OKW," WiRüAmt/Wi Iva to AA, RFM, RWM, November 24, 1941. By early 1941 trains with sleeping cars left Geneva Eaux-Vives for Cerbère-Port-Bou every Tuesday and Friday; every Thursday a car was reserved for "emigrating Jews." At that time controls were made only in Annemasse. "Deutsche Delegation für Wirtschaft," to AA, Wiesbaden, January 31, 1941; microfilm NA T-77, roll 706.

2. "Rundschreiben OKW," RüAmt/Wi IVA to AA, RFM, RWM, November 24, 1941 (draft), in microfilm NA T-77, roll 706.

3. "Zirkularschreiben," no. 15, August 4, 1941, in microfilm NA T-77, roll 706.

4. "Bericht V-W 10 Schweiz-Schmuggelwahrnehmungen," Anlage to Ast. Stuttgart, No. 7073, October 29, 1941, in microfilm NA T-77, roll 706. The local stations in the Swiss border areas were managed by French companies and also sold tickets for long-distance travel.

5. John Lomax, *The Diplomatic Smuggler* (London: A. Barker, 1965), 131, 141–42; not understanding the situation, he insisted that it was merely a question of pressure to get Switzerland to provide Great Britain and Germany similarly with goods; Bern therefore was relieved that Lomax could not return from London because of the closing of the gap.

6. "Schreiben Reichsfinanzministerium" to OKW, WiRüAmt, Berlin, December 12, 1941, signed Hossfeld, in microfilm NA T-77, roll 706.

Chapter Seventeen

The Final Phase: Contacts with the Resistance and Final Rescue Attempts

Up to the last days before the invasion of unoccupied France on November 11, 1942, the German surveillance authorities had been unable to obtain more effective rights of control from French authorities. Allen W. Dulles, who traveled via Lisbon, Barcelona, and Port-Bou to Switzerland as head of the American Secret Service (OSS) in Central Europe just at the time when the gap began to close, has provided a graphic picture of the border controls at Annemasse. He had already been warned in Washington that "most likely a German Gestapo officer" would be present at the border. When Dulles was forced to leave the train in Annemasse together with all the other passengers, he saw a "suspicious looking man in civilian clothes" who monitored the French customs officers and must have been the German agent who conducted the agreed upon surveillance. He took down the information in Dulles' passport, and a short time later Dulles was informed by the French official that all American and British passengers were to be detained at the border; yet Vichy would make the decision. Nothing could be accomplished, neither by means of negotiation nor with a full briefcase. Dulles, who was already considering the possibilities of flight, reports:

> Finally, towards noon, shortly before the train was to continue towards Geneva, the gendarme reappeared and told me quickly to board the train. He whispered: "Allez, passez. Vous voyez que notre collaboration n'est que symbolique [Go through. You see, our collaboration is merely symbolic]." . . . [The presumed "Gestapo man" was nowhere to be seen.] I learned later that every day, exactly at 12 noon, he went to the nearest tavern down the street to drink a glass of beer and have his noon meal. Nothing, not even a landing operation in North Africa, could deter him from his routine. The French office had dutifully called Vichy. But when the Gestapo man disappeared for his lunch, the French could do more or less as they pleased. Within minutes I had legally crossed the Swiss border.[1]

The support which the French resistance movement in Axis-controlled territory secretly received from Switzerland has been insufficiently explored. Allen Dulles established an excellent network of contacts, in part also with French officers who worked for de Gaulle and his Free France organization.[2] For the time being it remains an open question how, after the German occupation and until liberation, the importance of this border section should be evaluated concerning the secret contacts to the organized resistance in the Savoy Alps.

One of Dulles' close contacts was Dr. Hans Thalberg, who succeeded in gaining safety by difficult paths through the gap shortly before the total cutoff of Switzerland. In the resistance he had worked for an independent Austria and later closely collaborated with Foreign Minister and Federal Chancellor Bruno Kreisky and, as ambassador to Bern (1975–1982), was especially concerned about the solidarity of the neutral nations. His memoirs, with which this study closes, show that German economic warfare came considerably closer to closing the gap than has generally been assumed, yet without achieving more than partial success. The sealing off of Switzerland, which Hitler and Mussolini in June 1940 had tried in vain to achieve with military means, succeeded only with the invasion of unoccupied France in November 1942. However, not only those who were isolated were affected by the disappearance of the gap, as Thalberg demonstrates:

> Until October 1942 I lived hidden in southern France (Le Lavandou) where I was in close contact with the French resistance. However, after the landing in North Africa by the Americans, my situation became most precarious due to the expected German occupation. My friends strongly urged me to leave and pointed to the gap near Geneva as the only and last chance in Europe to escape the Germans. Using a false safe-conduct I traveled to Megève, where my family owned property at that time. A neighbor, Servan-Schreiber, familiarized me with an escape route into nearby Switzerland. On difficult paths across the Col de Balme I reached the Swiss border during the first week in October—just barely one month before the German invasion of Vichy France—where they wanted to send me back. After difficult negotiations I was brought at 3:00 a.m. to Martigny. In the house of the French farmer who had hidden me for a few nights and who then showed me the path across the mountain, several Gestapo agents (presumably collaborators of Klaus Barbie) were already present whose merry drinking sessions I could follow from my straw bed in the attic. I sent plans about my escape path back to my friends in Le Lavandou through Megève. One of them, the writer Peter Kast, also succeeded in his escape. He lived into the 60s in East Berlin where a street is named for him. Another friend, the Austrian writer Emil Alphons Reinhardt, a friend of Thomas Mann and Joseph Roth chose to remain in Le Lavandou for personal reasons. He died shortly before the end of the war in the concentration camp of Dachau.

Railroad Map "Switzerland – France" (Upper Savoy)

Thalberg adds the following conclusion to his report: "I did not want to neglect to mention these facts that reveal the importance of the failure fully to enclose Switzerland. The 'gap' near Geneva contributed to the outcome of the war. Thus Hitler's rage was not unjustified."[3]

NOTES

1. Allen Dulles and Gero v. S. Gaevernitz, *Unternehmen "Sunrise." Die Geschichte des Kriegsendes in Italien* (Düsseldorf: Econ Verlag, 1967), 22.

2. Allen Dulles, *Im Geheimdienst* (Düsseldorf: Econ Verlag, 1963), 43–44.

3. Letter of Ambassador Dr. Hans Thalberg to the author, dated Blonay, June 28, 1990. This information, for which I thank Dr. Thalberg sincerely, resulted from the article series "Juni 1940–Hitler's Krieg gegen die Schweiz hatte schon begonnen," which I published in the *Neue Zürcher Zeitung* nos. 131, 137, 143, June 9/10, 16/17, 23/24, 1990.

DOCUMENTS

Documents

The documents and the excerpts from diaries presented below again highlight the rapidly escalating posture of aggression against Switzerland that came to dominate the German leadership during the last days of the French campaign and led to actual preparations for an attack. This development emerged after the second air battle between German and Swiss pilots on June 8, 1940, when Hitler took the response to this clash into his own hands (document 1). The second and more dangerous phase began with the dramatic "race to the Swiss border" which was set in motion for political reasons during the night of June 16–17 and was characterized by patrol leader Dietrich as a "Husarenstück," as a daring coup. His report reprinted below also serves as vivid proof of the euphoria that victory induced at that time. The Swiss customs post which Dietrich had reached on June 17 at 8:20 a.m. was, as retired Division Commander Denis Borel discovered, most likely the border crossing at La Grosse Ronde (documents 2–4).

Hitler's secretly pursued plan of military action to achieve the full encirclement of Switzerland is disclosed by the interpreter's protocol and the memoirs of Wilhelm Keitel, then chief of the Supreme Command of the Armed Forces, regarding the meeting with Mussolini of June 18, 1940, in Munich (documents 5 and 6). This encounter was to force a complete reorientation. The manner in which the offensive of the "Group List" was set in motion and carried out can be traced by the entries in the war diaries kept by members of the general staff of the army. These also reveal that Halder was unable at first to understand the rationale of this enterprise; neither he nor the Italian general staff had been informed that on June 22 Mussolini had abandoned the occupation of Savoy.

On June 23, Hitler gave orders to the OKH: "Mental preparations for tasks of the 12th army" and assigned it two mountain divisions (document 7).

On June 24 followed instructions released by the top military leadership that were directed specifically against Switzerland. On that very morning, as his notes show, Otto Wilhelm von Menges had received orders to prepare an attack study (document 8). Prepared overnight, this study examines the possibilities of a surprise invasion of Switzerland and is printed in full (document 9). It should also be mentioned that the attempt to force the cutting off of Switzerland by means of an intervention from the OKW during the negotiations in Rome failed at 7:30 p.m. The preliminary order from the supreme commander of the army to the chiefs of the three army groups, also dated June 24, marks the transition to actual attack preparations. The letter, fully reproduced below, also shows the overall scope within which the order for Army Group C—"Preparations for a special task for which orders will be forthcoming"—was integrated. It is part of a historically significant document which announces to all three army groups the planned redistribution of tasks after the armistice had taken effect (document 10). Not reproduced here is the map, included in the advanced order, on which the future assembly area of the 12th Army is marked. This area included the entire region of the French border between Geneva and Basel. Dispositions made in conjunction with the definitive order of June 26 further expanded the staging region in the environs of Basel.

Halder's later notes once more look back to the evening of June 24 when Hitler had demanded the forced disruption of the rail line still operating (document 11). They also lead to another important piece of evidence: the terse explanations of Hitler's deliberations by Colonel i. G. Hans von Greiffenberg when high officers of the General Staff met in Versailles on June 28 (document 12). According to the strict rules for ongoing secret plans, this note, which had been enclosed only in the first copy of the meeting protocol, was removed in late October 1940 from the completed war journal of Army Group C and stored in a special file for highly confidential documents.

In his army orders no. 35 of July 3, 1940, General List gave the necessary instructions for the rapid replacement of Guderian's group by the 12th Army. Six of its nine large units assumed staging areas in close proximity to the western border of Switzerland. The quarters for the army corps as well as the locations of the staffs of the high command are indicated in Roman numerals as well as the positions for the individual divisions (document 13). There were slight changes in its execution as the 52nd and 5th Divisions exchanged their quarters and command positions on June 6; the General Command XVIII for the two mountain divisions and the 5th Division placed their command post not in Pontarlier, but rather further south in Malbuisson. General Command XXVII and the headquarters for Army Group C were in Dijon.

As the requests of the 12th Army and the response of the OKH of July 11 and 13, 1940 show, preparations for "Special Task Switzerland" continued. There were to be discussions about it with Hitler at the Berghof (document 14). The OKH had just learned about the documents found in Dijon which disclosed the secret Swiss-French military agreements to the German leadership.

After the withdrawal of the mountain divisions needed for the preparations of the landing operation "Seelöwe" [Sea Lion] against England, more intensive planning was begun which would make it possible to reestablish attack readiness within a short period of time. How far these preparations advanced in the OKH is evident from the detailed attack draft of August 12, 1940, reproduced here despite of its size in its entirety (document 15). Its evaluation is made easier by the three maps pertaining to this draft reproduced as illustrations VIII-XI. At that time the OKH considerably overestimated the total strength of the Swiss army; because of partial demobilization it had been reduced to fewer than 150,000 men and not, as assumed, to 220,000 men. The Department of Foreign Armies West corrected this mistaken estimate on August 28 by assuming 120,000 men ready for action. The shifting disposition from "Case North" into the pre-alpine and alpine regions was not sufficiently recognized until October 1940 which, given the studies of officers and historians such as Werner Roesch, Alfred Ernst, Hans Rudolf Kurz, and Hans Senn do not need further discussion.

The operational draft of August 12 forms the core of the German attack plans and is, in the light of the above given details, particularly impressive for its realistic assessment. Based on the available forces, the preparatory dispositions identify the units to be used against Switzerland in mid-August. They contain precise estimates about the means and the time needed for deployment as soon as orders were given. Even the individual tasks were specified in advance. Compared to the study of June 25, this attack plan was based on an increased need of forces; instead of the original nine, it called for ten divisions to which were added two "rapid" regimental units as well as airborne troops. Remarkable is the addition to item 10f at the end of the first part which mentions an alternative with the remark "if there is time before August 31." The goal of attack readiness within one week is identical—as Walter Schaufelberger discovered—with the timing given in plans worked out by Italy.

The documents are reproduced verbatim, yet obvious spelling errors have been quietly corrected and the graphic representation has been made uniform. Abbreviations are explained in the list given at the beginning of the book, yet without all the variations of punctuation used in the original. As the selection of documents assumes familiarity with the preceding text, the individual documents generally have not been further annotated.

NO. 1

*Hitler takes charge of the further response to the air incidents: Note, AA, Pol.
I M g, Berlin, June 9, 1940, signed Kramarz.*

PAB, AA, Büro des Staatssekretär, Akten betreffend: Schweiz, Bd. 1: 14 May
1938–30 June 1941.

                                                              Pol. I M g
NOTE

Concerns: Violation of Neutrality in Switzerland

According to a report by Captain *Gregor*, Air Force Command Staff, the
Führer himself has taken charge of a further response in this matter. Any material received by the air force command staff with regard to air fights with
Swiss pilots is to be sent to the Führer. The Führer has, among others steps,
ordered the commanding general of the primarily concerned Air Corps 5 to
appear for an oral report.

The above message has been transmitted by telephone to Mr. Sonnleithner,
special train.

                                                    Berlin, June 9, 1940
                                                            Kramarz

Distribution:
St.S.
Büro RAM
U.St.S.Pol.
Dg.Pol.
Pol. II.

NO. 2

"Reach Swiss border still today. Immediate report important for political reasons": Urgent Radio Message, Group Guderian, Ia, to 29th Division, June 16, 1940, 9:40 p.m.

BA-MA, RH 26–29/3, Inf. Division [mot.], Ia. Anlagenheft 2 zum Kriegstagebuch No. 3, Anlagen Nr.. 415–560, 15–19 June 1940.

NO. 3

"Race to the Swiss Border," Report of Lieutenant Dietrich (Leader of the Armored Reconnaissance Unit Dietrich), Reconnaissance Unit 29th mot. Division, no date.

BA-MA, RH 26–29/3, 29. Inf. Division [mot.], Ia, Anlagenheft 2 zum Kriegstagebuch No. 3, Anlagen Nr. 415–560, 15.-19. Juni, 1940.

Reconnaissance Unit 29
Lieutenant Dietrich

RACE TO THE SWISS BORDER

After the crossing of the Marne had been forcibly achieved and thus the last cohesive resistance broken, we were able to make an unstoppable advance towards the Swiss border across the Plateau of Langres, regardless of any French troops which came towards us or which we surprised. Armed transport trains and columns were quickly disarmed, any resistance instantly broken. There was a stop in this hurried advance only at the Saône, as rapidly assembled French troops had blasted all Saône crossings and occupied the opposite bank.

Already half a day later, after a short hard fight, it was possible to cross the first armored reconnaissance troops which were cautiously to approach the Doubs sector; a few hours later, advance units were able to storm forward across bridges to the Doubs, but at the Doubs most of the bridges had also been blown up, however, what joy, one bridge was captured undamaged.

There, near St. Vit, the reconnaissance unit under Lt. Dietrich, consisting of 1 light armored reconnaissance vehicle with cannon, 1 armored radio station, and 1 armored reconnaissance vehicle got the order on June 17, 1940, at 1:30 a.m. to advance as one of the first across the bridge and to reach the Swiss border near Pontarlier as fast as possible. It was added that this order was politically important. For the last part of the drive no maps could be handed out.

After giving short orders, the drive into the unknown of the night began. We had not been able to fill our tanks as the fuel supply vehicles had not yet arrived. We rode totally without light; the gunner had orders only to shoot if we were shot at. I rode ahead in the gun vehicle, followed by the light armored vehicle, and the armored radio vehicle brought up the rear.

We could still get information from the most advanced security units; the enemy is said to have just withdrawn.

On a small rural path along the Doubs we roll into the uncertainty of the night. It is pitch dark, nothing can be seen, but we move on and keep cheating our way forward, as these small paths are not marked on our large maps. Suddenly we get onto a real road, eerie movements are everywhere; my gunner calls to me: "The French!" "Leave them be, just no shooting!" We roar by the stopped French columns, peaking forward and backward to see if the second vehicle is following. They are following, further onward, the darkness and dawn have to be used to advantage; there are still 80 km to the border. We rush into the darkness. In front of us is a light. Ha: A French soldier wants to make us join a resting column. "Keep going!" The French soldier stumbles. Only no stop! I am checking things out: Heavy French artillery is stopped along the road. Dawn is breaking, it is getting brighter by the minute. Now French vehicles approach from the opposite direction. Just let them go! We cannot do anything against these masses. Our armored vehicles rush at full speed towards the border, every place is occupied by Frenchmen. At the front of our vehicle the large swastika flags are flying, the Frenchmen yield in horror. The people look at us thunderstruck. "The Germans are coming!"

We are already past Salins, it is already full daylight, we are approaching Pontarlier. The roads have been narrowed by half-blockades. We can already see into Pontarlier. Two enemy marching columns are joining, we want to detour to the right or left, but no path leaves the road. "Keep going! Between the marching columns!" I shout to my driver. "A few shots into the marching column!" In horror they disperse in all directions. Scared, some French officers who are standing at the road flee into a house. Several Frenchmen get in front of our wheels, but it does not matter. "Simply don't stop!" Forward, or everything is lost. I am worried as I look back, but the second armored vehicle rushes in between the marching columns. We have to pass yet another marching column. "Full Speed!" Finally, a path goes off to the left. I have no idea where it will lead, as we have no maps. We reach a small forest and stop. The last few minutes were too exciting; now only a brandy can cheer us up.

However, it does not take long until some Frenchmen show up again, this time infantry who sneak up on us shooting. Thus, forward, onward! No sense to stay here, we must look for the border. We move on through field paths. I am looking through my binoculars: Frenchmen are crawling around everywhere. We are already looking forward to their horrified faces. We drive on into rough and creepy territory. Suddenly a French customs house appears before us. It is occupied! Wire obstacles and road blocks have been constructed everywhere. We continue into a narrow and broken valley. Suddenly we see a sign "Frontière à 500 m" [To Border 500 meters] and already we have reached the barrier formed by a huge tree trunk. The border has to be here! Right, there is the barbed wire of the border. It is almost impossible to turn around on this narrow forest path. There are steep slopes on both sides. We still don't know exactly where the border is. Two of us climb over the blocking tree trunk and rush onward on foot. "There is a house!" I look through the binoculars and we are immensely pleased. "Douane Suisse," the Swiss customs station is in front of us. We run back happily. The message "Swiss border reached!" can now be sent in feverish hurry to the unit.

Shooting now erupts from the heights to our right and left. We cannot see anything, but the French have to be very close as we can hear them talk. We cannot stay here, as the French can burst out on us from impenetrable woods. The bullets smash hard on the tank. Nothing helps. With great difficulties we back up on the narrow forest path. Finally, we reach a slightly wider part and with repeated back and forth movement and the removal of trees we are able to turn around. The French don't let go, they are shooting wildly. However, we are rolling towards the exit from this inhospitable valley and are waiting anxiously for the enemy antitank guns, finger ready at the trigger, hand grenade and fogger in hand! Yet—it is hard to believe—we are getting out of this bottleneck.

We had barely reached another position when the shooting started anew; Frenchmen everywhere! Thus onward! With engines turned off we are rolling along slowly; there! before us a French outpost. A horrified guard dares to aim at us. Our machine gun is shooting. The sentry is scared away. Their resistance is broken. We keep on rolling. Another outpost appears in front of our machine gun; its men had been warned. But they also flee from our shots.

There was not a corner without Frenchmen. Between the French bunkers we ambled towards the Swiss border. We could not stay here, in spite of the fact that we only had a few liters of fuel left. Our attempt to break into a gas station near Pontarlier was actually successful, but the gas station was empty, so we were unable to refill our almost empty tanks.

We again approach Pontarlier, hoping before it to be able to turn off towards the right in order to try to hide there in the forest. It is teeming with Frenchmen everywhere; before we know, we are meeting a French motorized column. A wild ride ensues, only high speed can help us—the French watch us horrified and shoot at us wildly from the rear. Now, a large bus wants to ram us; we are strafing it, all goes well again! The wild ride continues. We are looking for roads going off to the left and right. Finally, after 5 km riding against this column, a road leads off to the left. We rush off into a terrain of underbrush and can hide there while the columns below us continue to move on.

Our armored vehicle had only enough fuel for another 2–3 km. Radio contact to our unit had been cut. We had no other choice but to wait there temporarily. The terrain was also suitable for defense, as it was still teeming with French everywhere. We stayed there for the night and the following morning we moved on to get fuel from French vehicles. This was successful, and soon we were again with our unit.

Signed: Dietrich

NO. 4

"Swiss border reached 0820." Urgent radio message, 29th Division to
XXXIXth Army Corps, June 17, 1940, 8:58 a.m.

BA-MA, RH 26–29/3, 29th Inf. Div. [mot.], Ia Anlagenheft 2 zu Kriegstagebuch No. 3, Anlagen Nr. 415–560, 15–19 June 1940.

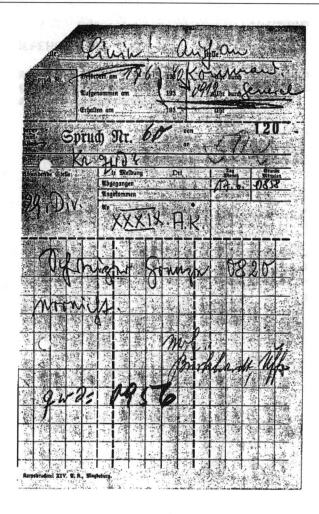

NO. 5

Notes on the meeting between the Führer and the Duce on June 18, 1940, in Munich, as it took place in the presence of the Reich foreign minister, of Count Ciano, of General Keitel, and General Roatta.

Excerpt from the section on Switzerland in Andreas Hillgruber, Hrsg., *Staatsmänner und Diplomaten bei Hitler. Vetrauliche Aufzeichnungen über Unterredungen mit Vertretern des Auslandes 1939–1941* (Frankfurt a. Main: 1967), 140–41.

The Führer then began to talk in detail about the armistice conditions. He explained with special thoroughness the occupation demands aided by a map. Thus the occupation of French territory would be arranged in such a way that the whole Channel and Atlantic coast and the most important ports of Cherbourg, Brest, Nantes, and Bordeaux would be protected by a broad strip of occupied territory against any outside influence. Internally the occupation would be arranged in such a way that in any case the rail connection to Spain via Irun would be totally within the occupied zone. In addition, as suggested by the Duce based on a remark by General Roatta, the Paris-Chambéry-Bourg-Modane line would have to be made secure by the French government for transports to Italy. Switzerland would also be fully cut off from France by a belt of occupied French territory and would thus be forced to assume a more accommodating position regarding transit questions as well as generally in its political attitude and its press. The area to be occupied by Italy from the Italian border to the Rhone, including Toulon and Marseille, was also discussed. Here too, on the suggestion of General Roatta, the Duce brought up the requirement of making the rail line Ventimiglia-Nice-Port-Bou-Barcelona available.

NO. 6

Meeting of Hitler and Mussolini in Munich, June 18, 1940: Excerpt from the Memoirs of General Field Marshal Wilhelm Keitel (1946)

BA-MA, N 54/5.

Already the next day[1] the Führer, Ribbentrop, and I had a meeting with Mussolini, Count Ciano, and the Italian Chief of the General Staff Roatta in southern Germany, I think in Munich. Apart from informing the Italians about our armistice and the important reasons for the lines of demarcation and the French regions (zones) to be demilitarized, the Führer wanted to induce Mussolini, by an Italian demand for the areas to be occupied by Italy—in unison with us—to cut off Switzerland from any connection with France. In fact this was not achieved—despite Mussolini's firm consent; the Italians never enforced the envisioned demands, and were also probably unable to do so after their military failures. Although an armistice soon ensued, the conditions were modest and peaked in a narrow occupied zone along the [Italian] alpine front; this did deliver the French border fortifications into the hands of the Italians; they had been unable, however, to conquer them.

1. The meeting took place on June 18, 1940, in Munich. Keitel moved it by mistake to the day after the conclusion of the German-French armistice negotiations, that is on June 23, 1940.

NO. 7

From the Notes of the Chief of the General Staff of the Army, June 19–24, 1940.

From Franz Halder, Generaloberst, *Kriegstagebuch*, Bd. I: *Vom Polen-feldzug bis zum Ende der Westoffensive (14 August 1939–30 Juni 1940)*, bearbeitet von Hans-Adolf Jacobsen in Verbindung mit A. Philippi. Stuttgart 1962.

June 19, 1940 [Wednesday]
 . . . In spite of the continued and in its speed unusual success, the Supreme Commander of the Army[1] is apparently greeted surly on the return of the High Master [Hitler] from his meeting in Munich, because some Frenchmen are still defending themselves in the NE region. . . .

 In the evening an "OKW directive" arrives which informs about a border with the French not to be crossed (generally Cher) and a line eastward of the Atlantic coast, and demands that we engage, on the one hand, parts of Kleist[2] with Army Group B across the lower Loire to take possession of the Atlantic coast and, on the other hand, advance parts of Kleist towards Lyon in order to get at the back [of the French front before] the Italian front. . . .

 The Italians report that they want to attack in 2 to 3 days along the alpine front. By that time we are supposed to have gotten at the back of the French through the Rhône valley. This will hardly be possible in the time available. The orders resulting from these "directives" will be finalized around midnight. . . .

June 20, 1940
 . . . As important events the morning reports mention the occupation of Nantes at the mouth of the Loire (with undestroyed bridges) and of Lyon. What else the high political leadership still demands of us and what wishes have remained unfulfilled, is to me incomprehensible, but as a subordinate one has to suffer the nervous exhaustion of the superiors.

 Subsequent to the morning discussions at the ObdH[3], orders for the creation of a group under OB 12[4] for a special task in the area of Chambéry and Grenoble are given out. Besides the XVIth Army Command, all temporarily

 1. General von Brauchitsch.
 2. General Edward von Kleist, Superior Commander of Tank Group 1, known as Tank Group Kleist.
 3. Supreme Commander of the Army.
 4. Supreme Commander of the 12th Army, General Wilhelm List.

motorized units are to be combined into fighting units, brought in from Army Group A, in addition, the strongest parts of mountain divisions on trucks from Army Group B.

According to my calculations, advance units from the environs of Lyon can get to Grenoble and Chambéry by the evening of June 21. However, the infantry cannot be expected there before June 25. Corps Hoepner[5] may certainly leave immediately, if that is desired.

[After 5pm] . . . With Colonel von Greiffenberg[6] the orders for Group List (attack from direction of Lyon on Grenoble and Chambéry into the back of the French alpine front) are worked out and the basic planning for the distribution of forces between coastal defenses and rear areas determined. . . .

June 21, 1940

. . . The Italians claimed that they will start today with their attack at the Little St. Bernard and south. The weather is so bad that the air force cannot help. It must thus be assumed that this attack will be limited to some patrol skirmishes. For us, a start from the area around Lyon will only be considered when the Italians have attacked seriously, thus not before June 22. Whether we will start on June 22 may be decided only after the conclusion of the armistice conditions. Practically this may not occur before June 23. . . .

[Evening] . . . The Italians demand that we start on June 22 in order to assist in the advance of their attack across the Little St. Bernard. We will not do that. Group List will only be ready to march on June 23. In addition, we first have to wait and see if this alleged attack by the Italians is more than a patrol skirmish. . . .

June 22, 1940

. . . At 6:50 p.m. the contract will be signed at Compiègne. During the day repeated telegram exchanges with the Italian General Staff which is urging that we advance from Lyon towards Grenoble and Chambéry in order to open the way for the Italians across the Alps. As our Group List will only be ready on June 23, the requests are treated in a dilatory fashion. In addition, the Führer has reserved for himself the right to give the permission for the start. The necessary orders for List are being prepared . . . .

. . . In the evening the decision is made that List is to attack on June 23, but not to proceed beyond Grenoble-Chambéry. . . .

5. General Erich Hoepner, commander of the XVIth Army Corps.
6. Colonel in the General Staff Hans von Greiffenberg, chief of the operational planning division of the General Staff of the Army.

June 23, 1940 [Sunday]

The war efforts of the day are limited to a further advance by the right wing (4th and 18th Armies) and the action by Group List. The latter started as planned and reached around noon the area northeast of Valence, northwest of Grenoble and Chambéry, and northeast of Aix-les-Bains. It faces barriers with antitank defenses and mountain infantry. I respond to an evening inquiry of Army Group A that additional pressure, which would entail higher losses for Germany, is not what the leadership has in mind. . . .

. . . The conference at the Führer during the afternoon included:. . . .

. . . d) mentally prepare the tasks of the 12th Army. List: Personnel Kuebler, Bergmann, Fahrmbacher, Schörner.[7]

June 24, 1940

Morning brings an interesting nuance. The Italians are stuck at the French fortifications and unable to advance further. However, for the armistice negotiations they want to designate an area as large as possible as having been occupied by them in France and have suggested to move in Italian battalions by air, in part through Munich and in part directly to Lyon, and to deposit them behind List's front to such points that are included in the Italian occupation claims. The whole thing is a fraud of the most vulgar sort. I have stated that I will not have my name associated with this affair.

All of this finally emerges as Roatta's suggestion, to which Marshal Badoglio has refused to give his approval. Now, OKW has to decide for itself how it fell for the proposals of a lower authority which the responsible Italian marshal, apparently the only decent soldier in this whole negotiating circle, has rejected as unworthy. The commander of the army is flying to the 7th army. His inner unrest pushes him towards preparatory measures in case the armistice negotiations with Italy should collapse and we are forced to undertake a serious attack into the back of the French alpine fortifications and at the same time an advance towards the Mediterranean coast.

Such an action can only be undertaken according to plan with the deployment of mountain troops and needs preparation. One cannot improvise this by hastily moving in motorized alpine battalions.

7. At the beginning of July 1940, with the exception of the 27th Infantry Division commanded by General Bergmann (1883–1941), all commanders mentioned were positionend with their troops as part of the 12th Army in the region facing Switzerland. Major General Ludwig Kübler (shot in Yugoslavia in 1947) was commander of the 1st Mountain Division which was moved to the region Salins-Morez; Lieutenant General Wilhelm Fahrmbacher (born 1888, after the war military advisor in Egypt) was positioned with his 5th Division east of Dijon whereas the 6th Mountain Division under Major m. d. F. Ferdinand Schörner (on April 5, 1945 still named General Field Marshall) subsequently was made especially part of the 12th Army in order to be moved into the environs of Pontarlier close to the Swiss Jura border.

This is again the same tortured game as when making contact with the Russians during the Polish campaign. The politician[8] would like Switzerland to lose its direct connection to France. A military mantle is supposed to be hung around this political demand. This will lead to much more unpleasantness.

10:20 a.m. Conversation with Tresckow,[9] Army Group A:

Introduction to the political picture and the resulting variations of military demands. Army Group A is supposed to consider the time needed for preparation of more serious combat actions against the Savoy front and continuation of operations against the French army with a strong left wing.

---

8. By "politician" or "political leadership" Halder consistently means Hitler, to mark a conscious distancing from his military leadership ambitions.

9. Lieutenant Colonel in the General Staff Henning von Tresckow, first General Staff Officer of the strategic operations division of Army Group A.

NO. 8

Private Note of Otto Wilhelm von Menges, June 24, 1940, Author of the First Three Drafts of Attack Prepared for the Division for [Strategic] Operations in the General Staff of the Army.

Private possession of Dr. Dietrich Wilhelm von Menges, Essen.

June 24, 1940

In the morning I get orders to make a study of an attack against a country. My first great independent task! . . .

8:50 p.m. we hear at the Casino that at 7:35 p.m. the French have signed the armistice with the Italians.

As of 1:35 a.m. suspension of hostilities. A great moment. We cannot be thankful enough to God and the excellent troops. The respective teletypes mean a lot of work; and in addition my study. All the same, immense joy. Unfortunately no champagne for celebration.

June 25 and 26, 1940

Work on my study with which the division chief is fully satisfied. Things are a bit more quiet. First orders regarding the restructuring of the army against England. . . .

NO. 9

OKH, Gen. Staff of the Army, Operations Division (I), 1st Presentation of Sketch of Attack against Switzerland, June 25, 1940, signed von Menges.

BA-MA, RH 2/465:Schweiz, Bd. C.

Op. Div. (I)   June 25, 1940

Secret Command Matter   *Chief's Matter!*   *Only by Officer!*

1.) Order Received:

The possibilities concerning a surprise invasion of Switzerland by German troops from France and Germany are to be explored in brief, under the condition that Italian troops will simultaneously attack Switzerland from the south.

2.) Execution:

In this enterprise it is imperative to achieve the following by a quick surprise invasion from several directions:

1.) Destruction of the enemy army in such a manner that a unified command and a build-up of further resistance of individual lines and an orderly escape into difficult mountain terrain (thus delaying the outcome of the war) is prevented.

2.) For political and morale reasons the rapid and undamaged occupation of the Capital and the region of the weapons industry around Solothurn.

3.) To gain the most important rail and road junctions as well as the numerous bridges in an undamaged state so that the country may be used as soon as possible as a transit area to Southern France for all transports.

Apart from 9 border guard brigades (about 100 battalions), Switzerland has 6 infantry divisions, 3 mountain divisions, 3 mountain brigades and, as corps troops, 3 light brigades. Added to this are 75 battalions of "territorial forces" (a type of riflemen). There are no armored units. The air force is weak, modernized only to a small extent; the antiaircraft forces in the initial stage of build-up.

According to the available reports, 6–7 divisions are deployed along the borders of the north and northeast. Only 1 1/2 divisions are at the French border (unless more forces are being shifted there now), the rest in the south and southeast.

The enemy has no way of going on the attack due to the necessity of protecting his long borders. He will defend his fortified positions near the border. The weakness of his current positioning is along the French border. A possible repositioning to that region can occur only at the expense of safeguarding the German border.

After losing his positions near the border, the enemy will try to regroup on a line Lake Geneva-Lake Neuchâtel-Lake Biel-Olten-Zurich-Sargans.

3.) Fortifications of Switzerland:

   a) Border with Germany:

Emphasis on reinforcement in the sector Basel-Constance-Rheineck-Sargans. Light reinforcement, only a few places medium reinforcement. Heavy reinforcement of the cornerstones Rheineck and Sargans, in between steep mountain slopes. Only weak safeguarding along southern shore of Lake Constance.

Thirteen Rhine bridges between Constance and Basel. Weaker points southwest of Basel, eastward to Waldshut and near Eglisau.

Rear positions: Apparently so far only barricade fortifications in narrow sections of valleys. Reinforcement planned for line Olten-Aarau-Zurich-Sargans.

   b) Border with France:

Reinforcement starting only early 1940, first only barricades at individual places and field-like firing positions.

Weak points of position: Around and west of Nyon, east of Pontarlier, north of La Chaux-de-Fonds; roads of mountain passes north and south of St. Maurice not fortified. Rear positions between the lake narrows have not yet been reinforced.

   c) Details: The shooting ranges are 6–8 m above ground, thus a good target; nothing known about antitank ditches. Everywhere road barricades are to be expected (prepared concrete blocks, to be overcome by blasting or by prepared bridging structures). Border guard houses without combat value.

4.) Own Forces: See Map.

   a) Use of Forces:

In this plan, motorized and tank divisions are envisioned for the rapid occupation of Bern, Lucerne, and Zurich and the blocking of the enemy's roads of retreat leading south, the few available mountain divisions only as far as absolutely necessary, infantry division for breaking through fortification line and for reaching the more nearby targets.

Use of a motorized instead of mountain division through Savoy Alps (= the southern most column in the Rhône valley) should be considered in spite of the difficult terrain in the second part.

Attack from the east should be avoided due to the difficult mountain terrain and the strong enemy fortifications.

For the infantry division deployed through Constance, the car ferry Friedrichshafen-Romanshorn might be used for the surprise landing of partial units for opening the fortifications from the south, while simultaneously using assault boats.

In case enemy defense measures still permit, airborne landings around Bern and, for the opening of the mountain exits from the south, of airborne troops around Olten and Solothurn should be undertaken, possibly also later to seal off retreat roads in southeastern Switzerland.

The occupation of the point around Chur-Davos should be left to the Italians due to the difficult terrain.

b) Required Forces:

One Army Supreme Command, 4 army corps (high number needed for reasons of terrain), 3 infantry divisions, 3 motorized divisions, 1 armored division, 2 mountain divisions = 9 divisions.

c) Deployment:

In southern Germany camouflaged for training purposes; in France some units at a distance, as motorization permits rapid transfer.

d) Time required for deployment cannot be predicted at this time due to current positioning.

e) Time required for operation: Occupation of Zurich, Lucerne, and Bern has to be possible no later than during the second day.

5.) *Tactical Command:*

Make use of the experience in Norway: Assignment of tanks, guns, and individual motorized troops to the vanguard; use of the mountain equipment of 7th Army; reinforcement of marching troops by machine gun company (motorized); increased use of infantry guns and grenade throwers; formation of strong advance units using the vehicles of the antitank gunner units, here not so necessary for antitank defense.

6.) *Details:*

a) Secrecy and Deception:

Discreet, increased closing of Swiss border. Corresponding press notices. Deceptive radio messages and radio silence for individual parts.

b) Use of spies to explore details of fortifications. What is the situation at rear positions? Are regroupings along the French border under way?

c) Improvement of the particularly bad maps. Production of maps 1:100,000. Acquisition of maps about road conditions, as much as possible on the open market in Switzerland. Preparation of a condensed military-geographical description of the country.

d) The chief of transports must be listened to about his requirements for deployment and about specially important, and thus rapidly to be occupied, traffic routes in Switzerland.

e) The use of forces west and south of Lake Geneva demands a shifting of the demarcation line as soon as possible, in order not to alert Switzerland too early of our intentions.

f) Given the momentary political situation in Switzerland it is possible that it might accede peacefully to our ultimatum demands, so that after a warlike crossing of the border a rapid transition to a peaceful invasion must be assured.

von Menges
Captain of the General Staff

NO. 10

"Preparation for a Special Task for which Orders Will Be Given:"

Vorbefehl vom 24. Juni, 1940. Sig. BA-MA: RH 19 III/141.

Supreme Command of the Army	H.Qu. OKH, June 24, 1940
Gen.Staff of the Army, Op.Div. (Ia)	3 copies
No. 374/40 g Kdos	3rd copy
Secret Command Matter	Army Group Command C
Chief's Matter! Only by Officers!	June 26, 1940, No. 230/40 g Kdos

To the Supreme Commanders of Army Groups A, B, and C

As provisional information for the Supreme Commanders, the following considerations, which are currently being worked out at the OKH, are communicated:

After the armistice with France has taken effect, the German armed forces will be regrouped for further warfare against England. For this purpose, only *parts* of the Army will be needed at first, so that a repositioning of the army is possible at the same time. Overall, the plans are as follows:

1.) Regarding Troop Deployment:
   a) In the West:
      Army Groups A and B will be committed along the Channel and Atlantic coasts.
      Tasks: Securing the coast,
            Preparation for continuation of war against England,
            Rearrangement and training of the units under their command.
      Army Group C will be used in the remaining occupied parts of France.
      Tasks: Reorganization and training of units under its command,
            Preparation for a special task for which orders will be given.

The enclosed sketch provides details about the intended groupings, but is only to be considered as a guideline.

   b) In the East:
      In the German East (East Prussia, area VIIIth, XXth, and XXIst Army Command, Generalgouvernement) 4–5 general commandos (among them higher commands) and about 15 divisions under Army Supreme Command 18 will be distributed.
      Tasks: Defense of country,
            Reorganization and training of units under its command.

c) In the North:
Five infantry divisions and 2 mountain divisions remain in Norway.
Command structure and tasks as before.

2.) As to Concerns of the Quartermaster General:
a) Military administration:
The military administration France will be separated from the command leadership and guided directly by the OKH through a military
governor. I reserve the use of executive power for myself. It is intended
to incorporate the military commander Paris into the authority of the
military governorship.
b) Provisions:
No changes in the provisioning of the troops by the command authorities. New regulations will be given in a timely fashion through special
directives.
c) Regarding the collection of *bounty*, repatriation of *refugees*, and use of
prisoners of war reference is made to orders already issued. Final regulations are being prepared.

3.) As to Organizational Concerns:
a) Within the course of regrouping, a number of organizational changes
will be initiated which aim to reduce the field army soon by about 1/4,
as well as preparatory measures for the later peace order. In addition,
older age groups will be separated from the field army and discharged.
These organizational changes will occur in part in occupied territories
and in part in our own country and in the East.
b) As soon as the railroad situation permits, leaves will be authorized.
However, no *larger* scope can be expected for the near future.

4.) In order to provide an overview of the entire plan and how it will be executed, there will be a conference this week with representatives of the command
and quartermaster departments of the army groups and army at the headquarters
of Army Group B. Army Group B is requested to prepare space accordingly.

Enclosure: 1 sketch   Signed: von Brauchitsch
                                                   For correctness:
                                                   von Greiffenberg
                                          Colonel on the General Staff

Distribution:
Staff
Army Group A-copy 1
Army Group B-copy 2
Army Group C-copy 3

NO. 11

Continuation of Notes (Excerpt) by General Halder

Franz Halder, *Kriegstagebuch,* Bd. I., June 25–28, 1940 (see No. 7).

June 25, 1940
1:35 a.m. cease-fire; ministerial activity is starting.

In the morning arguments with Supreme Commander of the Army: The political leadership wanted to make sure that the rail connection between Switzerland and France is cut off. For this reason a corresponding order has been given to List to destroy thoroughly the rail line La Roche-Annecy. Given the course the war has taken, this order could no longer be executed. The Supreme Command of the Army demands therefore that now, after the armistice has taken effect, a patrol task force of the army should execute this destruction. I object. After a cease-fire has been permitted to occur, such a military order is impossible. At best it could be executed by Canaris (that is by organization K).[1] After consultation with General Keitel I give the respective orders to Canaris . . .

June 27, 1940
. . . 12:30 p.m.–9 p.m. flight to Lyon, drive to XVIth Army Command and 3rd armored division in the area northwest of Grenoble (Voreppe) . . .

June 28, 1940
. . . 9:45 a.m. leave via Paris for Versailles: Meeting with Ia [First Officer of the General Staff] and O Qu. [quartermaster majors] of army groups and armies. First general discussions by me:

1. Thanks to the whole General Staff and my subordinates.
2. New tasks due to new situation.
3. Restructuring in the west. In the east dissolution and restructuring. The chiefs of operation, organization, and general quarters say a few words on this subject.
   Subsequently individual meetings of the chief of the operations division with the Ia's [officers of the General Staff], of the chief quartermaster general with the O Qu's [quartermaster majors].

---

1. K-Organization = War Organization of Defense Abroad, in this case in Vichy, France; the "KO-Schweiz [Switzerland]" was in 1940 first under the authority of Major Waag, then Lieutenant Colonel Erich Knabbe who were part of the German Embassy in Bern.

NO. 12

Message from Colonel on General Staff von Greiffenberg, Chief of Operations Division, General Staff of the Army, on the Occasion of Meeting in Versailles on June 28, 1940.

Anlage zur 1. Protokollausfertigung Ia Nr. 1119/40g.K. 29. Juni, 1940. BA-MA RH 19 III/128.

Secret Command Matter   Enclosure only with Ia no.
                                             1119/40, g.K. of June 26
1st copy with page 4.

Chief of Operations Division Declares:

Regarding the matter in question, the Führer has so far only stated that under certain conditions an occupation is to be considered. The case is at present not acute. For the time being no deployment and no preparations are to be made. Mental preparation for it. If the case becomes activated, forces from the north and northeast will also be deployed. Army Group C or 12th Army may present their ideas with map at a proper occasion, but in a wholly nonbinding form.

Suggestion: At some time discussion between Supreme Command Army Group C with Supreme Command 12th army. 12th Army appears inclined to tackle things aggressively.

NO. 13

12th Army Assumes the Task of "Securing the Swiss Border" as of July 6, 1940

Armeebefehl no. 35, AOK 12, gezeichnet List. BA-MA RH 20–12/23.

Army Supreme Command 12	A.H.Qu., July 3, 1940
Ia no. 700/40 g.Kdos	As of 4:00 p.m.
Secret Command Matter!	40 copies
	21st copy

Army Order 35.

1.) Enclosed blueprint 1:1,000,000 shows the new area of the 12th Army, defined according to departmental borders, with the now valid distribution of forces and command structure as well as corps headquarters.
   The assumption of command by the 12th Army, that is the general commands etc. will be ordered later.
2.) Starting July 6, 12:00 noon, the 12th Army assumes the safeguarding of the Swiss border from the road Geneva-Bellegarde (road included) to Delle.

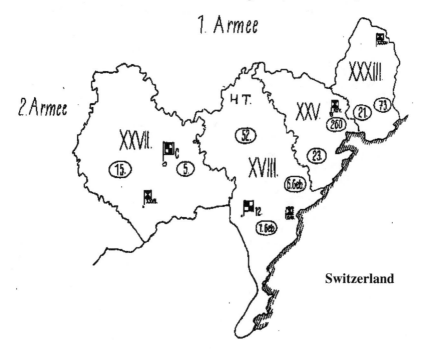

For this the General Commands XVIII and XXV must replace along their sectors by July 6, 12:00 noon those parts of Group Guderian which have been used along the Swiss border for blockading by advanced motorized forces of their divisions.

It is the task of the border guards to prevent any traffic across the border into Switzerland and from Switzerland.

The takeover of safeguarding the border is to be reported by General Commands XVIII and XXV by means of marked map 1:300,000 by July 7 to the 12th Army. Until the full assumption of command by A.O.K. 12, AOK 1 is responsible for safeguarding the Swiss border from Delle to the Rhine.

3.) Starting July 5, at midnight, a crossing of the line of demarcation southward and westward is prohibited to all troops and staffs who are located north of the line of demarcation! This prohibition must be right away generally promulgated.

The security forces stationed at the line of demarcation must be explicitly instructed and must most keenly monitor its observation. Violations must be reported!

4.) AOK 12 presumably in Salins les Bains and Besançon (here O.Qu) as of July 6.

1 blueprint   Supreme Commander of 12th Army
                                                                  List
                                                               General

NO. 14

Measures to Improve the Deployment Situation of Troops in the Frontier Region of Western Switzerland-Planning for the "Special Task Switzerland" Continues.

Request by the Chief of the General Staff of Army Group C (deputy Müller) to the Operations Section of the General Staff of the Army of July 11, 1940, as well as Note of July 13, 1940 to the Answer of Captain on the General Staff von Menges, Operations Section of the General Staff of the Army to Colonel on the General Staff Müller of July 13, 1940.

BA-MA, RH 19 III/141 and 129.

ARMY GROUP COMMAND C   H.Qu., July 11, 1940

Ia No. 239/40 g.K.   Chief's Matter
                                                    Only by Officers
Reference: Gen. St. of the Army Op. Sec. Ia no. 375/40 g. K.
 June 26, 1940, I item 1.b.).   6 copies
Re: Regrouping–Special task   copy

To O.K.H. General Staff of the Army–Operations Division

1.) AOK 12 requests the following changes in the line of demarcation:
 a) In the area south of Morez, inclusion of road Prémanon, Lamoura, Lajoux, Mijoux into the line of demarcation.
  Reason:
  The large road Morez-Gex, southeast of Morez, also forms the border for several km. All group movements there take place under the eyes of the Swiss customs officials.
 b) Inclusion of the rail line Pont d'Héry-Champagnole-St. Laurent-Morez into the line of demarcation.
  Reason:
  At present the road Salins, Champagnole, Morez is the line of demarcation along this stretch. The railroad crosses the road at several places and is thus unusable for us as well as the French.
2.) In the order of Bedeis [commander of rail units] to the Grukodeis C [Group Command C of Rail Units] a restoration of the destroyed rail bridges in the border region facing Switzerland is not mentioned. Thus at present railroad bridges there are not being repaired.

If the *special task for Army Group C* is still being considered, even for a time not yet determined, it is necessary to take the above two items into consideration as soon as possible and to give the respective orders.

For the Army Group Command
Chief of the General Staff
Deputy: (signed Müller)

Distribution:
Copy 1: OKH Op. Sec.
Copy 2: AOK 12 (for information)
Copy 3: Army Group Comm. C Bv.T.O.
Copy 4: Army Group C I b
Copy 5: Army Group C 0 1
Copy -: Army Group C Id (draft)

I a No. 1121/40 g. Kdos.   H.Qu. July 13, 1940
                                           1:00 p.m.
Secret Command Matter   2 copies
                                              -Copy

Colonel on the General Staff Müller from Captain on General Staff von Menges, Op. Sec.

1.) Regarding Request Army Group C for Demarcation Line at 12th Army:
  a) A new map will arrive from the Armistice Commission which puts the whole rail line Pont d'Héry-Champagnole-St. Laurent to AOK 12.
  b) A request has been made to the Armistice Commission to get the requested change in road assignment (Prémanon, Lamoura, Mioux) as requested.
  c) The chief of transports will get instructions regarding repair of the necessary rail bridges with the 12th Army.
2.) A meeting with the Führer is taking place today, during which the matter in question will also be discussed.

Captain von Menges has been notified that material has been found in Dijon which incriminates Switzerland for collaborating with the French. The material is en route to OKW.
O.B.-Chief
Distribution: 1 d = Copy 1
                0 1 = Copy 2
Ia informs Bv.T.O., Ic, AOK 12 [initial:] M(üller)

NO. 15

Third Updated Version of the Attack Draft of the Operations Division of the General Staff of the Army:

OKH, Op. Sec. (I), Revision due to New Information about Switzerland.
Part I: The German Attack on Switzerland; Part II: The Italian Attack, Aug. 12, 1940
signed: von Menges, Captain on the General Staff

BA-MA, RH 2/465; Switzerland, vol.C.

Op. Sec. (1)		Aug. 12, 1940
Secret Command Matter	Chief's Matter!	Only by Officers!
Part I		

Revision Due to New Information about Switzerland

THE GERMAN ATTACK OF SWITZERLAND

Orders Given:
The possibilities for a surprise occupation of Switzerland by German troops from France and Germany are to be examined assuming that Italian troops will attack Switzerland simultaneously from the south.

1.) Execution of Task:
In this enterprise it is imperative to achieve by a rapid surprise invasion from several directions:

    a) The smashing of the enemy army in such a manner that a unified command and structuring for renewed resistance on individual lines, as well as an orderly evasion into difficult mountain terrain (thus delaying the outcome of the war) is prevented.

    b) For political and morale reasons a rapid and undamaged occupation of the Capital and the region of the weapons industry around Solothurn and Zurich (Örlikon).

    c) Gaining the most important rail and road junctions as well as the numerous bridges and tunnels undamaged, in order to be able to use the country as soon as possible as a transit area to southern France for all transports.

2.) The Country of Switzerland: Appendix 1
Switzerland is truly a mountainous country. Central and southern Switzerland are regions of high mountains with glaciers in the Alpine sections of the

Valais, Bern, and Glarus. The Rhône and Rhine valleys are deeply cut in and narrow and thus easily blocked by the blasting of rocks.

The northern part of Switzerland is more flat. Its boundaries are Lake Constance, the Rhine (between Basel and Lake Constance it is 100–200 m wide) and the Jura mountains which are difficult to cross from the north. The industrial area of the country is northwest of Zurich as well as in the region of Fribourg-Bern-Solothurn.

3.) The Swiss Army:

a) According to the status of early August 1940, the Swiss army has a total strength of 220,000 men. It currently consists of: 6 infantry divisions, 3 mountain divisions, 3 mountain brigades, 1 border brigade, and border battalions. There is no armored force. The air force is weak and only partially modernized; the antitank forces are being built-up.

b) Demobilized are: the 3 light brigades (corps troops) and bicycle units, all territorial troops, the border brigades except for one along the southern border, and all rear services. For reasons of internal politics and due to joblessness, there are difficulties with further demobilization.

c) Mobilization may be preceded by measures in response to tensions (use of border forces). Mobilization itself requires only a short time. Ready to march are: parts of border patrols within 5 hours, corps staff, corps troops, and divisions on the second day of mobilization. Army staffs, light brigades, and border brigades on the first day of mobilization. Total strength of the mobilized army 278,000 men with 6 infantry divisions, 3 mountain divisions, 3 mountain brigades, and 9 border brigades (about 100 border battalions) and as corps troops 3 light brigades, and 75 battalions of "territorial troops" (type of riflemen).

d) Currently in internment camps in Switzerland (guarded by the 3rd and parts of the 7th divisions) are the following units, totaling 50,000 men, who came across the border during the western campaign:
   –the French 67th division, third wave, moderate fighting spirit
   –the 2nd Polish division (12,000 men) ⎫
   –parts of the fortification brigades ⎪ suffered little,
   Altkirch and Montbéliard ⎬ [all] good troops
   –1 Spahi [North African] brigade, 900 men ⎭
   –army supplies, artillery, and tanks.
   Switzerland would like soon to get rid of the Poles and Spahis—among other reasons—to have the 1 1/2 guard divisions available again.
   In case of war, a crossover to the Swiss side by the Poles, the Spahis, and possibly a small part of the French can be expected. Total strength

then about 1 division. The acquisition of the weapons and tanks taken from the interned troops is welcome to Switzerland.

If the interned units are not fighting and are still in the country, guarding them means a weakening of the Swiss fighting force.

4.) Fortifications of Switzerland: Exhibit 2
a) Border with Germany:

Emphasis on reinforcement in the sector Basel-Constance-Rheineck-Sargans. Lighter reinforcement, only a few places medium reinforcement. Heavy development of the cornerstones Rheineck and Sargans, in between steep mountain slopes. Only weak safeguarding along southern shore of Lake Constance.

Thirteen Rhine bridges between Constance and Basel. Weaker points southwest of Basel, eastward to Waldshut and near Eglisau.

Rear positions: Apparently so far only barricade fortifications in narrow sections of valleys. Reinforcement planned for line Olten-Aarau-Zurich-Sargans.
b) Border with France:

Reinforcement only starting early 1940, first only barricades at individual places and field-like firing positions.

Weakness of positions: around and west of Nyon, east of Pontarlier, north of La Chaux-de-Fonds; pass roads north and south of St. Maurice not fortified.

Rear positions between the lake narrows have not yet been developed.
c) State of Reinforcements:

Since July work on fortifications is at a standstill, except for those which have been started above ground. Work on fortifications and barricades along the northwest border continues without reduction. [See] Appendix 3
d) Details:

The shooting ranges are 6–8 m above ground, thus a good target; nothing known about antitank ditches. Road barricades to be expected everywhere (prepared concrete blocks, to be overcome by blasting or by prepared bridging structures). Border guard houses without combat value.

5.) Swiss Deployment and Fighting Strength:

According to the sparse reports currently available, 5 1/2 divisions are deployed along the German-Swiss border in the north and only 2 1/2 divisions in the west. Thus, no increase along the western border can be detected since last month; the divisions are only somewhat more removed from the border. The remainder are deployed in the south and southeast.

Fighting strength: A suitably organized, rapidly deployable, war[-ready] army. The state of training seems higher due to long-time mobilization. Only theoretically trained command. Methodical command. Deficiency in weaponry (artillery, tanks and antitank defenses, air force, flak). The individual soldier is a tough fighter and good rifleman. The mountain troops are said to be better than their neighbors to the south. The fighting value of the Swiss living in the west (French type) is moderate, while those who live south of Constance (Communists) will be bitter enemies. Conclusion: Army suitable for defense only, which is totally inferior to the German army.

6.) Swiss Possibilities for [Strategic] Operations:
The enemy has no way of going on the attack due the necessity of protecting his long borders. He will try to defend his fortified positions near the border.

The weakness of his current positioning is along the French border. A possible repositioning to that region can occur only at the expense of safeguarding the German border.

After losing his positions along the border, the enemy will try to regroup on a line Lake Geneva-Lake Neuchâtel-Lake Biel-Olten-Zurich-Sargans.

Then, the possibility remains to defend in the high mountains.

7.) The Neighboring Country of Liechtenstein.
Liechtenstein is an independent country which closely cooperates with Switzerland politically and financially (customs union). The prince is said to live mainly in Vienna. There is no army.
Own Deployment   Appendix 4 and 5

8.) Basic Ideas Regarding Deployment of Forces:
   a) The aim is,
       to destroy the enemy army as soon as possible,
       to occupy the capital and the industrial areas around Bern and Zurich rapidly and undamaged,
       to gain the most important rail lines, tunnels, and roads undamaged (see also above 1 a-c).
   b) General Deployment:
       It has to be done so fast that Switzerland is really surprised by the attack. Thus, moving in: the motorized units only at the last minute, the infantry divisions at a distance from the border, of these the divisions designated for the attack from the north camouflaged as being in training.
   c) The center of the attack has to come from France. Here are the weakest border fortifications, here is the weak point of the enemy deploy-

ment, from there it is possible to get most rapidly to the nearest large cities and industrial areas and, finally, the rear positions on both sides of Lake Neuchâtel have apparently not yet been reinforced.

d) Little deployment should be used for the attack across the Rhine. It is difficult and requires a lot of bridge convoys. There should only be deceptive maneuvers there along a wide front by one division. Parts of this division should be deployed at weak points of the enemy near Waldshut and Eglisau up to and beyond Zurich.

e) An attack from the east should be avoided due to the difficult mountain terrain, the strong enemy fortifications, and the unfavorable deployment possibilities.

f) For reasons of terrain, the invasion of the corner around Chur-Davos should be left to the Italians.

g) Attack possibilities for the Italians see page 4, Part II "The Italian Attack."

Appendix 6

It is most favorable for us if the Italians use their forces, inclusive of the Rhône valley, in such a way that a clear frontier of interests between Germans and Italians across the crest of the Bernese and Glarus Alps can be drawn. This solution should be aimed for, hoping that the Italians will proceed rapidly and forcefully in the Rhône valley.

(It is less favorable for us if the Italian-Western wing is only deployed to and including the Simplon pass. In that case, German forces would have to advance also in the very important Rhône valley. The frontier of interests between Germany and Italy would then run south of the Rhône valley. The Italians would not have a lateral connection between their attack groups within Switzerland. Their attack groups, furthermore, could not deploy their full strength. Thus, this solution should only be considered in case of need.)

h) Threat from the Air:

We are far superior in the air so that the use of motorized and panzer divisions with the assignment of corresponding antiaircraft units will be possible without misgivings in spite of the narrow, deeply cut-in roads.

9.) Available Forces:

With deployment of some of the motorized, panzer, and mountain divisions assigned to "Seelöwe":

a) The AOK 12 is to be charged with the overall command, for preparations it remains within Army Group C.

At the start of the attack, the AOK 12 will be put under the direct command of the OKH to shorten the chain of command.

b) The motorized and panzer divisions are used for the rapid occupation of Bern, Lucerne, and Zurich and for the blocking of the enemy's roads of retreat leading south. They are to be drawn from the area of the 2nd army. The approach distance is measured as 200–350 km as the crow flies.

c) SS "A.H." [Adolf Hitler] and I.R. [infantry regiment] "Grossdeutschland" are to be used as rapid reinforcement of the I.D. [infantry division].

d) There is a lack of mountain divisions (1st and 6th mountain divisions are stationed at the Pas de Calais). At least one mountain division is needed for crossing the Jura mountains and for possible later use in central and southern Switzerland. Replacing it by an infantry division with mountain equipment is impossible as this equipment is already fully in use for "Seelöwe." For this reason deployment of the 1st mountain division should be requested.

e) Infantry divisions are to be used for breaking through the line of fortifications and for closer targets. Available are:
For the attack from the west and northwest: 5th, 73rd, then as reserve 23rd division (from the 12th army in their current, advantageous areas), for attack from the north: 260th div. (from 12th army near Belfort, foot march), the 262nd div. (from 1st army southwest of Saarbrücken, by rail).
(Their use is preferred compared to the divisions on leave to be called back within ten days and which have to be retrained—88th near Rothenburg, 95th near Frankfurt am Main.—Their recall is also hard to camouflage.)

10.) *Employment and Orders in Detail:*   Appendix 4 and 5
   a) Overall command: AOK 12
   Orders for AOK 12: "AOK 12—for preparation under Army Group C, from start of attack under direct command of OKH—starts on orders by the OKH on day X at hour Y with concentric attack on Switzerland from the west (center of action), north, and northeast, in order rapidly to occupy Switzerland north of the demarcation of interests [Germany and Italy]. For this purpose it breaks through the enemy border fortifications and takes possession, as soon as possible, of the capital as well as the industrial areas around Bern and Zurich.
   The goal is to defeat the Swiss army rapidly and decisively, before it can escape southward into the high mountains, while simultaneously blocking its retreat routes from the south and southwest, as well as north of the Glarus Alps by the use of parachute troops. Traffic routes

should be taken with the least amount of damage possible. It is agreed that an Italian army will simultaneously attack south of the demarcation line of interests line from the south, centering across the Simplon and Splügen passes."

b) I) Should the German-Italian demarcation line of interest run south of the Rhône valley: (Appendix 4: line b-b)
"1st attack group"
Forces: Reinforced 20th motorized division, 1 machine gun battalion, motorized (from 2nd army)
Command: Directly under AOK 12.

Approach: via St. Laurent, St. Claude, Gex.
Putting on standby in the area around Ferney (south of Gex). The approach road runs in part west of the [French] line of demarcation, as the road from Morez towards Gex is fully used by the left adjoining division (29th motorized, see page 11), which is on standby in the area northwest of Gex for attack in the direction of Nyon. The approach through unoccupied territory west of the line of demarcation takes place without advance notification of the French during the night before the attack to the area of Geneva so that the division reaches the Swiss border only shortly before the start of the attack.

Orders: "Division—under the direct command of the AOK 12— makes a surprise seizure of Geneva on day X, hour Y, in order to advance from there in two attack groups, centered above Martigny, into the Rhône Valley in the direction of the St. Gotthard, and to open the Simplon pass to the Italians from the north, and later, to establish the connection in direction Schwyz and Brienz with the northern attack groups. Fort St. Maurice is to be seized from the north and the south."

II) Should the German-Italian demarcation of interests line run across the Bernese and Glarus Alps: (appendix 4 line a-a).
If the demarcation of interests runs across the Bernese and Glarus Alps, this attack group is to be omitted. Instead, parts of the division (29th motorized-southern wing of the 2nd attack group; see below) placed formerly only north of Lake Geneva adjoining advance via Geneva, hard along the south of Lake Geneva, Aigle towards Thun.

c) "2nd Attack Group":
Forces: XVth army corps (motorized) 5th division (of 12th army), 29th motorized div. (of 2nd army), 4th armored division (of 2nd army), corps troops: 1 heavy field howitzer unit.

Approach: 5th division is already there. Motorized and panzer divisions no difficulties.

Orders: "XVth Army Corps breaks on day X, hour Y through enemy border fortifications between Nyon and Vervières (including towns), rapidly takes possession of the capital and blocks the enemy's retreat into the area of Lake Thun to the south.

The army corps stands ready possibly, on orders of the AOK 12, to attack with sections from the region of Bern in a generally northern direction in order to open to its left neighbor the path through the Jura mountains from the south."

Command of the Attack:
29th motorized attacks with strong units from the area east of Gex towards Nyon, as the mountain ridge there has already been passed before the border and there are apparently no enemy fortifications. Use here one motorized division in order to rapidly block the road of retreat near Thun.

4th tank as core group to Bern. Use only after parts of the 5th division have broken through the border fortifications.

Later use of the 5th division for the occupation of Bern, of the industrial area situated there and of the area seized by the XVth Army Corps appears necessary. Use of a small secondary section through Neuchâtel towards Bern may ease the breaking through the mountains near La Chaux-de-Fonds for the adjoining division. Putting it later under the command of the XVIIIth Army Corps is to be planned.

d) "3rd Attack Group":
Forces: XVIIIth Army Corps (from 12th Army), 1st mountain division (from 16th Army) 73rd mountain division (from 12th Army), infantry regiment "Grossdeutschland" (from 12th Army) SS. "A.H." (from 1st Army). Corps troops: 1 heavy field howitzer unit, 1 armored rifle battalion 4.7 cm (from army troops).

Approach: General Command XVIII and 73rd divisions are already in their areas.

1st mountain division arrives with its fighting parts on a truck transport regiment (made available by quartermaster general), its columns by rail transport. The purpose of this transport has to be camouflaged (use along line of demarcation). Corps troops: Approach on foot.
No difficulties for infantry regiment "Grossdeutschland" and SS.

"A.H." For reason of camouflage and because of their later use, they will be brought up last.

Orders:
"XVIIIth Army Corps takes Lucerne on day X, hour Y—after breaking through the border fortifications and Jura in the sector Le Locle-Basel (including towns)—by rapidly advancing units from north and west and prevents the evasion of the enemy along a line Bern-Lucerne-Schwyz towards the south."

Command of the Attack:
Basel is to be bypassed on the west.
Infantry regiment "Grossdeutschland" and SS "A.H." should be sent forward as soon as possible after the first breakthrough. Use of paratroopers near Olten to open the mountain exits from the south should be considered.

e) "4th Attack Group:"
Forces: XIIth Army Corps (from 1st Army), 260th division (from 12th Army), 1 machine gun battalion (motorized) (from 2nd Army), 262nd division (from 1st Army).
Corps troops: 1 heavy field howitzer unit, 1 engineer battalion and bridge columns, 1 smoke mortar unit, 1 armored rifle battalion 4.7 cm (from army troops).

Approach: General Command XIIth Army Corps: foot march, 260th division: foot march for 140 km from area of Belfort to area Waldshut/Rhine, 262nd division: embarkation around Saarbrücken. Rail transport to area of Constance and Friedrichshafen. Corps troops: march on foot.

Orders: "XIIth Army Corps-assembling on day X, hour Y—destroys the enemy in the area Zurich-Sargans-Lake Constance-Waldshut. For this purpose break through enemy fortifications between Waldshut and Romanshorn and, in cooperation with paratroopers having landed along the Lindt Canal and near Sargans, prevent evasion by the enemy via Schwyz-Sargans towards the south.
Between Basel-Constance (excluding towns) an attack across the Rhine on a wide front is to be feigned."

Command of the Attack:
A very desirable attack in itself across Rheineck (shortest path to the enemy flank) promises no success due to the very heavy enemy

fortification. For the division deployed via Constance, the use of the car ferry Friedrichshafen-Romanshorn is envisioned for opening the fortifications there from the south and for the surprise landing of units with simultaneous use of assault boats.

  f) Reserves:

are necessary behind the core sectors:

    a) for taking rapid advantage of success, presumably of the XVth Corps (for this SS "T" [Totenkopf/Skull] from the 2nd Army) in the area south of Besançon,

    b) for breaking possibly especially heavy resistance in the mountains west of Basel (for this 23rd division of 12th Army). In the area of Belfort it is to be kept mobile on the truck transport regiment which had earlier brought in the 1st mountain division.

They are under the command of the AOK 12.

11.) Total Forces Required: (the divisions marked by* are planned for use in "Sea Lion").

1 AOK: 12th

3 army corps: XVth* (motorized), XVIII and XII

5 infantry divisions: 5th, 23rd, 73rd, 260th, 262nd

1 mountain division: 1st*

3 motorized divisions: 20th* mot., 29th* mot., SS "T"*

2 motorized regiments: infantry regiment "Grossdeutschland,"* SS "A.H."*

1 panzer division: 4th *

Army Troops:

a) engineering battalions and bridge columns for XIIth Army Corps

b) machine gun battalions mot. for 20th mot. and 260th infantry divisions

c) 1 flak unit for each army corps,

d) 1 armored rifle unit 4.7 cm each for XVIIIth and XIIth Army Corps

e) 1 smoke mortar unit for XIIth Army Corps,

f) for each army corps a heavy field howitzer unit.

Total:

AOK: 1

Army corps: 3

Divisions: 10

Mot. regiments: 2

Army troops

Air force (see No. 12)

12.) Air Force:

    a) Tasks of the operative air force:

        Smashing of the enemy air force. Destruction of rail lines and bridges initially is not permitted!

    b) Use of fighter planes in conjunction with army: for total attack XVth Army Corps and for breaking through fortifications with XVIIIth and XIIth Army Corps.

    c) Airborne troops:

        For use of parachute troops see "4th Attack Group".

    d) Flak important on the few deeply cut-in roads. Assignment, to the extent that the situation across from the British coast permits at this time (see also items 8 h and 11). One flak unit for each army corps is to be requested.

    e) Reconnaissance planes:

        1 reconnaissance squadron for each AOK, army corps, mot., and panzer division.

13.) Tactical Command and Composition:

Make use of the experience made in Norway: Assignment of tanks, artillery and individual motorized troops to the vanguard; reinforcement of the marching units by machine gun company (motorized); increased use of infantry artillery and grenade throwers; formation of strong advance units, using vehicles of the antitank gunner units, here not that necessay for antitank defense.

14.) Time Requirement:

    a) For approach:

        I) of the furthest motorized units from the area of the 2nd Army: 2 days,

        II) of the infantry divisions: march on foot: 2–3 days, of 260th div. up to 4 days,

        III) of 1st mountain div.: truck and rail transport: 3 days,

        IV) of 262nd div. by rail transport: 3 days.

        Added to this for III) and IV) 3 days advance warning for preparing rolling materials: $3 + 3 = 6$ days. No later than 7th day before attack, advance warning has to be given to railroad.

    b) for operations: Seizure of Bern, Lucerne, and Zurich has to take place no later than in the course of the 2nd day. Reaching the line of demarcation depends on the success of the first 2 days and the results of the battles around the St. Gotthard. In about 3–4 days the part of Switzerland assigned to us can be occupied (if demarcation line of interests runs across Bernese and Glarus Alps), otherwise in 4–5 days. The time requirements for the Italians depends on the type of their attack.

15.) Time of Year:

Summer is favorable. October through March brings snowfall in the mountains and delays in marching times; fog prevents, among other things, the use of the air force. September is particularly favorable for the air force.

16.) Requirements:

    a) Secrecy and Deception:
       Discreet, reinforced closing of the Swiss border, also along the Italian and, to the extent possible, the French section. Corresponding press notices. Deceptive radio traffic and radio silence for individual units.

    b) Use of spies to explore details of fortifications. What is the situation at rear positions? Are regroupings going on along the French border?

    c) Improvement of particularly bad maps. Acquisition of maps about road conditions, possibly on the open market in Switzerland. Preparation of a condensed military-geographic description of the country.

    d) The chief of transport must be listened to about his requirements for deployment and about especially important, and thus rapidly to be occupied, traffic routes.

    e) The Armistice Commission has rejected the shifting of the demarcation line Champagnole-St. Claude-Collonges-west of Martigny (including towns). As the advantages of a German and Italian attack south of Lake Geneva are great, request should now be made by the German political leadership that it permit the march of German and Italian troops through unoccupied territories and the fifty-kilometers zone (along the Italian/French border), that is create the precondition for it. The sooner the French/Swiss border segment Lake Geneva-Three-Country Corner (at the Great St. Bernard) is closed, the better, in order to cut off any movement from and to France.

    f) Switzerland's request to be able soon to repatriate Poles and Spahis from their country should be granted expeditiously in order to prevent a possible reinforcement of the Swiss army (see No. 3d).

17.) Given the momentary political situation in Switzerland, it is possible that it might accede peacefully to ultimatum demands, so that after a warlike crossing of the border, a rapid transition to a peaceful invasion must be assured.

von Menges
Captain on the General Staff

Additional Comments to Item 10 f) Reserves:
Added to the duplicate copy in Vol. A: "Switzerland (Drafts, Situation Reports). Microfilm NA T-78, roll 649, 2097/441.

Mobility must also be requested of the 260th division or of the 23rd division. (If a mountain division is used instead of the 23rd, the 23rd division would be the reserve instead of the 260th division.)

The following possibilities exist:
  a) Involving instead of the 260th or 23rd division: 2nd or 13th motorized division, which are both available at home as of August 31.
  b) Replacement of the 29th (motorized) division by another panzer division (8th), so that the 29th (motorized) will become the reserve.
  c) Release of a truck transport regiment for 23rd or 260th division for about 14 days by the quartermaster general. In the view of the Organization Division, this might be the best possibility because of the constantly improving rail situation.
  d) Creation of a transport space based on captured vehicles in the area of Army Group C, which would presumably only be sufficient for 1/3 of a division. Given the variety of vehicles, a rapid and reliable loading use is doubtful.
  e) Release of 2 supply columns each from the division, 2nd and 4th wave, of Army Group C, to the extent that they are not participating in "Seelöwe," provides transport space for 1/2 division. It is doubtful that these columns are not already otherwise taken and used by the quartermaster general.
  f) The 5 armies not designated for "Seelöwe," each form until September 1 a supply column unit from captured vehicles = 5 units = more than 1 truck transport regiment. The armies make these or, as a replacement, a corresponding number of columns available for the Division to be moved.

Final Assessment:
  a) is best if the time is before Aug. 31, followed by b) and c).
  d)–f) have the disadvantage that these vehicles are not designed for loads and are very light, thus the need for many vehicles and long columns.
    For the transport of the Mountain Division this Truck Transport Regiment could then also be used in order subsequently to load the respective reserves at the disposal of AOK 12.

Operations section (I)
Secret Command Matter.   Chief's Matter!   Only by officer!

Part II

THE ITALIAN ATTACK.   Appendix 6
1.) The attack possibilities for the Italians against Switzerland are condi-
    tioned by:
    a) the passability of mountains and passes,
    b) the Italian deployment possibilities by rail,
    c) the weak points of the Swiss fortifications,
    d) the enemy deployment.

Concerning a): The Lower Engadin with its few roads and small population, as well as the Valais Alps have to be ruled out for major operations
due to altitude and impassability (except for the road across the Great St.
Bernard to Martigny). For this reason, the mass of the Italian army should
not be deployed on the outermost wing.

Concerning b): Possible for the deployment are the continuous rail lines
across the Bernina Pass, St. Gotthard and Simplon Pass, as well as the
railroad leading to Chiavenna. On all lines it is important to occupy the
long tunnels on Swiss territory undamaged.

Concerning c): The Swiss fortifications have mountain and high mountain
characteristics. They have been blasted into the rock, partly built into the
stone. They are old, little modernized, but bomb-proof constructions. The
weak points are: the old construction of the forts, the mortar-built infantry
positions and the machinery of the armored turrets that can be lowered.
The core of the fortifications is at the St. Gotthard. There are several fortification groups which command all the passes towards east, south, and
west. Added to this are the barricade fortifications south of this near
Lugano and Locarno.
There are lesser fortifications on all the remaining passes of the southern
front, of these (to the extent known) remarkably weak ones at the Splügen and Simplon passes. Both of those have the shortest routes to the
Rhine and Rhône valley. It is then possible to cut off the eastern corner of
Switzerland from Chur.
Evaluation of the fortifications thus seems to indicate that an attack in the
direction of the St. Gotthard from the south would be difficult and time
consuming, while there are better conditions at the Splügen and Simplon
passes.

Concerning d): The Swiss deployment shows a core formation at the St. Gotthard with 1 1/2 divisions and strong border patrol (including mountain brigades), apparently only border patrol along Splügen and Simplon passes. The enemy apparently plans defense near the border (only in eastern Switzerland removed somewhat towards the west) and, after a breakthrough of this line, defense around Sargans and the St. Gotthard.

The weakness of his position in the south and on the St. Gotthard itself provides the possibility for encircling from the Splügen and Simplon passes. If the enemy evades early from the border to the St. Gotthard, it will be unable to resist long a concentric attack from south, east, and west.

2.) It is important for the Italians to occupy as rapidly as possible the valleys of the Lower Rhine and Upper Rhine and the Rhône in order to
   a) cut off the eastern part of Switzerland east and south of Chur,
   b) advance on the roads leading north and towards the German forces (direction Sargans, Schwyz, and Lake Brienz).

The Italians reach these goals fastest across the Splügen and Simplon passes. The Italian border is closest at this point; a deployment by rail to the area of the border is possible. In order to tie down the enemy frontally at the St. Gotthard and to occupy the undamaged rail line, an advance via Lugano-Locarno is necessary. An advance across the Bernina pass only appears appropriate if the rail line there should be seized particularly quickly.

An advance across the road at the Great St. Bernard and massed from Chamonix towards Martigny favors a rapid seizure of the Rhône valley, if a German column is not to be used in the Rhône valley. The latter may possibly make faster progress than an Italian column. When German and Italian troops meet in Brig, certain difficulties as to cooperation and the pursuit of goals may occur. In both cases, German or Italian troops would have to march through the demilitarized zone (a 50 km wide strip along the west of the Italian border) and be assembled in the area around Chamonix (France). (See also page 3, part I, item 8g).

3.) Thus, follows for the Italians:
   Deployment of the following troops:
   a) possibly a small group across the Bernina pass, direction Davos,
   b) a strong group across Splügen, direction Reichenau (on the Rhine), in order to cut off from there the eastern corner of Switzerland and to advance in the direction of the St. Gotthard to encircle the enemy,
   c) a group on both sides of the Lago Maggiore direction St. Gotthard,
   d) a strong group across the Simplon pass, Brig, direction St. Gotthard to encircle the enemy there and to seize the road to Brienz,

e) possibly a group (instead of a German one) from Chamonix via Martigny to Brig. It then has to march through the French-Italian demilitarized 50 km zone!

4.) From this follows that the demarcation line of interests between Germany and Italy has to run north of the Rhône valley south of Sargans, on the crest of the Glarus-Bernese Alps north of Martigny. This border is also to be recognized by the air force.

 With a German attack in the Rhône valley, the demarcation line of interests between Germany and Italy would have to run as follows: north slope of the Valais Alps—directly south of Brig-north slope of St. Gotthard—Arosa-Schiers. The latter line is only an emergency solution!

Appendix 4

5.) A unified supreme command of German and Italian forces is not necessary, but rather a communications staff for each with the German and Italian army supreme command.

6.) A radical closure of the Italian and Swiss border is already now necessary for reason of camouflage.

von Menges
Captain on the General Staff

Enclosures 1–3: Maps regarding Swiss defense, not reproduced
Enclosure 4: Illustration XI
Enclosure 5: Illustrations VIII/IX
Enclosure 6: Illustration X

Bibliography

UNPRINTED PRIMARY SOURCES

Manuscripts and Microfilms

Archiv für Zeitgeschichte [Archive for Contemporary History],
Eidgenössische Technische Hochschule [ETH], Zürich [AfZ]

Heinrich Büeler Papers:
17: Franz Riedweg, MD.
18: Einzelne Strafverfahren und Prozesse: Georg Freiberger.

Peter Dietz Papers:
21, 23: "Die italienisch-französischen Waffenstillstandsverhandlungen," 23./24. Juni
1940.
25–29: "Die deutsch-französischen Waffenstillstandsverhandlungen von Rethondes,"
21./22. Juni 1940.

Hans Hausamann Papers:
Berichte Juni 1940; Materialien zur Biographie.

Archives of the Neue Zürcher Zeitung:
Wirtschaft: Schweiz. "Allgemeine Verkehrsprobleme, Transithandel," 1924–1941.
Wirtschaft: Einzelne Länder. "Frankreich, Bahnen, 1925–1981."

Bundesarchiv–Militärarchiv [Federal Archive–Military Archive], Freiburg
i. Breisgau [BA-MA]

RW 4 Oberkommando der Wehrmacht/Wehrmachtführungsstab:
RW 4/v.41: "Kriegstagebuch Wehrmachtführungsstab. Notizen des Hauptmanns Deyhle,"
1940/1941.

RW 4/v.43: "Notizen zum Kriegstagebuch des Wehrmachtführungsamtes, mit Anlagen."

RW 4/521: "Führerweisungen und -befehle," Juli 1940–Dezember 1941.

RW 4/574: "Chefsachen 'Attila' (Besetzung Südfrankreichs)," 1940–1942.

RH 2 Oberkommando des Heeres / Generalstab des Heeres

RH 2/129: "Besprechungsnotizen von Generalstabsbesprechungen und dergleichen," 27. September 1939–16. Oktober 1942.

RH 2/427: "Chefsachen," 1941, vol 1.

RH 2/465: "Schweiz," Bde. A, B, C.

RH 2/465; "K 1–19; Karten."

RH 2/768; "Handakte des Chefs des Generalstabs des Heeres, Generaloberst Franz Halder," 1939–1942.

RH 2/2972: "Kriegstagebuch," Operations-Abteilung des Generalstabs des Heeres, 10. Mai–25. Juni 1940."—"Lagekartenatlas," Oberkommando des Heeres, Generalstab des Heeres, Operationsabteilung, Westen, 1940.

RH19 III Heeresgruppenkommando C

RH 19 III/7: "Handakte des Chefs des Generalstabes der Heeresgruppe C, General der Infanterie Felber," 27. Februar–3. Juli 1940.

RH 19 III/10: "Chefsachen Westen," Bd. 3, 28. August 1939–29. Juli 1940.

RH 19 III/128: "Heeresgruppenkommando C, Entnommene Anlagen aus Kriegstagebuch gemäss Verfügung Oberkommando des Heeres, Generalstab des Heeres, Operationsabteilung (III)," Nr. 9130/40, geheim, 29. Oktober 1940.

RH 19 III/132: "Einsatz von Eisenbahnpionieren im Bereich der Heeresgruppe C," September 1939–2. August 1940.

RH 19 III/139: "Anlage 2c zu Oberkommando des Heeres, Generalstab des Heeres, Operationsabteilung (III)," Nr. 385: "Kommandos vom 12. Juli 1940."

RH 19 III/139: "K 1–3; Unterkunftskarten."

RH 20–12 Armeeoberkomando [AOK] 12

RH 20–12/23: "Unterstellung, Umorganisation und Bereitschaftsräume in Frankreich, Armeebefehle," Nrn. 33, 34, 30. Juni–4. August 1940.

RH 20–12/41: AOK 12–Ia. "Bericht über den Einsatz des Pionierregimentes 107," 8. Juni–26. August 1940.

RH 20–12/42: "'Aufmarsch E': Umgliederung des Heeres," 24–26. Juni 1940.

RH 20–12/383: "Kodeis 12 (Eisenbahnpioniere), Westfeldzug 1940," 6. Juni–7. Juli 1940.

RH 21–2 Panzerarmeeoberkommando 2

RH 21–2/41 D: "Kriegstagebuch Nr. 3 (Gruppe Guderian)," 9. Mai–24. Juni 1940.

RH 21–1/43b: "Anlage zum Kriegstagebuch Nr. 3," Bd. 1, 9. Mai–28. Juni 1940.

RH 21–2/v. 51a, b: "Anlagen zum Kriegstagebuch Nr. 3 (Gruppe Guderian)," 2–14. Juni 1940; 14–21. Juni 1940.

RH 21–2/v. 57: "XIX. Armeekorps (Gruppe Guderian)," Ia, 2. Abschnitt, Akte XV. "Verschiedenes," 31. Mai–23. Juni 1940.

RH 21–2/v. 58: "XIX. Armeekorps (Gruppe Guderian)," 2. Abschnitt, Akte XVI.

RH 21–2/v. 61: "Anlagen zum Kriegstagebuch Nr. 3 (Gruppe Guderian)," Bd. 19. Juni–Juli 1940.—"Kriegstagebuch Nr. 3, XXXIX. Armeekorps," E 63/3, 1. 24 Juni 1940.

RH 24–18 Generalkommando XVIII. Gebirgs-Armeekorps
RH 24–18/46: "Kriegstagebuch Nr. 6, XVIII. Armeekorps," 27. Juni–6. November 1940.
RH 24–18/50: "Anlagen zum Kriegstagebuch Nr. 6," Bd. 1, 6. Juli–6. August 1940.
RH 24–18/156: Abteilung Ic, "Tagesmeldungen," 10. Juli–4. November 1940.

RH 26–29 29. Infanterie Division (motorisiert)
RH 26–29/3: Ia, "Anlagenheft 2 zum Kriegstagebuch Nr. 3, Anlagen Nrn. 415–560," 15–19. Juni 1940.
RH 26–29/4: Ia, "Anlagenheft Nr. 3 zum Kriegstagebuch Nr. 3, Anlagen Nrn. 562–641," 19–25. Juni 1940.
RH 26–29/5: "Sonderanlagenheft zum Kriegstagebuch Nr. 3," 4–7. Juni 1940.

RH 28–1 1. Gebirgsdivision
RH 28–1/11: Bd. 3, Teil I: "Führungsbefehle der Division," 21. Juni–5. Juli 1940.
RH 28–6 6. Gebirgs-Division
RH 28–6/1a: "Kriegstagebuch der 6. Gebirgs-Division," 3. Juni–23. Juli 1940.
RH 28–6/1b: "Kriegstagebuch der 6. Gebirgs-Division," 24. Juli 1940–12. Februar 1941.
RH 28–6/2: "Anlagen zum Kriegstagebuch, Nr. 2," Bd. I: Befehle und Meldungen, 4. Juni 1940–15. Januar, 1941.
RH 28–6/6: "Anlagen zum Kriegstagebuch Nr. 2," Bd. IV: "Besondere Anordnungen für den Nachrichtenbetrieb," 15. Januar 1940–29. Juli 1941.

N 463 Friedrich Dollmann Papers
N 463/v. 3: "Album Bau-Battalion 54."

N 67 Hans Felber Papers
N 67/2: "Kriegserinnerungen. Handschriftliche Aufzeichnungen des Generalleutnants Hans Felber über die Ereignisse vom 16. April 1939–3. September 1940: Vorbereitung und Einsatz im Polenfeldzug 1939 und Westfeldzug 1940."

N 51 Erich Hoepner Papers
N 51/1: "Erfahrungen aus den Feldzügen in Polen 1939 und Belgien-Frankreich 1940, Aufzeichnungen Juli 1940."

N 54 Wilhelm Keitel Papers
N 54/5: "Lebenserinnerungen" (maschinenschriftliche Ausarbeitung 1946), Bd. 5:4. Februar 1938–10. August 1940.
N 54/6: "Lebenserinnerungen," Bd. 6: "Vorgeschichte, Einleitung, Vorbereitung und Beginn des Krieges," 1940–1941.

N 527 Wilhelm List Papers
N 527/48: "Vom Rhein zur Rhone. Die Operationen der 12. Armee im Kriege gegen Frankreich 1940."
N 527/49: "Mit dem XIII. Armeekorps im Westen, 9. Mai–25. Juni 1940. Kriegstagebuchaufzeichnungen des Generalkommandos XIII. Armeekommando über Vormarsch und Kämpfe in Südbelgien und Frankreich."

Diverse Registers of Papers (Limited Relevance)
N 194: Wilhelm Fahrmbacher
N 69: Alfred Jodl

N 145: Wilhelm Ritter von Leeb
N 60: Ferdinand Schörner

Institut für Zeitgeschichte [Institute for Contemporary History], München
Kartei [Index Cards] Adolf Hitler, 19.–25. Juni 1940.

National Archives, Washington DC

Microfilms of Files from the Bundesarchiv-Militärarchiv [BA-MA], Freiburg im Breisgau
T-77/Roll 706: Oberkommando der Wehrmacht [OKW], Wi/IF 1/6–8: "Schweiz. Schiffahrt, Geleitscheinfrage; Grenzkontrolle; Personalfragen."
T-77/Roll 707: OKW, Wi/IF 1/9, 1/12, 1/17: Wehrwirtschafts-und Rüstungsamt im OKW [WiRüAmt]: "Schweiz, 1938–1942."
T-77/Roll 709: OKW, Wi/IF 1/26, WiRüAmt, 3 i 27: "Attaché Berichte Bern," I: 1939–1940.
T-77/Roll 902: OKW/1095, Amtsgruppe Ausland: "Wirtschaftliche Kriegsmassnahmen in der Schweiz 1940–1943" (Sig. BA-MA: RW 5/v. 347)
T-77/Roll 1434: OKW/1000/1, Amtsgruppe Ausland (Deutsche Gesandtschaft Bern), "Berichte," Oktober–November 1943 (Sig. BA-MA: RW 5/684, 685).
T-78/Roll 351: OKW/162: "Kriegstagebuch, Nrn. 2, 3, Führerhauptquartier," 10. Oktober 1939–31. Juli 1940. Heeresarchiv Potsdam, Nr. 70/34709 (Sig. BA-MA: RW 47/v. 5).
T-78/Roll 649: H 22/397: OKH, Generalstab des Heeres, Operationsabteilung/Gruppe IIa: "Schweiz (1940/41): Handschriftlicher Operationsentwurf 'Tannenbaum.'" Bd A: "Entwürfe, Lageberichte." Bd. B: "Operationsentwurf Heeresgruppe C 'Tannenbaum.'" Bd. C: "Studie Schweiz" (Sig. BA-MA: RH2/465).
T-79/Roll 15: OWK VII/412: "Sonderakt 'Bregenz'", 2. Februar–11. Juli 1940 (Sig. BA-MA: RH 53–7/v. 224)
T-311/Roll 46: Heeresgruppe Nord, W 6671/38 :Meldungen Kodeis," 10. Juli–5. August 1940. "Anlage 16 zum Kriegstagebuch IV, Heeresgruppe C" (Sig. BA-MA: RH 19 III/132).
Heeresgruppe Nord, Oberkommando Heeresgruppe C, Ia., "Anlage 22 zum Kriegstagebuch Nr. 4, Akte 'Sonderchef III,'" März–Mai 1940 (Sig. BA-MA: RH 19 III/11).
Heeresgruppe Nord, W 6671/45: Heeresgruppen Kommando C, Ia: "Anlage zum Kriegstagebuch IV," 24. Juni–2. August 1940 (Sig. BA-MA: RH 19 III/141).
Heeresgruppe Nord, W 6671/46: Heeresgruppen Kommando C, Ia: "Anlage 24 zum Kriegstagebuch IV, Karten," Juli 1940 (Sig. BA-MA: RH 19 III/134k).
T-311/Roll 214: Heeresgruppe Mitte 8755/7: Heeresgruppen B/Ic/Armeekommando, "Lageberichte, Oberkommando des Heeres [OKH], West," 15. Juni–16. September 1940 (Sig. BA-MA: RH 19 II/266).
Heeresgruppe Mitte, 8755/9: Heeresgruppen B/Ic/Armeekommando, OKH "Lageberichte, West," 22. September–20. Dezember 1940 (Sig. BA-MA: RH 19 II/297).
T-312/Roll 25: AOK 1, 31729: "Akte Studie Schweiz," September-October 1940 (Sig. BA-MA: RH 20–1/368, 368K)
T-312/Roll 427: AOK 12, E 346/1: AOK 12–Ia: "Tages- und Abendmeldungen West," 10. Mai–24. Juni 1940 (Sig. BA-MA:RH 20–12/34).
AOK 12, E 346/2: AOK 12–Ia: "Armeebefehle Nr. 3–34 Westen," 10. Mai–2. Juli 1940 (Sig. BA-MA: RH 20–12/33)

T-312/Roll 431: AOK 12, W 3503/b: AOK 12, Ia: "Anlagenband Teil 1 zum Kriegstagebuch Nr. 4," 21.–24. Juli 1940 (Bruchstück) (Sig. BA-MA: RH 20–12/47).

AOK 12, W 5314/g: AOK 12, Ia: "'Aufmarsch E': Umgliederung des Heeres"; Armee-Oberkommando [AOK] (BA-MA: RH 20–12/42).

AOK 12, W 6024, Ia: AOK 12 Ober Quartiermeister [O.Qu] "Kriegstagebuch Quartiermeister," 1:1. Januar–12. September 1940 (Sig. BA-MA: RH 20–12/251)

T-312/Roll 432: AOK 12, W 6024/3; "Anlage 3 zum Kriegstagebuch, AOK 12, O. Qu g. Kommandosache," 1. Januar–10. September 1940 (Sig. BA-MA: RH 20–12/253)

AOK 12, W 6024/4; "Anlage 4 zum Kriegstagebuch, AOK 12, O. Qu. Nrn. 1–64/1940, g. Kommandos," 1. Januar–10. September 1940 (Sig. BA-MA: RH 20 12/254, 255)

T-312/Roll 433: AOK 12, W 6024/9: "Anlage 9 zum Kriegstagebuch AOK 12 O. Qu. 3–tägige, bezw. tägliche Meldungen vom General Quarter," Januar–September 1940 (Sig. BA-MA: RH 20–12/261, 262, 263)

T-312/Roll 435: AOK 12, W 6410: AOK 12, O.Qu./Qu 2. "Kriegstagebuch der Oberquartiermeister Abteilung, AOK 12," 1. Januar–16. September 1940 (Sig. BA-MA: RH 20–12/340)

AOK 12, W 6410a: AOK 12, O.Qu./Qu 2. "Anlagen 1–95 zum Kriegstagebuch," 1. Januar–16. September 1940 (Sig. BA-MA: RH 20–12/341/342)

AOK 12, W 6469: "Kriegstagebuch Nr. 1, Dienststelle des Armeefeldpostmeisters beim AOK 12," 16. Oktober 1939–24. Juni 1940 (Sig. BA-MA: RH 20–12/360)

T-312/Roll 441: AOK 12, 10926/5: "Chefsache. Armee-Oberkommando 12," Ia Stoart, 3. April 1940–31. Dezember 1940 (Sig. BA-MA: RH 20–12/414)

T-312/Roll 446: AOK 12, 12729/1: "Kodeis 12. (Eisenbahnpioniere) Westfeldzug 1940," 6. Juni–10. Juli 1940"(Sig. BA-MA: RH 20–12/383)

T-312/Roll 475: AOK 12, 75099: "Gruppe Guderian." Ia and Ic Sachen, Mai–Juli 1940.

Microfilms of Files from the Politisches Archiv des Auswärtigen Amtes [Political Archive of the Foreign Office], Bonn

T-120/Roll 177: Auswärtiges Amt [AA], Büro des Staatssekretärs: "Schweiz," Bd. 1, 14. Mai 1938–30. Juni 1941.

T-120/Roll 1990: AA, Handelspolitische Abteilung [HaPol], Wiehl: "Schweiz," Bd. 8: Januar 1940–August 1942.

T-120/Roll 2423: Deutsche Gesandtschaft Bern: "Bern Geheimakten 1940," Bd. 2/1, 2/2, 2/3.

T-120/Roll 3672:AA, HaPol. Handel 13: –"Schweiz. Akten betreffend Handelsvertragsverhältnisse zu Deutschland," Bd. 9: Juli–Dezember 1940. AA, HaPol. Verträge, 8:–"Schweiz. Akten betreffend deutsch-schweizerisches Verrechnungsabkommen vom 9. August 1940," Bd.1:9. August 1940–Juni 1944.

For various microfilms I thank Dr. Daniel Bourgeois, Bern; Mr. Koch, Militärische Führungsschulen ETH Zürich, Au/Wädenswil; Werner Rings, Ascona. A complete set of the microfilms listed above is in the Archiv für Zeitgeschichte, Eidgenössische Technische Hochschule, Zürich.

Papers of Dr. Dietrich von Menges, Essen
Private Aufzeichnungen Otto Wilhelm von Menges, 20. Oktober 1939–12. Januar 1941.

Papers of Georges Wüthrich, Zürich
Fort de Vallorbe
Kopienbestand und anderes, Bundesarchiv-Militärarchiv Freiburg im Breisgau.

Oral and Written Communications

Oral:
Hermann Böhme, General, Munich, 1968.
Dennis Borel, ret. Division Commander, 1991.
Werner Gloor, Geneva, 1990.
Dr.h.c. Hans Hausamann, Teufen and St. Gallen, 1968–1970.
Dr. Dietrich Wilhelm von Menges, Essen, 1990.
René Nordmann, Zürich, 1990.
Dr. Hans Thalberg, ret. Ambassador Wien/Blonay, 1990.
Walter Warlimont, General, Gmund, 1968–1970.

Written:
Franz Halder, General, Aschau, 1970–1971.
Dr.h.c. Hans Hausamann, Teufen and St. Gallen, 1968–1970.
Dr. Dietrich Wilhelm von Menges, Essen, 1990.
René Nordmann, Zürich, 1990.
Dr. Hans Thalberg, ret. Ambassador Wien/Blonay, 1990.
Walter Warlimont, General, Gmund, 1968–1970.

PRINTED PRIMARY SOURCES

General

Akten zur deutschen auswärtigen Politik (ADAP) *1918–1945*, ser. d, vols. 9–13. 1. Frankfurt a. M.: Keppler, 1962–1970.
Bericht des schweizerischen Bundesrates an die Bundesversamlung über seine Geschäftsführung im Jahre 1940, 1941, 1942, 1946. Bern.
Boberach, Heinz, Hrsg. *Meldungen aus dem Reich. Die geheimen Lageberichte des Sicherheitsdienstes der SS 1938–1945.* Bd. 4. Herrsching: Pawlak Verlag, 1984.
Boelcke, Willi A., Hrsg. *Deutschlands Rüstung im Zweiten Weltkrieg. Hitler's Konferenzen mit Albert Speer 1942–1945.* Frankfurt a. M.: Akademische Verlagsgesellschaft Athenaion, 1969.
———. *Kriegspropaganda 1939–1941. Geheime Ministerkonferenzen im Reichspropagandaministerium.* Stuttgart: Deutsche Verlags-Anstalt, 1966.
Bonjour, Edgar. *Geschichte der schweizerischen Neutralität. Dokumente.* Bde. 7–9. Basel: Helbing & Lichtenhahn, 1974–1976.
Der Prozess gegen die Hauptkriegsverbrecher vor dem Internationalen Militärgerichtshof Nürnberg, November 14, 1945–Oktober 1, 1946, Vol. VI Nürnberg: 1947.
Die Wehrmachtsberichte 1939–1945. Vol. 1: *September 1, 1939 to December 31, 1941.* Reprint, Munich: Deutscher Taschenbuch Verlag, 1985.
Domarus, Max. *Hitler. Reden und Proklamationen 1932–1945.* Bd. II, 1. Halbband: *1939–1940.* München: Süddeutscher Verlag, 1965.
Eidgenössische Zentralstelle für Kriegswirtschaft, Hrsg. *Die schweizerische Kriegswirtschaft 1939/1949. Bericht des Eidgenössischen Volkswirtschaftsdepartmentes.* Bern: 1950.
Funk, Walther. "Wirtschaftliche Neuordnung Europas!" *Südost-Echo,* Nr. 20, 26. Juli, 1940.

Guides to German Records. Microfilmed at Alexandria, Va. Edited by the American Historical Association, Committee for the Study of War Documents. Washington, DC: National Archives and Records Service, 1958.

Guisan, Henri, General. *Bericht an die Bundesversammlung über den Aktivdienst 1939 1945.* Bern: Eidgenössische Drucksachen und Materialienzentrale, 1946.

Heiber, Helmut, Hrsg. *Hitlers Lagebesprechungen. Protokollfragmente aus Hitlers militärischen Konferenzen 1942–1945.* Stuttgart: Deutsche Verlags-Anstalt, 1962.

Hillgruber, Andreas, Hrsg. *Staatsmänner und Diplomaten bei Hitler. Vertrauliche Aufzeichnungen über Unterredungen mit Vertretern des Auslandes.* Bd. 1: *1939–1941.* Bd. 2: *1942–1944.* Frankfurt am Main: Bernard & Graefe Verlag, für Wehrwesen, 1967, 1970.

Hoffmann, Heinrich, Hrsg. *Mit Hitler im Westen.* München: Zeitgeschichte-Verlag, 1940.

Hubatsch, Walther. *Hitlers Weisungen für die Kriegsführung 1939–1945. Dokumente des Oberkommandos der Wehrmach,* 2. Auflage. Koblenz: Bernard & Graefe Verlag, 1983.

I Documenti Diplomatici Italiani. Nona Serie: *1939–1943,* Vol. V: *11 Giugno–28 Ottobre, 1940.* Ministero degli Affari Esteri. Roma: Liberia dello Stato, 1965.

Jochmann, Werner, Hrsg. *Adolf Hitler. Monologe im Führer-Hauptquartier 1941–1944. Die Aufzeichnungen Heinrich Heims.* Hamburg: Albrecht Knaus Verlag, 1980.

Kriegstagebuch des Oberkommandos der Wehrmacht (Wehrmachtführungsstab) 1940–1945. Geführt von Helmuth Greiner und Percy Ernst Schramm. Bd. I: *1. August, 1940–31. Dezember 1941.* Zusammengestellt und erläutert von Hans-Adolf Jacobsen. Frankfurt a. Main: Bernard & Graefe Verlag für Wehrwesen, 1965.

Picker, Henry. *Hitlers Tischgespräche im Führer Hauptquartier 1941–1942.* Hrsg. Gerhard Ritter. Bonn: Athenäum-Verlag, 1951.

———. *Hitlers Tischgespräche im Führer Hauptquartier.* Vollständig überarbeitete und erweiterte Auflage. Stuttgart: Seewald Verlag, 1977.

Rihner, [Fritz]. *Bericht des Kommandanten der Flieger- und Fliegerabwehrtruppen an den Oberbefehlshaber der Armee über den Aktivdienst 1939–1945.* Bern: 1946.

Rovighi, Alberto. *Un secolo di relazioni militari tra Italia e Svizzera 1861–1961.* Roma: Stato Maggiore dell'Esercito, Ufficio Storico, 1987.

Tessin, Georg. *Verbände und Truppen der deutschen Wehrmacht and Waffen-SS im Zweiten Weltkrieg 1939–1945.* Bde. 1–6. Frankfurt am Main/Osnabrück: Biblio Verlag, 1972.

Diaries, Notes, Memoirs

Barbey, Bernard. *Fünf Jahre auf dem Kommandoposten des Generals. Tagebuch des Chefs des Persönlichen Stabes General Guisans 1940–1945.* Bern: Verlag Herbert Lang, 1948.

———. *Von Hauptquartier zu Hauptquartier. Mein Tagebuch als Verbindungsoffizier zur französischen Armee, 1939–1940.* Frauenfeld: Verlag Huber, 1967.

Below, Nicolaus von. *Als Hitlers Adjutant 1937–1945.* Mainz: von Hase & Koehler Verlag, 1980.

Breker, Arno. *Im Strahlungsfeld der Ereignisse 1925–1965.* Preussisch Olendorf: Schütz, 1972.

Ciano, Galeazzo. *Diario.* Vol. I: *1939–1940.* Tertia edizione. Milano: Rizzoli Editore, 1946.

———. *Tagebücher 1939–1943*. Bern: Alfred Scherz Verlag, 1946.

Dulles, Allen. *Im Geheimdienst*. Düsseldorf: Econ-Verlag, 1963.

Dulles, Allen und Gero von Gaevernitz. *Unternehmen "Sunrise." Die geheime Geschichte des Kriegsendes in Italien*. Düsseldorf: Econ-Verlag, 1967.

Fröhlich, Elke, Hrsg. *Die Tagebücher von Joseph Goebbels. Sämtliche Fragmente*. Teil I, Bd. 4: *1. Januar, 1940–8. Juli, 1941*. München: K. G. Saur, 1987.

Frölicher, Hans. *Meine Aufgabe in Berlin*. Bern: Privatdruck, 1962.

Giesler, Hermann. *Ein anderer Hitler. Bericht seines Architekten. Erlebnisse, Gespräche, Reflexionen*. Leoni am Starnberger See: Druffel-Verlag, 1977.

Groscurth, Helmuth. *Tagebücher eines Abwehroffiziers 1938–1940. Mit weiteren Dokumenten zur Militäropposition gegen Hitler*. Quellen und Darstellungen zur Zeitgeschichte, Bd. 19. Stuttgart: Deutsche Verlags-Anstalt, 1970.

Guderian, Heinz. *Erinnerungen eines Soldaten*, 11. Auflage. Stuttgart: Motorbuch Verlag, 1978.

Halder, Franz. *Kriegstagebuch. Tägliche Aufzeichnungen des Chefs des Generalstabes des Heeres 1939–1942*. 3 Bde. Bearbeitet von Hans-Adolf Jacobsen. Stuttgart: W. Kohlhammer Verlag, 1962–64.

Hassell, Ulrich von. *Die Hassell-Tagebücher 1928–1944*. Erweiterte Ausgabe, Hrsg. Friedrich Freiherr Hiller von Gaertringen. Berlin: Siedler Verlag, 1988.

Hill, Leonidas E., Hrsg. *Die Weizsäcker-Papiere 1933–1950*. Frankfurt am Main: Propyläen Verlag, 1974.

Kelly, David. *The Ruling Few, or The Human Background to Diplomacy*. London: Hollis and Carter, 1952.

Kesselring, Albert. *Gedanken zum Zweiten Weltkrieg*. Bonn: Athenäum-Verlag, 1955.

Kordt, Erich. *Nicht aus den Akten. . . . Die Wilhelmstrasse in Frieden und Krieg. Erlebnisse, Begegnungen und Eindrücke 1928–1945*. Stuttgart: Union Deutsche Verlagsgesellschaft, 1950.

———. Hrsg., unter Mitwirkung von Karl-Heinz Abshagen. *Wahn und Wirklichkeit*. Stuttgart: Union Deutsche Verlagsgesellschaft, 1947.

Liss, Ulrich. *Westfront 1939/40. Erinnerungen des Feindbearbeiters im Oberkomando des Heeres*. Neckargemünd: Vowinckel, 1959.

Lomax, John. *The Diplomatic Smuggler*. London: A. Barker, 1965.

Lossberg, Bernhard von. *Im Wehrmachtführungsstab. Bericht eine Generalstabsoffiziers*. Hamburg: H. H. Nölke Verlag, 1949.

Menges, Dietrich Wilhelm von. *Unternehmensentscheide. Ein Leben für die Wirtschaft*. Düsseldorf: Econ Verlag, 1976.

Meyer, Georg. *Generalfeldmarschall Wilhelm Ritter von Leeb. Tagebuchaufzeichnungen und Lagebeurteilungen aus zwei Weltkriegen*. Stuttgart: Deutsche Verlags-Anstalt, 1976.

Müller, Vincenz. *Ich fand das wahre Vaterland*. Hrsg. Klaus Mummach. Berlin: 1963.

Rintelen, Enno von. *Mussolini als Bundesgenosse. Erinnerungen des deutschen Militärattachés in Rom 1936–1943*. Tübingen: Wunderlich, 1951.

Schmidt, Paul. *Statist auf diplomatischer Bühne 1923–1945. Erlebnisse des Chefdolmetschers im Auswärtigen Amt mit den Staatsmännern Europas*. Bonn: Athenäum-Verlag, 1949.

Schneeberger, Ernst. *Wirtschaftskrieg und "anderes," als Diplomat erlebt in Bern und Washington D.C. 1940–1948*. Wädenswil: Stutz & Co. AG, 1984.

Speer, Albert. *Erinnerungen*. Frankfurt am Main: Propyläen Verlag, 1969.

Speidel, Hans. *Aus unserer Zeit. Erinnerungen*, 4. Auflage. Berlin: Propyläen Verlag, 1977.

Thomas, Georg. *Geschichte der deutschen Wehr- und Rüstungswirtschaft (1918–1943/45)*. Hrsg. Wolfgang Birkenfeld. Schriften des Bundesarchivs, Bd. 14. Boppard am Rhein: Harald Boldt Verlag, 1966.

Warlimont, Walter. *Im Hauptquartier der deutschen Wehrmacht 1939–1945. Grundlagen, Formen, Gestalten.* Dritte Auflage. München: Bernard & Graefe Verlag, 1978.

SECONDARY SOURCES

Ackermann, Josef. *Heinrich Himmler als Ideologe*. Göttingen: 1970.

Adam, Jost. *Die Haltung der Schweiz gegenüber dem nationalsozialistischen Deutschland im Jahre 1940*. Dissertation Mainz. Bielefeld: 1972.

Azeau, Henri. *La Guerre franco-italienne, Juin 1940*. Paris: Presses de la cité, 1967.

Beck, Roland, ed., *Kriegsmobilmachung 1939*. Zürich: 1989.

Boelke, Willi A. *Die deutsche Wirtschaft 1930–1945. Interna des Reichswirtschafts-ministeriums*. Düsseldorf: Droste Verlag, 1983.

Böhme, Hermann. *Der deutsch-französische Waffenstillstand im Zweiten Weltkrieg*. Bd. 1: *Entstehung und Grundlagen des Waffenstillstandes von 1940*. Quellen und Darstellungen zur Zeitgeschichte, Bd. 12. Stuttgart: Deutsche Verlags-Anstalt, 1966.

Bonjour, Edgar. *Geschichte der schweizerischen Neutralität. Vier Jahrhunderte eidgenössischer Aussenpolitik*. Vols. IV-VI: *1939–1945*, 3. Auflage. Basel: Helbing & Lichtenhahn, 1971–1976.

Borel, Denis. *Parcelles peu connues de l'histoire du service actif 1939–1945*. Typoskript. Neuchâtel: 1991.

Bourgeois, Daniel. "Documents sur la subversion nazie en Suisse pendant l'été et l'automne 1940," *Relations internationales*, no. 3 (Juillet 1975): 107–32.

———. "La neutralité de la Savoie du Nord et la question des zones franches. Rappel historique, présentation des sources, indications de recherche," in *Studien und Quellen* 8, ed. Schweizerisches Bundesarchiv (Bern: 1982), 7–48.

———. *Le Troisième Reich et la Suisse 1933–1941*. Neuchâtel: Éditions de la Baconnière, 1974.

Braunschweig, Pierre-Th. *Geheimer Draht nach Berlin. Die Nachrichtenlinie Masson-Schellenberg und der schweizerische Nachrichtendienst im Zweiten Weltkrieg*. Zürich: Verlag Neue Zürcher Zeitung, 1989.

Buchheit, Gert. *Der deutsche Geheimdienst. Geschichte der militärischen Abwehr*. München: List Verlag, 1966.

Bücheler, Heinrich. *Carl-Heinrich von Stülpnagel; Soldat–Philosoph–Verschwörer*. Frankfurt a. M.: Ullstein Verlag, 1989.

Buck, Gerhard. *Das Führer-Hauptquartier 1939–1945*, 3rd Edition. Leoni am Starnbergersee: Druffel Verlag, 1983.

Burdick, Charles B. *Hubert Lanz 1896–1982. General der Gebirgstruppe*. Osnabrück: Biblio-Verlag, 1988.

Cattani, Alfred. "Der grosse Schock vom Sommer 1940. Vor 50 Jahren entfesselte Hitler den Krieg im Westen," in *Neue Zürcher Zeitung*, Nr. 107, 10. Mai, 1990.

Das Deutsche Reich und der Zweite Weltkrieg, Hrsg. Militärgeschichtliches Forschungsamt. Bd. 2: *Die Errichtung der Hegemonie auf dem Europäischen Kontinent*. Bd. 3: *Der Mittelmeerraum und Südosteuropa*. Stuttgart: Deutsche Verlags-Anstalt, 1979, 1984.

Ernst, Alfred. "Die Bereitschaft und Abwehrkraft Norwegens, Dänemarks und der Schweiz in deutscher Sicht," in *Neutrale Kleinstaaten im Zweiten Weltkrieg*. Schriften der Schweizerisichen Vereinigung für Militärgeschichte und Militärwissenschaften, Heft 1 (Münsingen: buchverlag Tages-Nachrichten, 1973): 7–73.

Ernst, Alfred. *Die Konzeption der schweizerischen Landesverteidigung 1815–1966*. Frauenfeld: Verlag Huber, 1971.

Felice, Renzo de. *Mussolini l'alleato*. Vol. I: *L'Italia in Guerra 1940–1943*. Torino: Giulio Einaudi editore, 1990.

Fink, Jürg. *Die Schweiz aus der Sicht des Dritten Reiches 1933–1945. Einschätzung und Beurteilung der Schweiz durch die oberste deutsche Führung seit der Machtergreifung Hitlers. Stellenwert des Kleinstaates Schweiz im Kalkül der nationalsozialistischen Exponenten in Staat, Diplomatie, Wehrmacht, SS, Nachrichtendiensten und Presse*. Dissertation. Zürich: Schulthess Polygraphischer Verlag, 1985.

Fuhrer, Hans Rudolf. *Spionage gegen die Schweiz Die geheimen deutschen Nachrichtendienste gegen die Schweiz im Zweiten Weltkrieg 1939–1945*. Frauenfeld: Allgemeine Militärzeitschrift, Verlag Huber, 1982.

Gautschi, Willi. "Guisan und Wille im gefährlichen Sommer 1940," *Neue Zürcher Zeitung*, no. 193, 20./21. August, 1988.

———. *General Henri Guisan. Die schweizerische Armeeführung im Zweiten Weltkrieg*. Dritte Auflage. Zürich: Verlag Neue Zürcher Zeitung, 1990.

Görlitz, Walter, Hrsg. *Generalfeldmarschall Keitel, Verbrecher oder Offizier? Erinnerungen, Briefe, Dokumente des Chefs OKW*. Göttingen: Musterschmidt-Verlag, 1961.

Greiner, Helmuth. *Die oberste Wehrmachtführung 1939–1943*. Wiesbaden: Limes Verlag, 1951.

Hauschild, Reinhard, Hrsg. *Der springende Reiter. 1. Kavallerie-Division–24. Panzer-Division im Bild*. Gross-Umstadt: Dohany, 1984.

Heiniger, Markus. *Dreizehn Gründe. Warum die Schweiz im Zweiten Weltkrieg nicht erobert wurde*. Zürich: Limmat Verlag, 1989.

Heusinger, Adolf. *Befehl im Widerstreit. Schicksalsstunden der deutschen Armee 1923–1945*. Tübingen: Wunderlich Verlag, 1957.

Hillgruber, Andreas. *Hitlers Strategie, Politik und Kriegsführung 1940–1941*, 2. Auflage. Frankfurt a. M.: Bernard & Graefe Verlaf für Wehrwesen, 1982.

Hoffmann, Peter. *Die Sicherheit des Diktators. Hitlers Leibwachen, Schutzmassnahmen, Residenzen, Hauptquartiere*. München: R. Piper & Co. Verlag, 1975.

Homberger, Heinrich. *Schweizerische Handelspolitik im Zweiten Weltkrieg*. Erlenbach: Eugen Rentsch Verlag, 1970.

Inglin, Oswald. *Der stille Krieg. Der Wirtschaftskrieg zwischen Grossbritannien und der Schweiz im Zweiten Weltkrieg*. Zürich: Verlag Neue Zürcher Zeitung, 1991.

Irvin, David. *Göring*. München: Albrecht Knaus Verlag, 1987.

Jäckel, Eberhard. *Frankreich in Hitlers Europa. Die deutsche Frankreichpolitik im Zweiten Weltkrieg*. Quellen und Darstellungen zur Zeitgeschichte, Bd. 14. Stuttgart: Deutsche Verlags-Anstalt, 1966.

Jacobsen, Hans-Adolf und Hans Dollinger, Hrsg. *Der Zweite Weltkrieg in Bildern und Dokumenten.* Vol. 1: *Der europäische Krieg 1939–1941.* München: Verlag Kurt Desch (Lizenzausgabe) R. Löwit, 1963.

Jodl, Luise. *Jenseits des Endes. Leben und Sterben des Generaloberst Alfred Jodl.* Wien: Verlag Fritz Molden, 1976.

Jost, Hans Ulrich. "Bedrohung und Enge (1914–1945)," in *Geschichte der Schweiz und der Schweizer.* Bd. III (Basel: Helbing & Lichtenhahn, 1983), 101–89.

Jouvet, Robert. *Le problème des zones franches de la Haute Savoie et du Pays de Gex.* Genève: Georg & Co., 1943.

Keilig, Wolf. *Das deutsche Heer 1939–1945.* 3 Bde. Bad Nauheim: Podzun Verlag, 1963.

Kreidler, Eugen. *Die Eisenbahnen im Machtbereich der Achsenmächte während des Zweiten Weltkrieges.* Studien und Dokumente zur Geschichte des Zweiten Weltkrieges, Bd. 15. Göttingen: Musterschmidt-Verlag, 1975.

Kreis, Georg. *Auf den Spuren von La Charité. Die schweizerische Armeeführung im Spannungsfeld des deutsch-französischen Gegensatzes 1936–1941.* Basel: Helbing & Lichtenhahn, 1976.

Kurz, Hans Rudolf "Die militärische Bedrohung der Schweiz im Zweiten Weltkrieg," in *Allgemeine schweizerische Militärzeitschrift,* Nr. 11 (November 1951).

———. *Die Schweiz in der europäischen Strategie vom Dreissigjährigen Krieg bis zum Atomzeitalter.* Zürich: Bachmann, o. J.

———. *Die Schweiz in der Planung der kriegführenden Mächte während des zweiten Weltkrieges.* Biel: Schweizerischer Unteroffiziersverband, 1957.

———. *Dokumente des Aktivdienstes.* Frauenfeld: Verlag Huber, 1965.

———. *Nachrichtenzentrum Schweiz. Die Schweiz im Nachrichtendienst des Zweiten Weltkrieges.* Frauenfeld: Verlag Huber, 1972.

———. *Operationsplanung Schweiz. Die Rolle der Schweizer Armee in zwei Weltkriegen.* Thun: Ott Verlag, 1974.

Lehmann, Rudolf. *Die Leibstandarte.* Bd. I. Osnabrück: Munin, 1977.

Lemelsen, Joachim et al. *29. Division.* Bad Nauheim: Podzun Verlag, 1960.

Lévêque, Gérard. *La Suisse et la France Gaulliste 1943–1945.* Genève: Imprimerie Studer, 1979.

Liss, Ulrich. "Noch einmal: La Charité 1940," in: *Allgemeine schweizerische Militärzeitschrift,* Nr. 12 (1967): 729–33.

Lüönd, Karl. *Spionage und Landesverrat in der Schweiz.* 2 Bde. Zürich: Ringier, 1977.

Maier, Klaus A. et al., *Das deutsche Reich und der Zweite Weltkrieg.* Vol. 2: *Die Errichtung der Hegemonie auf dem europäischen Kontinent.* Stuttgart: 1979.

Martin, Bernd. *Friedensinitiativen und Machtpolitik im Zweiten Weltkrieg 1939–1942.* Düsseldorf: Droste Verlag, 1974.

Matt, Alphons. *Zwischen allen Fronten: Der Zweite Weltkrieg aus der Sicht des Büros Ha,* 2. Auflage. Frauenfeld: Verlag Huber 1969.

Matter, E. und E. Ballinari, "Eidgenössisches Kriegs-Transport-Amt," in *Die schweizerische kriegswirtschaft 1939/1948. Bericht des eidgenössischen Volkswirtschaftsdepartementes* (Bern: 1950), 109ff.

Medlicott, W. N. *The Economic Blockade,* 2 vols., 1952, 1959. London: Kraus Reprint, 1978.

Messenger, Charles. *Hitler's Gladiator. The Life and Times of Oberstgruppenführer and Panzergeneral–Oberst der Waffen SS, Sepp Dietrich.* Exeter: Brassey's Defence Publ., 1988.

Mitcham, Samuel W. Jr. *Hitler's Legions. The German Army Order of Battle, World War II.* New York: Dorset Press, 1987.

Neugebauer, Karl-Volker. *Die deutsche Militärkontrolle im unbesetzten Frankreich und in Französisch-Neuwestafrika 1940–1942. Zum Problem der Sicherung der Südwestflanke von Hitler's Kontinentalimperium.* Boppard am Rhein: Harald Boldt Verlag, 1980.

Ochsner, Richard. "Transit von Truppen, Einzelpersonen, Kriegsmaterial und zivilen Gebrauchsgütern zugunsten einer Kriegspartei durch das neutrale Land," in *Schwedische und schweizerische Neutralität im Zweiten Weltkrieg.* Hrsg. Rudolf L. Bindschedler et al. (Basel: Helbing & Lichtenhahn, 1985), 216–35.

Plan, E. Général et Eric Lèfvre. *La Bataille des Alpes 10–25 Juin 1940. L'armée invaincue.* Paris: Charles-Lovauzelle, 1982.

Rings, Werner: *Kollaboration und Widerstand. Europa im Krieg 1939–1945.* Zürich: Ex Libris Verlag, 1979.

———. *Raubgold aus Deutschland. Die "Golddrehscheibe" Schweiz im Zweiten Weltkrieg.* Zürich: Artemis Verlag, 1985.

———. *Schweiz im Krieg 1933–1945. Ein Bericht.* Zürich: Ex libris Verlag, 1974.

Roesch, Werner. *Bedrohte Schweiz. Die deutschen Operationsplanungen gegen die Schweiz im Sommer/Herbst 1940 und die Abwehrbereitschaft der Armee im Oktober 1940.* Dissertation Zürich. Frauenfeld: Allgemeine Schweizerische Militärzeitschrift, Verlag Huber, 1986.

Ruef, Karl. *Gebirgsjäger zwischen Kreta und Murmansk. Die Schicksale der 6. Gebirgsdivision.* Graz: Stocker, o. J.

Schaufelberger, Walter. "Die militärische Bedrohung der Schweiz im Zweiten Weltkrieg," in *Neue Zürcher Zeitung,* Nr. 265, 14. November, 1989.

———. "Militärische Bedrohung der Schweiz 1939/1940," in *Kriegsmobilmachung 1939. Eine wissenschaftlich-kritische Analyse aus Anlass der 50. Wiederkehr des Mobilmachungstages von 1939.* Hrsg. Roland Beck. Abteilung Militärwissenschaften, Eidgenössische Technische Hochschule (Zürich: 1989), 39–47.

———. Hrsg. *Sollen wir die Armee abschaffen? Blick auf eine bedrohliche Zeit.* Frauenfeld: Verlag Huber, 1988.

Senn, Hans. "Schweizerische Dissuasionsstrategie im Zweiten Weltkrieg," in *Schwedische und schweizerische Neutralität im Zweiten Weltkrieg.* Hrsg. Rudolf L. Bindschedler et al. (Basel: Helbing & Lichtenhahn, 1985), 197–215.

———. "Die Haltung Italiens zum 'Fall Schweiz' im Jahre 1940," in *Neue Zürcher Zeitung,* Nr. 111, 14./15. Mai, 1988.

———. *Der Schweizerische Generalstab.* Bd. VII. Basel: Helbing & Lichtenhahn, 1995.

Shirer, William L.. *Der Zusammenbruch Frankreichs. Aufstieg und Fall der Dritten Republik.* München: Droemersche Verlagsanstalt Th. Knaus Nachfahren, 1970.

Stadelmann, Jürg. "Auf der Flucht vor deutschen Panzern. Internierung von 50 000 Personen in der Schweiz im Juni 1940," in *Neue Zürcher Zeitung,* Nr. 137 16/17. Juni, 1990.

Tanner, Jakob. *Bundeshaushalt, Währung und Kriegswirtschaft. Eine finanzsoziologische Analyse der Schweiz zwischen 1938 und 1953.* Dissertation Zürich: Limmat Verlag, 1986.

———. "Hand in Hand mit den Nazis," in *Bilanz,* Nr. 10 (1989): 346–52.

Trepp, Gian. "Warum Hitler eine neutrale Schweiz brauchte," in *Die Wochen-Zeitung*, Nr. 23 8. Juni, 1990.

Umbreit, Hans. *Der Militärbefehlshaber in Frankreich 1940–1944*. Militärgeschichtliche Studien, Bd. 7. Boppard am Rhein: Harald Boldt Verlag, 1968.

Urner, Klaus. "Die schweizerisch-deutschen Wirtschaftsbeziehungen während des Zweiten Weltkrieges," in *Neue Zürcher Zeitung*, Nrn. 734, 745, 756, November/Dezember 1968.

———. "Economie et neutralité," in *Revue d'histoire de la deuxième guerre mondiale*, Nr. 121 (Janvier 1981): 35–69.

———. "Neutralität und Wirtschaftskrieg 1939–1945," in *Schwedische und schweizerische Neutralität im Zweiten Weltkrieg*. Hrsg. Rudolf L. Bindschedler et al. (Basel: Helbing & Lichtenhahn, 1985), 259–92. Reprinted in *Der Zweite Weltkrieg und die Schweiz* Hrsg. Kenneth Angst (Zürich: Verlag Neue Zürcher Zeitung, 1997), 47–86.

Vetsch, Christian. *Aufmarsch gegen die Schweiz. Der deutsche "Fall Gelb"–Irreführung der Schweizer Armee 1939/40*. Olten: Walter-Verlag, 1973.

Vogler, Robert Urs. *Die Wirtschaftsverhandlungen zwischen der Schweiz und Deutschland 1940 und 1941*. Dissertation Zürich. Basel: Helbing & Lichtenhahn, 1983.

Walde, Karl-J. *Guderian*. Frankfurt am Main: Ulstein, 1976.

Wangel, Carl-Alex. "Verteidigung gegen den Krieg," in *Schwedische und schweizerische Neutralität im Zweiten Weltkrieg*. Rudolf Bindschedler et al., eds. (Basel: Helbing & Lichtenhahn, 1985).

Wehrli, Edmund. *Wehrlose Schweiz–eine Insel des Friedens?* Beiheft Nr. 9 zur *Allgemeinen Schweizerischen Militärzeitschrift*. Frauenfeld: Verlag Huber, 1973.

Weinberg, Andreas. *Das gelbe Edelweiss. Wege und Werden einer Gebirgsdivision*. München: Zentralverlag der Nationalsozialistischen Deutschen Arbeiter Partei, 1943.

Wetter, Ernst. *Duell der Flieger und der Diplomaten. Die Fliegerzwischenfälle Deutschland-Schweiz im Mai/Juni 1940 und ihre diplomatischen Folgen*. Frauenfeld: Verlag Huber, 1987.

Witmer, Jürg. *Grenznachbarliche Zusammenarbeit. Das Beispiel der Grenzregionen von Basel und Genf*. Dissertation Universität Zürich. Zürich: Schulthess Polygraphischer Verlag, 1979.

Wüthrich, Georges. "'Höchste Dringlichkeit: Noch heute Schweizer Grenze erreichen!'" in *Sonntags-Zeitung*, Nr. 25, 18. Juni, 1989.

———. "Vallorbe: Das 'Unterseeboot' an der Schweizer Grenze," in *Sonntags-Zeitung*, Nr. 25, 18. Juni, 1989.

Index

accommodation and tempering of Hitler through good behavior, 9
"Adler" sabotage mission, 20
Africa: North, 37, 99, 102n2; plans of German Reich, 17
airplane clashes between Germany and Switzerland, 18–19, 133, 136
air service to and from Switzerland, 80n3; after the armistice, 81
Algeria, landing of American troops in, 37
Allies: arms and war materials exports from Switzerland, 7, 82, 85; blockade agreements, 77; secret passages of contact with, x. *See also* Great Britain; United States
Alsace-Lorraine, 11, 69, 119–20
Alsatians and Swiss-French collusion regarding their free movement, 120
American Secret Service (OSS), 127
Annecy, 47, 48
Annemasse: border controls at, 127; passenger traffic, 119
armaments and war materials, Swiss, 124; Hitler's interest in purchase of only after attack in the West, 11; purchase of by Allies, 11, 82, 94; shipment of aircraft canons, 110; supply of, 7, 82, 85, 105. *See also* watch components and precision instruments
Armed Forces High Command for Conducting Economic Warfare, 93

armistice, German-French, of 1940, x, 3, 27, 31, 33; economic transition phase after, 81–82; Gotthard transit route, 12; Munich meeting of Mussolini and Hitler, 27–29, 37, 133, 142, 143; non-use of Switzerland by Germany for transit because of, 63; possible continuation of war in southern France after armistice, 38; protective effect of relative to invasion of Switzerland, 63, 66; Swiss retaining of transit route, 33
Armistice Commission, 66, 69, 118
Army. *See* German Army; Swiss Army

Badoglio, Marshal, 28–29, 31, 146
Bank for International Exchange (Basel), 12
Battle in the Alps, June, 1940, 29–31
The Battle in the Alps June 10–25, 1940 (Plan and Lefévre), 31
Bedrohte Schweiz (Roesch), 4
Belgian Rexist movement, 49
Belgium: capitulation of on May 28, 1940, 15; occupation by Germans, 3
Bellegarde-Geneva railway line: blocking of, 96–97, 106; export transit through, 87–88; Great Britain, 106; reopening of in August 1941, 115; restriction of passenger transit traffic to, 118
Below, Nicolaus von, 20–21
Berghot conference, 65–66

191